ALSO BY RICHARD NIXON

SIX CRISES (1962)
RN: THE MEMOIRS OF RICHARD NIXON (1978)
THE REAL WAR (1980)
LEADERS (1982)
REAL PEACE: A STRATEGY FOR THE WEST (1983)
NO MORE VIETNAMS (1985)
1999: VICTORY WITHOUT WAR (1988)
IN THE ARENA (1990)

SEIZE
THE
MOMENT

America's Challenge
in a
One-Superpower World

RICHARD
NIXON

SIMON & SCHUSTER
NEW YORK   LONDON   TORONTO
SYDNEY   TOKYO   SINGAPORE

SIMON & SCHUSTER
SIMON & SCHUSTER BUILDING
ROCKEFELLER CENTER
1230 AVENUE OF THE AMERICAS
NEW YORK, NEW YORK 10020

SIMON & SCHUSTER AND COLOPHON ARE REGISTERED TRADEMARKS
OF SIMON & SCHUSTER INC.
DESIGNED BY EVE METZ
MANUFACTURED IN THE UNITED STATES OF AMERICA

3   5   7   9   10   8   6   4   2

LIBRARY OF CONGRESS CATALOGING IN PUBLICATION DATA
NIXON, RICHARD M. (RICHARD MILHOUS). 1913–
SEIZE THE MOMENT: AMERICA'S CHALLENGE
IN A ONE-SUPERPOWER WORLD/RICHARD NIXON.
P.   CM.
INCLUDES INDEX.
1. UNITED STATES—FOREIGN RELATIONS—1989–   I. TITLE.
E881.N59   1992   91-37743
                                                                              CIP
ISBN 0-671-74343-0
ISBN 0-671-77874-9 LTD. ED.

To the democrats

CONTENTS

1

THE REAL WORLD

IN TOASTING THE BEGINNING of a new relationship between China and the United States in the Great Hall of the People in Beijing twenty years ago, I quoted from a poem in which Mao Zedong exhorted his followers to work for the victory of communism: "So many deeds cry out to be done always urgently. The world rolls on. Time passes. Seize the day. Seize the hour." Today, as we celebrate the defeat of communism in Eastern Europe and the Soviet Union and the defeat of aggression in the Persian Gulf, many deeds remain to be done abroad and at home. We must seize the moment to win victory for peace and freedom in the world.

For the past half century, we have lived in a world dominated by the clash of two superpowers inspired by two conflicting ideologies. The East-West struggle was the defining characteristic of the era. The Soviet Union and the United States confronted each other across the front lines in Europe and Asia, backed rival clients in regional conflicts in the Middle East and South Asia, and sparred with each other in civil wars throughout the underdeveloped world. But today one ideology—communism—has been discredited beyond resurrection. And one superpower—the Soviet Union—has a new noncommunist government so preoccupied with its massive problems at home that it can no longer play a dominant role abroad.

We now live in a world in which the United States is the only superpower. We must recast our foreign policy to cope with this radically new situation. For many on the American left and right, the knee-jerk response to the decline of the Soviet Union as a credible superpower is to withdraw into a new isolationism. But in fact American world leadership will be indispensable in the coming decades.

During the last three years, the world took a roller-coaster ride from soaring hopes to shattered illusions to unbounded euphoria. In 1989, our expectations climbed as one great historic event was quickly overtaken by another. Communist regimes in Eastern Europe collapsed. The Berlin Wall fell. Soviet president Mikhail Gorbachev adopted significant political reforms. Superpower cooperation increased. Regional conflict in the underdeveloped world decreased. The conventional wisdom in the prestige media, in the universities, and in the think tanks was that we were witnessing the beginning of a new world order of peace and freedom.

In 1990, the changes of the previous year began to reverse themselves. The new democracies of Eastern Europe confronted the pains of reform. The Communist reactionaries in the Soviet Union caught their second wind. Gorbachev slammed the brakes on reform. Iraqi president Saddam Hussein invaded and pillaged Kuwait. America and its coalition partners were forced into a major ground war in the Persian Gulf. Regional conflicts in the underdeveloped world continued to defy easy resolution. The vision of a more peaceful world turned out to be a mirage. While the cold war had kept the peace between the two superpowers, its demise did not end the threat of hot war involving smaller powers.

In 1991, these developments were overtaken by two events. The decisive victory of the United States and its allies over Iraq and the expulsion of Saddam Hussein's forces from Kuwait in February restored America's confidence in its role as a world leader. This was eclipsed by one of the watershed events of the twentieth century: on August 24, the forces of freedom in the Soviet Union won victory without war over the forces of communism. Just as the Russian Revolution of 1917 raised the curtain on this century's totalitarian horrors, the new Soviet revolution dropped the closing curtain on the final act of a failed ideology and totally discredited system of government. While Gorbachev is still a Communist, the ministers in the new government are noncommunists.

These starkly contrasting events should remind us that the real world revolves not around wishful thinking about "peace breaking out all over" but around the enduring realities of geopolitics. While we should celebrate the current turn of events, we should not give in to euphoria. In a world of competing states, clashing interests and national conflicts are inevitable. The skillful use of American power represents the best hope for advancing freedom and preserving peace. Only if we learn the right lessons from the dramatic developments of the last three years will we succeed in securing our interests and promoting our values.

For half a century, the principal cause of world conflict has been Communist aggression. The cold war started before World War II ended. Acting under cover of the infamous Hitler-Stalin Pact in 1939, Moscow annexed Lithuania, Latvia, Estonia, and large parts of prewar Poland and Romania. As the war ended, Stalin installed Communist puppet governments in Poland, Czechoslovakia, Hungary, East Germany, Bulgaria, and Romania. Soviet armies "liberated" Eastern Europe from Nazi Germany, but Communist liberation meant a new tyranny for these nations. To his subservient clients, Stalin exported the brutal tactics he had used in the Soviet Union before World War II—show trials, political purges, forced-labor camps, and mass terror. As the iron curtain descended, Eastern Europe was enveloped in totalitarian darkness.

Eastern Europe was only the first theater of the cold war. Over the ensuing years, the Soviet Union annexed four Japanese islands in 1945, attempted to dismember Iran in 1946, sponsored Communist guerrillas in Greece and Turkey in the late 1940s, helped to establish a Communist regime in North Korea in 1948, tried to subjugate Josip Tito's independent Communist regime in Yugoslavia in 1948, blockaded West Berlin in 1948, helped Mao Zedong's Communist revolution prevail in China in 1949, backed Communist North Korea's attack against South Korea in 1950, suppressed a workers' uprising in East Germany in 1953, supported Beijing in two crises with the U.S.-supported Republic of China in Taiwan over Quemoy and Matsu in 1955 and 1958, triggered the Middle East arms race with sales to Egypt in 1955, slaughtered hundreds of Hungarian freedom fighters in the streets of Budapest in 1956, backed Gamal Abdel Nasser's seizure of the Suez Canal in 1956, helped to establish Fidel Castro's regime in Cuba in 1959, assisted Communist revolutionaries in the Congo in 1960, built the Berlin Wall in 1961, attempted to place offensive nuclear missiles in Cuba in 1962, supplied arms to India in wars against Pakistan in 1965 and 1971, supported Nasser's adventurism throughout the Arab world in the late 1950s and 1960s, backed the Arab powers in their war against Israel in 1967, crushed the Czechoslovakian reform movement in the "Prague Spring" in 1968, supported Syria and radical Palestinians in their effort to topple the government of Jordan in 1970, provided indispensable assistance for North Vietnam in its war against South Vietnam, Laos, and Cambodia in the 1960s and 1970s, supplied and supported Syria and Egypt's war against Israel in 1973, backed a Communist coup in Ethiopia in 1974, installed Communist regimes in Angola and Mozambique in 1975, helped the Communist Sandinistas take power in Nicaragua in 1979, supplied Communist guerrillas in El Salvador with arms since the late 1970s, invaded Afghanistan in 1979, backed the Communist government's repression of Solidarity and imposition of martial law in Poland in 1981, trained and supported scores of international terrorist groups, engaged in state-sponsored terrorism through its clients in East Germany, Bulgaria, and Afghanistan, and conspired in dozens of other attempted coups and revolutions in every corner of the world.

While other sources of conflict existed during the cold war, none rivaled Moscow's expansionism in scope and intensity. Without ever issuing a formal declaration of war, the Soviets engaged in an unprecedented campaign of direct and indirect aggression. Despite Moscow's occasional calls for "peaceful coexistence" or "détente" in its diplomacy and propaganda, the leaders in the Kremlin continued to march to the ominous drumbeat of Communist expansion.

All this appeared to change in 1989. Everywhere we looked, dramatic events seemed to overturn settled realities. In the Soviet Union, Gorbachev initiated major reforms. He eased controls on the press and triggered a flood of criticism of the Soviet system. He permitted partially free elections that led to humiliating defeats for the Communist party. He opened up some limited opportunities for private economic activity that created hopes for a more prosperous future. He adopted changes in long-held foreign policy positions, accepting deep cuts in Moscow's massive superiority in conventional arms in Europe and unprecedented on-site inspection provisions in the Strategic Arms Reductions Treaty (START) talks. More important, these changes soon acquired a momentum of their own as independent political movements demanded that Gorbachev press forward more aggressively with reforms.

In Eastern Europe, the upheaval was even more dramatic. In the 1980s, the tectonic plates of East European nationalism and Soviet-imposed communism had built up tremendous pressure, making a political earthquake inevitable. Once Gorbachev's reforms at home had discredited communism abroad, the first fissures appeared in the Soviet bloc. Polish Communist leaders, trapped between foreign sanctions and domestic political gridlock, concluded that they had to legalize Solidarity, the anticommunist labor movement. After partially free elections produced a total defeat for the Communists, they ceded power reluctantly to democratic forces. In Hungary, after the party split between hardliners and moderates, even reformist Communists were swept from office through the ballot box. Hungary soon became a path to freedom for thousands of East Germans fleeing into West Germany. As the exodus bled the red Germany white, the Communist leadership accepted the necessity for democratic change, thereby signing its own death warrant. When Moscow failed to intervene to save the citadel of its imperial power—East Berlin—mass demonstrations swept the Kremlin's clients from power in Bulgaria, Czechoslovakia, and Romania. Within one year, the East European political temblor left only Albania's Communist regime intact, and the following year the aftershocks of this political earthquake hit Albania, toppling its hard-line Communist leaders from power.

In the underdeveloped world, the tide of Soviet expansionism in the 1970s receded in the 1980s. The ill-equipped, U.S.-supported Afghan resistance fought the Red Army to a standstill, forcing Moscow to accept a humiliating withdrawal and shattering the myth of the irreversibility of communism. In Angola, after tens of thousands of Cuban troops and Soviet advisers failed to suppress the U.S.-supported UNITA freedom fighters, Luanda grudgingly accepted an agreement demanding the withdrawal of foreign forces and free elections. In Southeast Asia, Vietnam withdrew its forces from Cambodia, as international mediation advanced toward a political settlement of its civil war. Under pressure from the U.S.-supported contras, the Sandinista regime in Nicaragua accepted a plan for free elections, which, to the shocked surprise of the Kremlin and most liberal observers in the United States, would propel noncommunists into power in early 1990. And the leader of the last Communist holdout in the Western hemisphere, Fidel Castro, was forced to impose wartime austerity measures in Cuba to stave off a total economic collapse.

Even in China—a country with few significant democratic traditions—a million demonstrators gathered in Tiananmen Square to demand political reform. Initially composed of only students and intellectuals, the crowds swelled dramatically when workers joined their ranks in calling for democratic change, and the protests quickly spread to over two hundred provincial cities. Mesmerizing Western television audiences, the tumultuous scenes outside the bastion of Chinese communism even eclipsed Gorbachev's historic visit to China and the rapprochement between Moscow and Beijing. The ensuing violent crackdown by Chinese leaders in Tiananmen Square dashed democratic hopes and outraged the world. Yet considering the dramatic democratic triumphs of 1989, most observers viewed this brutal repression as a tragic but temporary aberration.

The changes of 1989 extended beyond the Communist world. After a decade of grueling trench warfare and 1.2 million casualties, the Iran-Iraq war came to an end. Namibia was granted independence and elected a new government. South Africa's leaders accepted the need to create a nonracial society and moved decisively to relegate the policy of apartheid to the archives. U.S. intervention in Panama overthrew Manuel Noriega's dictatorship and put the legitimately elected government into power. Elsewhere, new democratic governments in South Korea, the Philippines, and Latin America stabilized themselves and strengthened their long-term prospects for progress.

The balance sheet for 1989—nine democratic revolutions liberating 122 million people—created expectations that we were entering a new era of world history. These high hopes, though understandable, were unfounded. The world was moving into uncharted waters. Never before has there been a successful transformation of a Communist command economy to a free-market economy. All lasting change is incremental, based on unfolding traditions and developing institutions. Revolutionary upheavals may change how the world looks but seldom change the way the world works. Lasting historical change comes not through tidal waves but through the irresistible creeping tide.

The events of 1989 gave rise to three myths that dominated the debate about the future of U.S. foreign policy:

The myth of the end of history. Many argued that the defeat of communism, the triumph of liberal democracy, and the end of the cold war buried the idea of history as the armed rivalry of opposing ideologies. Market economics and representative government, they claimed, were now universally accepted as superior to central planning and dictatorship. The march of technology, not armies, and battles over markets, not ideas, would become the central dynamics of history. America, they concluded, should declare victory and come home.

This facile notion of an end of history is illusory. While communism has suffered several devastating defeats, Communist regimes continue to rule twelve countries with 1.3 billion people. Communism is a discredited ideology, but Communists are still effective in using force to gain and retain power. Moreover, the waning of the cold war does not mean an end to international conflict. Age-old struggles based on tribal, ethnic, national, or religious hatreds continue to fuel dozens of civil and regional wars. Nuclear powers have never fought each other, but the clash between Muslim Pakistan and Hindu India over the disputed Kashmir territory could erupt into the world's first war between nuclear powers. As East-West tensions fade, the reins on potential regional aggressors—such as Saddam Hussein—will also loosen.

Since the end of World War II, 22 million people have lost their lives in "small wars"—8 million more than the number killed in World War I. Most of those killed in those wars would have perished had there been no superpower conflict. While it may not be dominated by ideological conflict, the "new era" in world history could become even more violent than its predecessor.

Those who proclaimed the end of history overstated the triumph of the ideas of liberal democracy and market economics. Never before has capitalism been so broadly accepted as the foundation of sustained growth and elections been so widely heralded as the basis for limited and accountable government. But rival ideas have not been driven from the field. Advocates of the cradle-to-grave welfare state and of "socialism with a human face" still carry clout at the elitist dinner parties in Washington and other Western capitals. Marxism is alive and well in many American universities, and radical ideologies such as Pan Arabism and Islamic fundamentalism have enormous appeal in the Middle East.

We should never underestimate the unpredictability of history. Previous proponents of "the end of history" have been proved wrong. Over two hundred years ago, Immanuel Kant foresaw an imminent "perpetual peace" as a result of the spread of democracy around the world. But Lenin's communism, Mussolini's fascism, and Hitler's Nazism were only a few of the surprises that confounded his predictions. However illogical and inhumane these ideologies were, the leaders who espoused them did take power and proceeded ruthlessly to use that power to advance their twisted ideas. Rationality and politics have parted ways before. We cannot disregard the possibility that they might do so again. As Paul Johnson observed, "One of the lessons of history is that no civilization can be taken for granted. Its permanency can never be assured. There is always a dark age waiting for you around the corner, if you play your cards badly and you make sufficient mistakes."

The myth of the irrelevance of military power. After the Soviet defeat in Afghanistan and the "velvet revolutions" in Eastern Europe, it became fashionable to argue that military power no longer serves as the key instrument of statecraft or represents the bedrock of foreign policy. Some say that interdependence among the great powers has rendered the use of force irrelevant. Others hold that the costs of waging war, in terms of both resources and world opinion, have become prohibitive. Still others contend that, as the cold war waned, the importance of economic power and "geo-economics" has surpassed military power and traditional geopolitics. America, they conclude, must beat its swords not into plowshares, but into microchips.

Though economic interdependence constricts every country's freedom of action, it does not make military power irrelevant. While the end of the cold war has substantially reduced security concerns in Western Europe, our NATO allies know that a transatlantic security pact and a credible U.S. nuclear and conventional presence in Europe are essential to guarantee peace and security in a period of unprecedented instability in the Soviet Union and Eastern Europe.

If an issue affects vital national interests, a major power will throw even the strongest economic ties overboard in order to prevail. In both world wars, nations that traded with each other killed each other's citizens by the millions. At the height of the cold war, many argued that trade with the Soviet Union would sate the Kremlin's appetite for expansion. While trade can serve as an important added restraint on potential aggressors, it can never substitute for hard-headed deterrence based on military power. None of the West's credits and investments in the 1970s dissuaded the Kremlin from ordering the invasion of Afghanistan in 1979.

Those who propound the irrelevance of military power vastly overstate the influence of economic power. The world's rising economic giants—Germany and Japan—have exploited their huge foreign exchange reserves and industrial competitiveness. They have gained control of foreign markets, dominated key bilateral trade relationships, and have set the pace for the economic integration of Europe and the Pacific rim. But on political and security issues, economic power does not amount to geopolitical leverage. The collapse of communism in East Germany, rather than Berlin's economic payoffs to Moscow, led to the unification of Germany. Despite Germany's and Japan's critical need for Gulf oil for economic survival, both countries were impotent in the Gulf crisis, totally dependent on the United States and our allies in the Persian Gulf War to protect their interests. Saddam Hussein, after all, could not have been bribed to leave Kuwait.

This does not mean that economic power is irrelevant. As the cold war has waned, military security threats have diminished, thereby elevating the *relative* importance of economic issues. But matters of national security retain a higher priority in *absolute* terms. Economic power contributes only indirectly to a nation's security by generating wealth to channel toward that end. While an essential prerequisite, economic power still represents only one of several necessary variables in the equation of national power.

The myth of the decline of America. The image of the United States as a declining great power remains dear to the hearts and minds of many academics. They argue that America, hamstrung by domestic budget and foreign trade deficits and obsessed with consumer consumption, stood on the sidelines during the great events of 1989. Their premise is that all great powers experience periods of expansion, stability, and decline. They have traced this pattern through the rise and fall of Spain, Austria-Hungary, France, and Great Britain and claim to have detected the telltale symptoms that the United States is on the same path of inevitable decline.

While drawing such comparisons may be an interesting exercise in intellectual gymnastics, it creates false parallels and reveals shallow reasoning. With the discrediting of Marxism, we should reject all other arguments based on economic determinism. Great powers have risen and fallen for reasons other than economic ones. International influence depends not only on economics, but also on such intangibles as leadership, political skill, ideological and cultural appeal, domestic unity and will, and even blind luck. History does not move according to a fixed trajectory, but rather ebbs and flows. Many great powers consigned to the ranks of declining powers have risen from their deathbeds.

Those who advance this myth ignore the fact that the United States retains a dominant position in the world economy. It still has the highest overall productivity, has the strongest scientific and technological base, and ranks near the top in per capita income. The often-cited decline in America's share of the global economy—from 50 percent in 1950 to 25 percent in 1990—misreads reality. After World War II, Europe, the Soviet Union, and Japan lay in ruins, while the United States continued on its wartime boom. U.S. dominance represented a temporary distortion of normal economic balances, certain to be corrected as the world recovered from the war. In fact, America's current 25 percent share of world GNP—an impressive achievement by any measure—mirrors its proportion before World War II. U.S. GNP today is almost twice as great as Japan's, three times as great as the Soviet Union's, and four times as great as Germany's.

Many who discern a declining America are guilty of wishful thinking. They do not want to see the United States play a leadership role, promote its values and ideals, or serve as an example for others to follow. They should ask themselves this fundamental question: If the United States does not lead, who should? The only other nations with the potential resources to do so are Japan, China, the Soviet Union, and Germany. The United States not only has the resources to lead, but also has what all the others lack—the absence of any imperialistic aspirations or designs on other nations.

Today, as the only country that possesses global economic, military, and political power, the United States stands at the apex of its geopolitical power. If its status as the world's only superpower erodes, that will result from choice, not necessity.

The high expectations of a new era of peace and freedom in 1989 were crushed by the hard realities of 1990. The world saw its hopes for a more peaceful phase in world history dashed by a cascade of events from renewed repression in the Soviet Union to aggression in the Persian Gulf. Though developments around the world dealt severe blows to the dreams of 1989 in a new world order, these hopes were finally buried in the sands of Kuwait in 1990.

After playing off the reformers against the hard-liners and vice versa for five years, Gorbachev decisively rejected accelerated reform and allied himself with holdovers from the old regime in 1990, choosing reaction over reform. An improviser, not a strategist, he could not bring himself to bite the bullet on allowing private ownership of property and instead pursued the impossible objective of creating a halfway house between a market and planned economy. Having broken faith with the reformers, who then rallied to his rival, Russian federation president Boris Yeltsin, Gorbachev aligned himself with the reactionaries, who backed him not because of political loyalty but because they needed a front man to conceal their control of the levers of power.

The renewed ascendancy of the hard-liners quickly checked progress toward a more cooperative U.S.-Soviet relationship. After signing the Conventional Forces in Europe (CFE) treaty, Moscow brazenly violated its provisions, claiming that several armored divisions were exempt from treaty restrictions because they had been resubordinated to the Soviet Navy and Strategic Rocket Forces security units. In the START talks, Kremlin negotiators backpedaled on a succession of key compromises and obstructed the completion of the treaty for more than a year. Meanwhile, the relentless Soviet strategic forces modernization program continued unabated. More ominous, top Soviet leaders resuscitated Stalin-era rhetoric, accusing the United States of seeking to subvert their country. Though Gorbachev had denounced the "era of stagnation" under Brezhnev, he launched his own "era of reversion."

In Eastern Europe, euphoria gave way to a grim recognition of sobering realities. The odds against successful reform were stacked against the new democracies. A lack of domestic capital, willing foreign investors, modern technology, and well-trained managers was compounded by the loss of traditional markets and the danger of simultaneous hyperinflation and mass unemployment. To complicate matters further, all these problems had to be solved while politicians who had more experience in Communist prisons than democratic parliaments put into place entirely new political systems. While the anticommunist revolutions of 1989 represented a great step forward, they were only a first step on the long road to stable democratic government and market-based prosperity.

In third world regional conflicts, peace remained illusive. After the Red Army withdrew from Afghanistan, resistance forces liberated 80 percent of their country but failed to topple the Communist government in Kabul. Hunkered behind its Soviet-built fortifications and bankrolled with its $3-billion annual aid allotment, Kabul opted for stalemate instead of a just political settlement. In Cambodia, negotiations between the warring parties bogged down as their Communist leaders insisted on achieving through the fine print of an agreement what they had failed to win on the battlefield: uncontested power. In El Salvador, peace talks stalemated as the guerrillas tested U.S. staying power and escalated attacks and civil strife.

Elsewhere, promising developments went sour and hopeless situations grew worse. In the Philippines, the Aquino government betrayed its commitments to adopt market reforms and end corruption. The transition from the Marcos to the Aquino regime seemed only to replace one hand in the till with another. In Sri Lanka, ethnic warfare between the Tamils and the Sinhalese grew ever more violent. In South Africa, President Frederik W. de Klerk pressed ahead with reform, but the death toll from black-on-black violence climbed to more than five thousand, over five times the number of blacks killed by the apartheid regime in the past ten years. In Liberia, savage revolutionaries overthrew a brutal dictatorship and then turned on each other. In the West Bank and the Gaza Strip, communal violence continued, as Israeli military police killed over eight hundred Arabs and Arabs killed sixty-five Israelis. In Lebanon, the tortured life of a once-prospering country no longer even made the headlines.

Saddam Hussein dealt the final blow to the high hopes of 1989 for a new world order with his invasion of Kuwait in August 1990. His aggression violated every tenet of the "new era" in world affairs: a barbaric dictator flouted international law and world opinion by conquering and annexing militarily a weak neighbor. It brought back memories of Hitler and Stalin picking off small European countries one by one.

In 1991, we risked forgetting the hard lessons of 1990 amid the euphoria of the victory in the Persian Gulf and the defeat of communism in the Soviet Union.

President Bush masterfully orchestrated the world's response to Saddam Hussein's aggression. Sturdily supported by British prime minister Margaret Thatcher, he recognized the grave threat to Western interests and promptly deployed the military force needed to deter further Iraqi aggression. He skillfully forged a global coalition and won U.N. Security Council approval for the use of force. He mobilized sufficient forces to achieve a rapid and decisive victory and repeatedly articulated the rationale for U.S. actions in terms of our strategic interests and moral values. He set forth a clear list of political demands and explored every diplomatic channel from the Soviet Union to the Arab League to try to achieve them without war. When he ordered our troops into battle, he resisted the temptation to micromanage the military effort. After he achieved his fundamental military objectives and even after he shielded the Kurds from Saddam Hussein's wrath, he avoided the quagmire of playing kingmaker in

Iraqi internal politics. Though some believe he stopped too soon, it was a textbook case of superb presidential crisis management and wartime leadership.

Had we not intervened, an international outlaw would today control more than 50 percent of the world's oil. While the United States could survive if necessary without Persian Gulf oil, Western Europe and Japan could not. What happens to the economies of the other industrial democracies directly affects the health of our own economy. We therefore could not have afforded to allow Iraq to control access to Gulf oil and blackmail the world through its choke hold on our oil lifeline.

A far more momentous event than the Persian Gulf War followed five months later: Soviet communism committed suicide. Karl Marx once wrote that all great historical events happen twice, the first time as tragedy and the second time as farce. When the old Bolsheviks took power in the revolution of October 1917, they ushered in an era of unprecedented tragedy for the Russian and non-Russian peoples of the Soviet Union. When neo-Bolsheviks tried to overthrow Gorbachev in a coup in August 1991, they finally fulfilled one of Marx's prophecies: their putsch collapsed after a farcical three-day run on center stage.

The plotters were a Soviet version of the gang who could not shoot straight. When they decided to depose Gorbachev, they failed to understand how much his reforms had changed Soviet society. A freer press, laxer controls on social and political organizations, and free elections at the republic and local levels had toppled key pillars of the totalitarian order. Even the instruments of force—the army and the KGB—no longer responded to orders without questioning their legitimacy. The coup plotters were Stalinists who no longer commanded a Stalinist system.

They were not the only casualties of the revolution. Gorbachev as the central figure in Soviet politics and Moscow as the center of the Soviet empire also suffered devastating blows. The Soviet president, whose authority had eroded during six years of start-and-stop reform and economic deterioration, lost much of his remaining political standing by virtue of having appointed all the coup's ringleaders to their high positions. In the aftermath of the coup, Yeltsin and the leaders of the other Soviet republics eclipsed Gorbachev as the authors of the Soviet future, and virtually all of the non-Russian nations took advantage of the paralysis at the center to assert their political independence. They forced the center to take a series of steps—such as cutting nuclear arms and curtailing aid to client regimes—that the precoup government had opposed. Though Gorbachev returned and the central authorities survived, theirs was a hollow victory.

After the tumultuous events of 1989, 1990, and 1991, the time has come for America to reset its geopolitical compass. We have a historic opportunity to change the world. While many of our traditional security concerns have faded with the end of the cold war, many new political and economic issues have assumed a new importance. Our top priority must be to redefine America's global mission and reformulate its strategy.

After the Communist victory in Vietnam in 1975, many believed the United States could achieve nothing of value in the world. After the collapse of communism in Eastern Europe in 1989, many argued that we had nothing left to achieve. After the victory in the Persian Gulf in 1991, many concluded that we could achieve anything. After the new Soviet revolution in 1991, many asserted that America's leadership was no longer needed. All these views miss the mark. Today, for the first time, the United States stands as the world's only complete superpower. The key is how we choose to use this unprecedented power.

The Persian Gulf War highlighted America's unique position. No other country could have mobilized the world to defeat Saddam Hussein. Western Europe, economically powerful but politically fragmented, acted individually, not collectively. Japan, an economic heavyweight but military lightweight, only barely met its financial pledges. Germany, limited by its constitution and preoccupied with the bills for reunification, remained peripheral. The Soviet Union, struggling with its internal crises, reluctantly followed America's lead, but only diplomatically and not militarily. Only the United States, supported by Britain and France among the major powers, possessed the combination of economic, military, and political power needed to meet the challenge.

In the war's aftermath, two rival American traditions—isolationism and internationalist idealism—clashed again. Isolationists argued that the United States should quit serving as the world's 911 emergency number. Some of those on the isolationist left denounced aspirations to make America the world's policeman and demanded that resources be kept at home to solve pressing problems such as the underclass, drug addiction, and AIDS. Others argued that because of our faults at home, we were not worthy to lead abroad. Those on the isolationist right insisted that the defeat of communism eliminated the rationale for a global U.S. presence, that foreign aid wasted money on ungrateful foreigners, and that "America should come not just first but first, second, and third." In this unholy alliance, both counseled a retreat into comfortable isolationism.

The United States has too much at stake to heed that advice. Isolationists say, "Come home, America." But the security of our home in this politically, economically, militarily, and ideologically interdependent world is affected by changes everywhere. Walking away from global challenges will carry a dangerous price. History may once again produce nations aspiring to regional or global dominance. Proliferation of nuclear and ballistic missile technologies renders the oceans obsolete as buffers against aggression. With imports and exports comprising over 20 percent of our economy, our prosperity depends on international stability. Most important, an America withdrawn into isolationism would not be true to itself. Our values, derived from our religious tradition, demand public as well as private virtue. This does not imply an unlimited commitment to right every wrong, but does involve a moral imperative to use our awesome capabilities as the world's only superpower to promote freedom and justice in areas where our interests and our ideals coincide.

Idealistic internationalists argued that the United States enjoyed a unique opportunity to create a "new world order." Some insisted that we should launch a crusade to advance the democratic revolution around the world and that imposing democracy on Iraq through military force would have represented a vital initial step. Universal democracy, they argued, would not only guarantee the respect of human rights but would also ensure peace because a democratic state has never started a war. Others viewed the role of the United Nations as the key to victory in the Gulf War and called for the United States to make collective security and international law the centerpieces of its foreign policy. Their goal was not just a better world, but a perfect world.

These noble aspirations are unrealistic. Those who call for a global democratic crusade ignore the limits of our power.

Recognizing these limits does not mean that we should shrug off forces struggling to advance democracy or that we should give a green light to dictators poised to strike against fragile democratic regimes. But we do not have sufficient power to remake the world in our image. Even in the West, democratic government has existed for only two hundred years. Nations in Asia, Africa, and Latin America cannot develop overnight the traditions, cultures, and institutions needed to make democracy work. What works for us may not work for others. In these regions, democratic government does not necessarily mean good government. It could lead to majority repression of minorities and to mob rule that would make authoritarian rule enviable by comparison.

The advocates of a greater role for the United Nations ignore the abysmal record of collective security. Woodrow Wilson envisioned the League of Nations as the body that would make World War I the "war to end all wars." Yet within two decades the bloodiest war in history engulfed the world. In the more than one hundred wars since 1950, the U.N. adopted scores of resolutions condemning aggression, but took effective action in only two—the Korean War, when Moscow boycotted the Security Council debate and thus negated its veto power, and the Persian Gulf War, when all the major powers had a common interest in stopping Iraq. Because no great power will abdicate its right to defend its interests, the United Nations cannot operate successfully unless the major powers agree in advance. Though useful in slapping down minor aggressors, the U.N. will be paralyzed in any conflict that puts great powers on opposite sides.

Although President Bush has used the phrase "new world order," he does not share this woolly-headed idealism. In the Persian Gulf conflict, he used the U.N. rather than being used by the U.N. Moreover, as he explicitly stated, failure by the

U.N. to authorize "all necessary means" to liberate Kuwait would not have changed his course. Even without the U.N.'s blessings, the United States and its allies had the right to use force under the principle of a state's inherent right of individual or collective self-defense. President Bush clearly aspires to enlarge the constructive role of the U.N. as part of a "new world order." But he recognizes that no substitute exists for U.S. leadership and power. Where U.S. vital interests are threatened, the United States should act with the U.N. where possible but without it if necessary.

A new American mission in the world must be based not on the soft sand of unrealistic idealism but on the hard rock of enduring geopolitical realities. States have ideals and interests. To advance their interests, they acquire power, including military forces. In advancing interests, states often come into conflict. Without an umpire to settle disputes, such conflicts can—and almost certainly will—lead to war. These principles preceded the cold war and will survive the cold war. Unless the world transcends the current international system, we must accept them as immutable facts of life.

The sterile debate over whether we should have a policy of realism or one of idealism misses the mark. Idealism without realism is impotent. Realism without idealism is immoral. As Robert Kaufman has observed, *"Realpolitik* alone will not suffice to win the domestic support necessary to sustain an effective foreign policy. Americans must believe that U.S. foreign policy is right and legitimate as well as in our self-interest."

In charting our course, practical idealism and enlightened realism should guide our policies. The world has not changed to the extent that we can ignore the realities of power politics. But it has changed enough so that we can devote more resources and attention to issues other than security in the narrowest sense. Today, there are vast opportunities to paint on a wider canvas. The world, though not a blank canvas, is an unfinished work. We should make our mark, adding bold strokes and bright colors, not timid touches and pale pastels. Our motif should be the concept of practical idealism.

The first task is to distinguish between vital interests, critical interests, and peripheral interests. No country has the resources to defend all these interests with its own military forces all the time. As Frederick the Great observed, he who tries to defend everywhere defends nothing. Making strategy means making choices, and making choices means enforcing a set of clear priorities.

—An interest is vital if its loss, in and of itself, directly endangers the security of the United States. The survival and independence of Western Europe, Japan, Canada, Mexico, and the Persian Gulf states are vital to our own security. We also have a vital interest in preventing the acquisition of nuclear weapons by potential aggressors in the underdeveloped world. The United States has no choice but to respond with military force if necessary to turn back threats to these interests.

—A critical interest is one that, if lost, would create a direct threat to one of our vital interests. De Gaulle once observed that Central America is only an incident on the road to Mexico. Whittaker Chambers pointed out that the war in Korea was not just about Korea but also about Japan. Korea and Central America therefore are critical U.S. interests. We must recognize that the United States must sometimes treat critical interests as if they were vital as part of a prudent strategy of forward defense.

—A peripheral interest is one that, if taken by a hostile power, would only distantly threaten a vital or critical interest. While we would not want to see an aggressor seize a country such as Mali, we cannot conclude that such an event would endanger important American interests and require a military response.

Our overall security strategy must calibrate what we will do to protect an interest to its strategic importance. We should then match our capabilities—and the will to use them —to the threat we face. We should not send the Eighty-second Airborne Division to defend a peripheral interest in Mauritania, but we must not hesitate from doing so to defend a vital interest in the Persian Gulf.

Beyond its security concerns, the United States has a profound interest in the survival of democratic states, the expansion of economic prosperity through free trade and development, and the promotion of democratic forms of government. The level of commitment we make and the types of foreign policy instruments we use to pursue these values will vary widely. To secure our top priority among these values, the survival of threatened democratic states such as Israel or South Korea, we should be prepared to employ military force if necessary. But diplomacy, foreign aid, hardheaded negotiating, and sanctions will be the principal instruments to advance our lower-priority values. Our belief in these values is absolute, but our commitment to advance them in specific cases must be limited by our capabilities. The level of our response must be balanced against the costs, risks, and the possibility of success.

A policy of practical idealism may not be as emotionally satisfying as a clarion call "to bear any burden and fight any foe" to advance democracy or as a smug insistence on turning our backs to the complex problems of a troubled world. Americans usually respond to lifting rhetoric of idealistic crusaders, but just as often balk at staying the course when the crusade hits tough going. Practical idealism, with its limited objectives and measured commitments, offers a sustainable approach to global engagement. A world of opportunities exists today for major positive contributions by the United States. To take advantage of them, what is needed is not vast resources but creative ideas and sustained leadership.

—In the Soviet Union—where the Communist revolution of 1917 has been succeeded by the revolution of freedom in 1991—the noncommunist governments of the center and the republics are searching for a way to bring prosperity and progress to their long-suffering peoples. Our challenge is to help them find the way. We have a tremendous opportunity to shape the political system that will succeed the one built by Lenin and Stalin.

—In Europe—newly united after a half century of ideological division—we face the twin tasks of redefining NATO's mission and ensuring the success of the fragile new democracies of Eastern Europe. The most successful regional alliance in history, NATO should become the focal point of cooperative foreign policy initiatives by the world's industrial democracies. Helping Eastern Europe's postcommunist recovery must be a top priority, not only for its own sake, but also because the fate of reform there will profoundly affect the prospects for reform in the Soviet Union.

—Along the Pacific rim—the world's new economic locomotive—the lack of a comprehensive security framework keeps the region on edge. Moscow and Tokyo, estranged for more than fifty years, remain at loggerheads politically. Moscow and Beijing, after a wary rapprochement, remain divided by a long history of national and ideological rivalry. The region as a whole retains suspicions of Japan's ultimate geopolitical aspirations, particularly as Tokyo takes its first tentative steps in almost half a century on the world stage. Our role as the key balancer can enhance stability and ensure continued regional prosperity.

—In the Muslim world—turbulent, unstable, but vitally important—the forces of modernism, radicalism, and fundamentalism have been struggling to win the hearts and minds of the peoples of thirty-seven nations with a combined population of over 850 million. Whether they choose to follow the path of pro-Western modernism of Turkey, secular radicalism of Iraq, or obscurantist fundamentalism of Iran, the evolution of the Muslim countries will have enormous consequences for the entire world. How America and the West deal with the Muslim world will contribute significantly to which choice these countries make.

—In the underdeveloped world—where 78 percent of the human race lives—many nations face not dilemmas of development but crises of regression, as incompetent political leaders and senseless economic policies squander the resources and energies of some of the world's most capable people. We have the opportunity to take the lessons of the developing world's success stories—South Korea, Taiwan, Singapore, and Hong Kong—and help apply them to other societies, thereby creating the hope that future generations will escape the misery of grinding poverty.

—In the United States—the richest and strongest nation in the world—we confront pervasive domestic problems of crime, drugs, poor education, inadequate health care, racial discrimination, and urban blight. When Moscow's cold war expansionism threatened the survival of the West, foreign policy necessarily became our top priority. But today foreign and domestic problems should receive equal priority. Though they compete for our attention and resources, we need to engage ourselves on both fronts. Success abroad will bolster our confidence and unity at home, and success at home will enhance our prestige and leadership abroad. Above all, we must not allow our problems at home to blind us to the responsibilities and opportunities we have as the world's only complete superpower to provide needed leadership abroad.

Our mission was not completed with the defeat of communism. We must now work to ensure the success of freedom. Winning a revolution is not easy, but governing after winning is far more difficult. This is the challenge facing the new democracies in Eastern Europe and the new noncommunist governments in Moscow and the former Soviet republics. We must do everything possible to help them measure up to it. We should bear in mind that many East Europeans chose freedom primarily because they hated communism, not because they loved capitalism. Democracy, free markets, and private enterprise are on trial. If they fail, these nations could suffer massive disillusionment and even experience counterrevolutions, restoring not communism but other authoritarian or statist systems. Like coups, not all revolutions succeed. No revolution is permanent if it fails to produce a better life.

Just as the free world turned to America for leadership to confront the post–World War II Soviet threat, the world as a whole will look to America for leadership to grapple with the post-cold-war problems. For most of the world's people, the twentieth century has been a century of war, repression, and poverty. For the first time in history, there is a real chance to make the next century a century of peace, freedom, and progress. Today, only one nation can provide the leadership to achieve those goals. The United States is privileged to be that nation. Our moment of truth has arrived. We must seize the moment.

2

THE FORMER EVIL EMPIRE

A MULTINATIONAL EMPIRE, at its peak composed of more than a dozen nations, began to break apart. It was a relic of conquests accumulated over centuries, a mosaic of peoples with little in common except historical grievances against the imperial center and antagonisms toward each other. While Western capitals urged radical reform, a corrupt and dictatorial government—out of place in an increasingly democratic world—tried to pacify a sullen but increasingly assertive people. A rump parliament, partially elected but largely powerless, created more resentment than it defused. Doled out in half-measures, economic reform not only failed to cut the crushing fiscal burden of a huge standing army and parasitic bureaucracy but also increased prices for bread and other basic commodities while average wages dropped. Unable to collect taxes or enforce conscription, the center issued decree upon decree that vanished like water poured onto desert sands. As the center's power waned, disorder broke out in the provinces, prompting deployment of regular and special troops to suppress nationalists. With the leaders of the military and security forces gaining a decisive voice over government policies, the regime's base of support steadily narrowed. Within a few years, the empire collapsed as a result of a fatal crisis of legitimacy.

While this synopsis reads like recent news dispatches from the Soviet Union, it actually describes the demise of the Ottoman Empire in the late nineteenth and early twentieth centuries. As I visited the Soviet Union in March 1991, I sensed that I was witnessing the death throes of an old system and the birth pangs of a new one. When the coup by Communist hard-liners failed on August 23, 1991, the new "sick man of Europe" drew his last breath. The subsequent appointment of a noncommunist government and declarations of independence by a majority of the Soviet republics marked the passing of one of this century's great false faiths and most fearsome totalitarian systems. In the wake of the old regime came not the rise of a renewed Soviet Union but the birth of new nations, though it remains unclear whether they will be stillborn or develop into full members of the family of nations.

Any revolution contains as much potential for evil as for good. Soviet president Mikhail Gorbachev once said that the triumph of Lenin and the Bolsheviks in 1917 represented a "new dawn for humanity." In reality, it turned out to be the twilight before the fall of the totalitarian night. Just as the Chinese word for *crisis* is composed of the two characters for *danger* and *opportunity,* the situation we face combines both peril and promise. In toppling what President Ronald Reagan once called the "evil empire," the nations of the former Soviet Union have an opportunity to build a new order that is neither evil nor an empire. At the same time, they confront three dangers that could make the victory of freedom short-lived.

—The Soviet bureaucracy—the "system" that has ruled the country for seventy-five years—remains in the hands of members of the former Communist party. The danger is that they will use their power not to restore the old Communist order but to sabotage the new democratic order. By frustrating reform, they hope to create economic chaos that will lead to calls for a new authoritarianism based on a desire not for communism but for order.

—The Russian imperial tradition, the fundamental but unspoken pillar of support for the previous Communist regime, has retreated but not disappeared. The danger exists that at some point a demagogue will revive Russian imperialism by depicting the defeat of the Communist center as a defeat for the Russian nation. In such hands, the Kremlin might then use the ethnic Russian minorities in the former Soviet republics to try to reestablish Russian domination.

—Communism has been totally discredited, but socialism appeals to a broad spectrum of Soviet society. As a true believer in communism, Gorbachev consistently resisted genuine free-market reforms on ideological grounds. As democratic politicians, reformers may succumb to the allure of democratic socialism and may balk at the needed wrenching economic changes out of fear of the voters, who expect the security of fixed prices and guaranteed jobs and housing and fear the uncertainty of the market.

A wide range of views exists on what tack the West should take in responding to the Soviet crisis. Some urge that we pour in massive economic assistance to Gorbachev and the new noncommunist government to consolidate the victory of the reformers. Others contend that we must use aid to reverse the disintegration of the Soviet Union and prevent potential international "instability." Others say that we need a step-by-step aid program that will reward each increment of economic reforms with Western assistance. Still others hold that we should set our policy on cruise control, waiting for events to sort themselves out before we accelerate or hit the brakes on Western help to Moscow.

All of these arguments address only part of the issue. The key strategic question is not what kind of help we should give but what kind of successor to the Soviet Union we wish to see emerge from the current crisis. In this respect, we should seek to advance one key principle: democratic self-determination. We must not use aid to prop up the center—whether ruled by Gorbachev or Yeltsin—at the expense of the republics. With the death of communism, a stable order can be built only by recognizing the legitimate rights of nations to determine their own political destinies through democratic means. If the new noncommunist leaders in Moscow try to cobble together a new centralized union or federation, it will be an unstable one. If they allow each former Soviet republic to determine its relationship with the center—including the option of outright independence—the result will be a sturdy new commonwealth based on the natural economic ties mandated by proximity, interdependence, and market forces.

The Soviet revolution has opened up new vistas for constructive relations with the West. In the past, our conflicting values led us to look for the few areas where common interests permitted limited cooperation. Today, our growing common values have created almost limitless possibilities for developing cooperative projects that serve our mutual interests. The first item on our new agenda must be to resolve old business, the outstanding issues of the cold war, such as arms control and Moscow's aid to third world totalitarians. The second item must be to assist those former Soviet republics that take the needed and painful steps to transform their state-dominated economies into market-based ones. A policy of selective assistance that differentiates among republics on the basis of their commitment to economic and political reform will create powerful incentives for needed change.

While internal developments, not external aid, will determine what kind of system will replace the Soviet Union, its desperate economic crisis has given the United States unprecedented leverage over the course of events. The last of the world's great empires has now disintegrated. We should not assist those who seek to piece it back together. At the same time, we should recognize that the great victories of freedom will survive only if freedom succeeds. As the world's only superpower, we must not smugly enjoy the defeat of communism but rather roll up our sleeves to help ensure the victory of freedom.

I have traveled to the Soviet Union seven times since 1959, when I parried verbal jabs from Nikita Khrushchev in the Kitchen Debate. During my most recent trip in March 1991,

I met not only as I had in my previous visits with the top man—Khrushchev in 1959, Brezhnev in 1972 and 1974, and Gorbachev in 1986—but also with a wide range of government officials and political leaders. I had discussions with the head of the KGB, the interior minister, the defense minister, and other key players in the August coup. I met with Boris Yeltsin, who three months later would resoundingly win election as president of Russia and five months later would stand in heroic defiance against the coup plotters. I also discussed the course of events with former key members of Gorbachev's inner circle such as Eduard Shevardnadze, Alexander Yakovlev, and Leonid Abalkin, as well as with top officials and opposition leaders in Lithuania and in the republics of Russia, the Ukraine, and Georgia.

I discovered that before the coup three fundamental errors about the situation in the Soviet Union dominated the debate about Western policy. The first error was the idea that Gorbachev's government should be provided with massive economic assistance in order to support the course of reform. Some Western pundits and policymakers peddled the "grand bargain" under which foreign aid to the tune of $100 billion or more would underwrite the Soviet Union's transition to a market economy. But aid to Gorbachev's regime—which was dominated by the hard-liners who later tried to depose him—would have undercut, not advanced, the prospects for political and economic reform.

One newspaper editorialized that spurning aid to the Soviet president could deal "a mortal political blow to Gorbachev, in whose leadership the U.S. has invested so much hope for a continued improvement in East–West relations." Another argued, "Gorbachev and his country need help. It is fitting, and in America's interests, to join in supplying that help." Gorbachev played to this gallery. In his Nobel Peace

Prize speech in June 1990, he asserted that "the world needs *perestroika* no less than the Soviet Union," that "the Soviet Union is entitled to expect large-scale support to assure its success," and that if it fails "the prospects of entering a new peaceful period in history will vanish."

Moments after the hard-liners announced their seizure of power, the debate began over "who lost Gorbachev." Many in the West, including leaders such as German chancellor Helmut Kohl, claimed that the failure to shower Gorbachev with gifts of economic aid at the London summit had contributed to the Soviet president's ouster. That is fatuous nonsense. A helping hand to Gorbachev would have hurt the cause of democracy. Historically, the Russian and Soviet leaders have reformed only when under severe pressure domestically or internationally. Aid at that time would have been exploited by hard-liners to preserve the Communist system. As Andrei Sakharov said shortly before his death in 1989, "In the absence of radical reforms in the Soviet system, credits and technological aid will only prop up an ailing system and delay the advent of democracy."

Those who today claim that aid to Gorbachev would have prevented the coup ignore the fact that our aid would have gone to a cabinet dominated by the Soviet-style "gang of four":

—Valentin Pavlov, the prime minister, was steeped in the Stalinist practice of blaming external forces for domestic woes. In February 1991, he made groundless accusations that Western banks had conspired to try to undermine the ruble and thereby destabilize the Soviet economy. He then authorized the police and KGB to raid the offices of Western joint ventures without search warrants. When Gorbachev apparently bridged his differences with Yeltsin in April 1991, Pavlov fired a shot across the bow, independently asking the

Supreme Soviet to transfer powers from the president to the prime minister on the lame pretext that the head of state simply lacked the time to exercise these responsibilities.

—Dimitri Yazov, the defense minister, was an unapologetic advocate of reactionary defense and foreign policies. When I pointed out to him in our meeting that arms control could not go forward unless the Kremlin abandoned its attempt to evade CFE limits through the resubordination of three divisions to the naval infantry and other services, he replied that since the Soviet Union did not have a Marine Corps, it was entitled to such transfers to balance U.S. capabilities, breezily disregarding the fact that this still violated the letter of the treaty. In discussing the need to reduce the massive Soviet military budget, I observed that the Kremlin was spending at least 20 percent of its GNP on defense, while the U.S. allocated only 5 percent. He responded that the real Soviet figure was 12 percent of GNP, a patent falsehood based on vastly understated official figures. He then added that because the U.S. economy was "at least five or six times larger" than that of the Soviet Union, Washington was spending almost twice as much as Moscow on the military. As I listened, I was reminded of Khrushchev's earthy comment to me in 1959 that "statisticians are the kind of people who can melt shit into bullets."

—Boris Pugo, the interior minister and tough-minded former KGB chief in Latvia, was a throwback to the Brezhnev era. When I met with him, he engaged in a lengthy hard-line monologue. He blamed the "politicians" and "troublemakers" for generating the political and economic crisis. He insisted that the regime had to cut back on reforms in order to restore order and stability. He justified the use of force in the Baltic states—for which he fully accepted responsibility —as necessary to defend the ethnic Russian minorities living there, ignoring the fact that even the Russians voted over-whelmingly for independence a few days before we met. Until his suicide in the aftermath of the failed coup, Pugo continued to orchestrate bloody attacks by Soviet military and internal security forces against pro-independence republic governments and innocent civilians from the Baltics to Transcaucasia.

—Vladimir Kryuchkov, the steely head of the KGB, showed no sympathy for broader political reform. In the past, he had publicly accused reformers of taking their cues from the CIA and other Western intelligence services. In my meeting with him, he pulled no punches. While most hard-liners carefully cultivated the pretense of supporting reform, Kryuchkov did not bother. He blamed Gorbachev's reforms for a steep rise in crime and corruption. He called the revolutions in Eastern Europe "disastrous," not surprising coming from the man who had served as third secretary in the Soviet embassy in Budapest during the bloody suppression of the Hungarian uprising in 1956. When I raised the issue of Baltic independence, he dismissed it outright on the grounds that the United States would never entertain such an option for Puerto Rico! He also said that he had had "tough arguments" over reform with Gorbachev and did not know how long the Soviet president would keep him around because "he may get bored with me." Kryuchkov's vision for the Soviet future most resembled post–Tiananmen Square China: a mixed economy coupled with a totalitarian state. When I asked about the future of political reform, he bluntly replied, "We have had as much democratization as we can stomach."

If Western aid had started flowing before the August revolution, Pavlov, Yazov, and Kryuchkov would be sitting in power instead of sitting in jail. Those who touted the "grand bargain" failed to understand that without political reform, aid to Moscow would have been the "grand con job." Without genuine democracy, the choke hold of the Communist party apparatus on society would not have been broken, the people would have refused to accept the sacrifices inherent in the transition to the market, and the political process would have lacked the accountability needed to keep the reforms on track. Without democratic self-determination for the Soviet republics, political instability and the lack of an accepted framework of laws would have undermined even the best economic reform program.

While Gorbachev carries an American Express card, the idea that we should have given the precoup Soviet government a personal automatic-teller card to the U.S. Treasury has been thoroughly discredited by subsequent events. Such aid would have helped the very individuals who sought to return the Soviet Union to its Stalinist past and demoralized the reformers who ultimately prevailed in the August 1991 democratic revolution.

The second fundamental error in the conventional wisdom of Western analysts before the coup was that there was no better alternative to Gorbachev. That view might have been true in the first years of Gorbachev's rule. But it was outdated by 1991 and was totally refuted by the resistance to the coup. Although many Western diplomats and leaders were obsessed with supporting Gorbachev, reformers—led by Yeltsin but reinforced by key figures who had resigned from Gorbachev's inner circle and by new democratic nationalists in the republics—had already become a broad-based movement capable of governing the country.

When I received briefings on Yeltsin before my trip to the Soviet Union in 1991, I was reminded of the official assessments of Khrushchev in 1959. State Department and CIA briefers characterized Khrushchev as "oafish," dwelling on his habit of drinking too much in public, his poor Russian grammar, and the sartorial ineptitude of his floppy hats, short-sleeve shirts, and ill-fitting suits. But of all the leaders whom I have met in forty-six years of public life, Khrushchev had the quickest mental reaction time. He proved to be a strong leader, at times almost more than the West could handle. One of the briefers on Yeltsin in 1991 sounded like a recording of my 1959 briefing on Khrushchev. He was dismissed as an opportunistic lightweight who drank excessively, behaved erratically, spoke colloquial Russian, and was not in Gorbachev's league intellectually or socially.

After meeting for over an hour with Yeltsin, I found that some of my briefers had fallen victim to the tendency among many foreign policy analysts to mistake style for substance. While their observations might have been accurate factually, they were irrelevant politically. Politics is not learned from the pages of a textbook or a fashion magazine. It depends on ideas, organization, and charisma. Yeltsin was clearly a political heavyweight who could discuss complex subjects without aides present or notes for reference and who had an instinctive understanding of the people. He had proved his ability to marshal a nation-wide campaign, winning 60 percent of the vote in a multicandidate field. Both Gorbachev and Yeltsin possess genuine personal charisma—the intangible quality of leadership that no one can define but everyone can recognize—but each draws his support from a different audience. Gorbachev appeals to Wall Street, Yeltsin to Main Street. Gorbachev captures the elite in Georgetown drawing rooms, Yeltsin the workers at the Sverdlovsk factory gates. Gorbachev appeals to the head, Yeltsin to the heart. Gorbachev dazzles a crowd, Yeltsin moves a crowd.

Yeltsin is a better politician—in the Soviet setting—than

Gorbachev. Yeltsin is a combination of John Wayne and Lyndon Johnson. He is a two-pistol kind of man who radiates animal magnetism. He takes a no-nonsense approach and adopts categorical views. He expresses his opinions in earthy terms and can connect with the average person. Gorbachev is a Soviet version of Adlai Stevenson: intellectually brilliant, articulate on television, but unable to relate to the man in the street. He speaks tirelessly about abstract "processes in society" and "steadily unfolding phases of change" —rhetoric that thrills academics but that leaves people cold. Unlike Yeltsin, Gorbachev is profoundly uncomfortable in dealing with average Soviet people. Yeltsin likes retail politics, while Gorbachev likes boardroom politics.

Those Soviet experts who characterized Yeltsin to me as a demagogue who "believes in nothing but the desire for power" revealed shocking political superficiality. Yeltsin's views had grown, evolving to cope with the deepening Soviet crisis while Gorbachev's remained in the quagmire of Marxism-Leninism. Before the failed coup, Yeltsin had totally repudiated communism, while Gorbachev had not. Yeltsin supported private ownership of enterprises and land, while Gorbachev did not. Yeltsin supported immediate independence for the Baltic states, while Gorbachev did not. Yeltsin called for cutting off all aid to Cuba, Afghanistan, and other Soviet clients in the underdeveloped world, while Gorbachev did not. Yeltsin wanted to make major cuts in spending on the Soviet military, while Gorbachev did not. Yeltsin won office in a fully free election, while Gorbachev did not. Immediately after the coup, Yeltsin spoke of a bold democratic revolution, while Gorbachev spoke timidly of reforming the Communist party.

Yeltsin certainly aspires to power—as all politicians do— but that does not make him a demagogue. He wants power not for its own sake but for what he can achieve with it.

When I asked him whether he sought Gorbachev's job, he responded flatly that he did not, that ruling from the center would mean compromising principle. Shrewd calculation, as well as genuine conviction, clearly stood behind that decision. He knew that he could never win the support of the reactionaries who kept Gorbachev in power. To court their support, Yeltsin would have had to turn his back on democratic and market reform, a price that he refused to pay. Instead, he sought to defeat the center through an end run—winning power in the Russian republic, developing close political ties with other major republics that shared his values, such as Byelorussia and the Ukraine, and confronting Gorbachev with a reformist united front. It was the knowledge that Yeltsin's strategy was on the eve of success that prompted the Communist hard-liners to launch their coup.

Yeltsin's resolute leadership of the democratic revolution after the coup made him a world figure and exposed his critics in Western diplomatic and media circles as political amateurs. Because he proved them wrong, he has been pelted by a barrage of barbs and snipes in the press. One policymaker warned that he had "very serious questions about Yeltsin" and that the Russian leader displayed "undemocratic instincts." Another dismissed him as a politician with "an enormous ego" and "an instinct for what plays." Many criticized his decrees outlawing Communist party activities in Russia and his forceful exchanges with Gorbachev before a public session of the Russian parliament immediately after the coup. A major Western newspaper termed his behavior "worrisome" and condemned the way "he bulldozed a shaken Mr. Gorbachev in the autocratic style of the old apparatchiks." And a widely read columnist condescendingly sniffed at how he licked caviar and butter off his fingers at a state dinner in Washington.

Yeltsin is a victim of a blatant double standard. When

Gorbachev made 180-degree swings in his policies, western pundits and policymakers called it statesmanship. When Yeltsin made modest shifts in his positions, they called it opportunism. Those who call Yeltsin's democratic credentials into question have never scrutinized Gorbachev's. Their faith in Gorbachev has led them to overlook his often-reiterated fidelity to the communist ideology and to excuse his precoup alliance with the unrepentant reactionaries. When I was in the Soviet Union in March 1991, he called out more than fifty thousand troops to enforce his ban on demonstrations in central Moscow. But few of his Western supporters denounced him. Even though KGB thugs and Interior Ministry troops pummeled many of the five hundred thousand protestors who turned out despite his decree, the State Department spokesperson refused to reproach him. She argued that this situation was "no different than our own country," adding that if groups wanted to hold "a demonstration in Washington, D.C., they have to apply for a permit."

After the August coup, Western leaders who staked their political capital on a personal relationship with Gorbachev went bankrupt overnight. Those who belittled Yeltsin and who glorified Gorbachev made the critical error of confusing personal relations between leaders with political relations between great powers. Western policies toward Moscow should never have hinged so much on the fate of one man, even as remarkable a figure as Gorbachev. Fortunately for the Soviet people, the policy of backing Gorbachev "to the end," as one policymaker urged, turned out to be as futile as it was foolish.

Yeltsin has disproved Pushkin's observation in the nineteenth century that rebellions in Russia tend to be senseless and violent. While the Russian president unquestionably has the eloquence and charisma to incite a crowd to violence, he took power through ballots, not bullets. In the aftermath of the coup, he has sought to advance democracy through parliament, not through purges. In speaking of the violence of revolution, Lenin often remarked that you cannot make an omelette without breaking some eggs. If a few bruises to Gorbachev's ego were the cost of the peaceful triumph over the Soviet Communist system, it was a fair price to pay.

The third fundamental error prevalent in the Western policy debate before the August revolution was that nationalism in the Soviet republics was an unmitigated evil threatening to unleash instability and violence. In fact, the new nationalists not only gave the democratic movement in the Soviet Union its initial momentum but also provided indispensable strategic depth to the forces resisting the coup. The only fully free elections in Soviet history have been conducted not by Gorbachev and the center but by democratic nationalists in Russia and other republics. Moreover, if Yeltsin and the reformers in Moscow had been the only obstacle to the attempted Stalinist restoration, the coup leaders could have found enough card-carrying killers within the Soviet security apparatus to prevail. It was the fact that the democratic resistance commanded the loyalty of tens of millions across all fifteen republics that caused the Communist system to suffer a fatal breakdown of its political will.

In an age of nationalism, it was inevitable that loosening the Soviet Union's totalitarian order would produce an outburst of nationalist feelings. Communism was premised on the idea of a worldwide workers' revolution, in which the ideology transcended borders and nationalities. The failure of communism thus left the Soviet empire without a unifying ideology and gave the Soviet peoples an opportunity to reassert their national identities. Promoting democratic and market-oriented reforms while simultaneously fighting a rearguard battle to save the empire was impossible. The Soviet empire was put together and held together by force. The glue of the communist idea, which once enhanced unity, long ago lost its potency. Today, the new Soviet political order can remain intact only through the voluntary consent of the Soviet nations.

Before the coup, some Soviet spokesmen tried to sell the line that the West should help Gorbachev hold his country together. Just as Lincoln waged the Civil War to preserve the United States, they argued, Gorbachev needed to take whatever steps were necessary, including the use of force, to preserve the Soviet Union. Their analogy—which, tragically, even some leading Western statesmen parroted—was fundamentally flawed. While the United States is a multinational society composed of free individuals, the Soviet Union was a multinational state composed of captive nations annexed against their will. Legislatures in each of the thirteen colonies ratified the U.S. Constitution before it came into force, while Lenin and Stalin ratified the incorporation of fourteen republics into the Soviet Union through the use of force. In addition, while the union in the American Civil War fought for the higher moral cause of abolishing slavery, the secessionists in the Soviet crisis struggled for the higher principle of abolishing communism, another form of slavery.

The new sick man of Europe was doomed to die. The centrifugal nationalist forces within the Soviet Union did not stem from trivial origins. The Soviet nations opposed the center not out of a desire to fly their own flags or sing their own folk songs. They did so as a result of their profound traditions as sovereign nations—six of which had been either independent countries or part of another free country—and of the deep and abiding historical grievances of each against the brutality of the center's Communist rule:

—In the Ukraine, Stalin killed 5 million peasants during the collectivization of agriculture, 10 million through forced famines, and 3 million in suppressing the postwar guerrilla resistance, while more recently the Chernobyl disaster doomed an estimated 2 million people to premature deaths from cancer and other ailments.

—In Byelorussia, Stalin not only killed 100,000 people in purges and repression in the 1930s but also doomed 1.5 million people and 75 percent of the republic's cities and towns to death and destruction through his half-witted military strategies in World War II.

—In the Baltic republics, more than 150,000 Lithuanian, Latvian, and Estonian guerrilla fighters died resisting Soviet rule after World War II, while another 540,000 were killed in purges or exiled to Siberia.

—In Moldavia, a young Leonid Brezhnev orchestrated the postwar subjugation of the newly annexed Romanian territory, ordering thousands of executions and shipping off 30,000 people to Siberian labor camps.

—In the Caucasian republics, 100,000 Azerbaijanis, 30,000 Georgians, and tens of thousands of Armenians were imprisoned, tortured, or killed under Stalin, with Armenia's prisons so full at some points that basements of government buildings were converted into makeshift jails.

—In the Central Asian republics, Stalin crushed the anticommunist guerrilla forces that fought Moscow into the 1930s, while Khrushchev's "virgin lands" campaign triggered a massive influx of Russian colonists and Brezhnev's harebrained agricultural and development schemes wreaked ecological disaster throughout the region.

In light of the scope of these human tragedies—which have

no parallels in American history—it was totally unreasonable to expect these nations to use their growing political freedom under Gorbachev to seek a new union with Moscow as its dominant political center.

Reform leaders in the non-Russian Soviet republics have more in common with Walesa and Havel, who opposed communism from the outside, than with Yeltsin and Shevardnadze, who at first tried to reform the system from within. Lithuania's Vytautus Landsbergis, Latvia's Anatolijs Gorbunovs, Estonia's Arnold Ruutel, the leaders of the Ukrainian Rukh movement, and other democratic leaders at the republic level sought not only freedom but also independence for their nations. In the republics, strategies based on working within the system were discredited because to be part of the system was to betray the nation. As a result, the new republic leaders were not reform-minded Communists like Gorbachev but nationalists who led democratic popular fronts and who sought to free their nations through elections.

I must admit to a measure of skepticism when I was introduced to Lithuanian president Landsbergis, who had been a professor of musicology before entering the political arena. I tend to agree with the observation of an eighteenth-century European king who said, "The cruelest way to punish a province is to have it governed by professors." With notable exceptions, such as Woodrow Wilson, great professors are seldom good executives. I have found that they tend to become mired in irrelevant trivia, to flit from one intellectual fad to another, and to lack the decisiveness needed in politics. But I soon discovered in the course of our exchanges that this musician was a very strong leader who talked pianissimo but acted forte.

In our conversation, Landsbergis mentioned that his favorite literary quotation was a line from Ibsen's *Enemy of the*

People: "The strongest man in the world is he who stands most alone." The Lithuanian president personifies the concept better than almost any leader I have met. Like Charles de Gaulle in World War II, Landsbergis knew that his only source of power was his absolute inflexibility on matters of principle. His insight and personal will enabled him not just to navigate the perilous course that ultimately led to the restoration of his country's independence after fifty-one years of Soviet occupation. In concert with Yeltsin's Russia, he and the other democratic nationalists in the non-Russian republics served as the indispensable backstop in the victory of the August 1991 revolution.

It was ironic that many Americans, particularly within the foreign policy elite, viewed the new nationalists in the Soviet Union with disdain or contempt. That has not been our traditional—and historically vindicated—approach to nationalism. Few other forces inspire loyalties as strong as patriotism. International stability requires the great powers to accommodate legitimate nationalist aspirations while reproaching the excesses of extremists. With the death of communism as an ideology, the force of nationalism inevitably— and rightly—has become the decisive element in defining the future of the Soviet Union.

Since Woodrow Wilson, American presidents have recognized the legitimacy of nationalist movements around the world. At Versailles, Wilson helped oversee the birth of the new nations of Eastern Europe. Roosevelt and his immediate successors pressed Britain and France to grant their colonies independence. During the French war in Indochina, Truman and Eisenhower kept their distance in order to avoid tainting America with European imperialism. During the Suez crisis, Eisenhower forced the British, French, and Israelis to abandon their attempt to retake the canal by force. It makes no

sense for the United States to have pressed for the dismantling of the British and French empires, which were based on
the values of European civilization, and yet to have attempted to prop up the Soviet empire, which was based on
the ideology of communism.

These fundamental policy errors were rooted in a misunder-
standing of the Gorbachev era. Gorbachev has profoundly
changed the world and the Soviet Union. But to understand
him—and to comprehend why he failed—we must look not
just at his actions but at why he took them.

Many in Western media and diplomatic circles uncritically
embraced Gorbachev as the champion of world peace and
democracy. In 1990, *Time* magazine named him "man of the
decade," remarking, "He is the force behind the most momentous events of the 1980s and what he has already done
will almost certainly shape the future." One newspaper commented, "No single individual alive today has more impacted
the course of modern history and directly contributed to a
climate for world peace than has this Soviet President. Future
historians will divide the post–World War II era in terms of
'before Gorbachev' and 'after Gorbachev.' " Another editorialized, "Gorbachev has solidified his place as one of the
world's greatest peacemakers," adding, "perhaps the United
States could use a leader such as Mikhail Gorbachev." Still
another opined, "Gorbachev is a prophet." He was also
awarded the Nobel Peace Prize for his "decisive" contributions toward easing East-West tension and advancing disarmament. Former president Reagan called the Nobel
committee's choice "wonderful," while former prime minister Thatcher called it "terrific" and Chancellor Kohl remarked that he was "delighted."

For six years, Gorbachev stood at the center of the deepening crisis. A complex man who rose to power under Brezhnev and Andropov but who ultimately rejected much of their political and economic legacies, he has impressed the world with his personal grace, powerful intellect, and acute political sense. He has supreme self-confidence, iron self-control, and a healthy degree of self-esteem. Not as quick as Khrushchev, Gorbachev carefully thinks through a proposition before he speaks. He is an *homme sérieux,* in both the literal and broader senses. Khrushchev tried to cover up Soviet weaknesses by bragging outrageously about Soviet superiority. Brezhnev had without question achieved nuclear parity, but still never missed an opportunity to insist defensively that the Soviet Union and the United States were equals as world powers. Gorbachev was so confident of the Soviet Union's strengths that he was not afraid to talk about its weaknesses.

But Gorbachev was not, and is not, a closet democrat, secret capitalist, or furtive pacifist. Those who portray him as such miss the point. Gorbachev is not a one-dimensional personality. He is a troika: a loyal Communist, a patriotic Russian nationalist, and a brilliant pragmatic politician who likes power, knows how to use it, and will do whatever he believes necessary to keep it.

In overhauling Soviet foreign policy and launching domestic reforms, he acted not out of choice but necessity. In 1985, shortly after Gorbachev took power, I asked Hu Yaobang, then the general secretary of the Chinese Communist party, whether the new Soviet leader would adopt economic reforms similar to China's. "If he does not," he answered, "the Soviet Union will disappear as a great power by the middle of the twenty-first century." Hu was right: Gorbachev had no other option. To preserve the Soviet Union's status as a great power, he had to retrench abroad and reform at home.

For over seventy years, Soviet economic policy served Soviet foreign policy. Under Gorbachev, foreign policy served economic policy. But it was a change of the head, not the heart. He knew that without access to Western technology, capital, and markets the Soviet economy would remain dead in the water. In each reversal of policy, he knew that he had to make whatever sacrifices were necessary to create an economic lifeline to the West:

—In third world regional conflicts such as Afghanistan, Angola, and Nicaragua, Moscow was wasting tens of billions of dollars and thousands of lives—plus alienating all of the world's major powers—in order to advance at best peripheral interests. Gorbachev chose to scale back Moscow's direct engagement in those conflicts, even at the risk of losing his clients.

—When anticommunist revolutions erupted in Eastern Europe, Moscow faced the choice between preserving its Communist regimes through force but losing the goodwill of Western Europe or permitting the collapse of empire but winning new and wealthy allies in Western Europe. Gorbachev chose to lose his satellites in the East in order to win support and aid from the West.

—With a resurgent United States under President Reagan embarking on its high-tech Strategic Defense Initiative (SDI) —which threatened to neutralize the Soviet advantage in first-strike land-based missiles—Moscow confronted the need to ante up hundreds of billions of rubles to stay in the game. After doggedly trying and failing to stop SDI through arms control, Gorbachev recognized after checking with his banker that the Soviet Union had to fold its hand.

—In the Persian Gulf War, Moscow had to choose between supporting its traditional ally, Iraq, and retaining its newly won respectability in the West. Though the Soviet Union helped Saddam Hussein covertly with military advisers and spare parts and sought to save him from decisive defeat through last-minute diplomacy, Gorbachev ultimately endorsed the U.S.-led coalition's use of force to liberate Kuwait and to cut Iraq down to size. Gorbachev is not a stupid man. Faced with a choice of Iraq or the West, he chose the West.

As a pragmatic politician, Gorbachev sought to combat the apathy of the Soviet people by denouncing the Stalinist past, allowing criticism of the current system, and decentralizing some power to the republics. He also chose to shake up the Soviet establishment through *glasnost,* to seek leverage over the *nomenklatura* through the threat of further democratization; and to try to solve Soviet economic failings through *perestroika.* As a loyal Communist, however, he could not bring himself to cut his umbilical cord to the Communist party. He refused to institute genuine democracy— the Soviet people were still denied the power to change their central government through the ballot box—or to run in a competitive election himself. He rejected proposals to legitimize private property and to free prices. As a Russian nationalist, he refused to allow the non-Russian nations to exercise their constitutional right to secede, instead contriving a secession law harder to work than Rubik's Cube.

To ask whether Gorbachev was sincere begs the question. Unlike his predecessors, he recognized the fundamental inhumanity of the system founded under Stalin. But like his predecessors, he sincerely believed that the ideology of communism remained the solution, not the problem. "I am a Communist, a convinced Communist," he said in 1990. "For some that might be a fantasy. But for me, it is my main goal." He reaffirmed this view in early 1991, saying, "I am a Communist and adhere to the communist idea. And with this I will leave for the other world."

In November 1990, Gorbachev gave a candid speech to

Soviet intellectuals that provided great insight into his heart-felt views. He described a conversation he had had with Shevardnadze in March 1985, shortly after taking power. Reflecting on the course of Soviet history, Shevardnadze had said that since the 1917 revolution "everything had gone rotten." Gorbachev had stated that he concurred, that "we could not live as we had lived previously." But in the rest of the speech he indicated that on two principles—retaining socialism and keeping the Soviet Union intact—he would not budge. He said, "There are the founders of *Moscow News,* and they will say, 'President, stop assuring us and swearing that you are a follower of socialism.' But why should I stop if it is a profound conviction of mine? I will not stop; I will not stop as long as I have the opportunity of doing things precisely in such a way." On retaining the union, he insisted, "We must not split up. I came and said honestly at a Supreme Soviet session: 'We cannot split up, comrades. Whether we like it or not, this is how things have turned out for us. If we begin to split up, there will be a war, a terrible war.' "

Gorbachev's adamant refusal to abandon the discredited doctrine of socialism and to move away from the center's imperial domination of the republics soon isolated him from the growing Soviet pro-reform movement. Outpaced by his own reforms, he resorted to rhetorical inflation, praising "democracy" and "free markets" and eventually even calling communism "an outdated ideological dogma." But his actions did not measure up to his words. Increasingly, he appeared to become yesterday's man. His Communist beliefs and his Russian nationalism were blinders constraining his vision of the Soviet future. Like a circus performer on a high wire, he swayed from side to side, never too far one way or the other. He knew that if he fell, there would be no safety net to catch him.

A key turning point came in September 1990, when he rejected the Shatalin five-hundred-day plan to transform the Soviet system into a market economy. He then swung decisively to side with the reactionary forces of the Communist old guard—the *nomenklatura,* the economic central planners, the KGB, and the military top brass. Real reformers turned against him and called for accelerated change, not retrenchment, insisting only full democracy and free-market economics could save the country. The brightest and the best left him and joined Yeltsin. He was left with yes-men, second-raters, and hard-liners who used him rather than serving him. The problem was not just that Communist hard-liners occupied the seats in the cabinet room but that their ideas formed part of Gorbachev's mind-set. The hard-liners were not an incidental part of his administration but an integral part of his vision.

In making common cause with the reactionaries, Gorbachev rolled back some of his own reforms. He curtailed *glasnost,* sharply limiting the permissible criticism and opposition views presented in the media, particularly on television. Though he denied giving the orders, he endorsed after the fact the actions of security forces that led to the killing of twenty-one people by the brutal OMON internal security forces in Latvia and Lithuania. He denounced cooperatives even though they accounted for only 1 percent of GNP in 1990. He recentralized economic controls to strangle budding private enterprise. And in January 1991, he launched a much-heralded economic reform plan worthy of a Brazilian junta: its centerpiece was a confiscation of high-denomination currency that only served to further undercut confidence in the ruble.

In April 1991, Gorbachev appeared to recognize that he had turned down a dead end. Hard-line allies could guarantee his grip on power, but they provided no program to rebuild the country. Meanwhile, the reformers were gaining strength, with Yeltsin only weeks away from a massive mandate in the presidential election in the Russian republic. Gorbachev backpedaled toward the reformers. He initialed an agreement on the future of reform and a new union treaty with Yeltsin and the leaders of eight other republics, moving in some ways toward a more reformist line.

While Gorbachev had temporized, however, the reform movement had taken on a momentum of its own. Independent democratic political parties took root. The press refused to be shackled again. The Communist party suffered a hemorrhage of resignations, with 25 percent of its 20 million members breaking ranks in a pell-mell struggle to escape a sinking ship. Despite their minority status, pro-reform factions in the Supreme Soviet and the Congress of People's Deputies managed to hamstring some antidemocratic legislation. All fifteen republic governments declared their sovereignty and asserted the supremacy of their laws over those of the center. Six republic governments held free and fair elections, with their new leaders openly challenging the Kremlin in what Gorbachev called a "war of laws." Among the people, fear of the once-mighty regime evaporated. Massive pro-democracy rallies—numbering in the hundreds of thousands —took place in Moscow and other cities, some even in defiance of explicit decrees from Gorbachev. This trend culminated in June 1991 with the resounding victory of Boris Yeltsin in a free presidential election in the Russian republic.

When the Communist hard-liners temporarily ousted Gorbachev two months later, they soon discovered that the smooth overthrow of Khrushchev in 1964 could not be reenacted. Before Gorbachev, Soviet leaders could intimidate the entire country by repressing a few dissidents. But Gorbachev's reforms had corroded the system. While the coup leaders controlled the levers of power, those levers no longer flawlessly operated the machinery of repression. Kryuchkov, Yazov, and Pugo gave the orders to crack down, but their subordinates opted not to carry them out. Even if the coup had not collapsed within sixty hours, it would have soon degenerated into a replay of the downfall of the East German regime, with massive demonstrations and general strikes in Moscow and other major cities overwhelming the capacity of the state to suppress them with force.

Gorbachev failed at first to understand that he returned from captivity to a changed nation. Even before the coup, he had two political strikes against him. The first was his responsibility for the collapse of the Soviet economy. No Western democratic leader could possibly survive the fallout after a 15 percent drop in the economy over one year. The second strike was his position atop the Communist establishment. He won no friends by ruling the house that Stalin built and perpetuating the system of parasitical privileges for the Soviet elite. Yet while down in the count, he was not yet out. He could have gotten ahead of the pitcher if he had resigned from the party, accepted genuine democracy, accelerated market-oriented reform, and permitted self-determination for the republics immediately upon his return to Moscow. Instead, by proclaiming that he would "fight to the end for the renewal of the party," he went down without swinging.

Just as history has bypassed communism, it has also bypassed Communists. Gorbachev will now have to face not only the polls but also a near certainty that he will lose. Before the coup, Gorbachev's only constituency was the Communist party. After the party betrayed him and the reformers scorned him, he was left with a constituency of one —himself. In viewing Gorbachev as indispensable, many in the West assumed that any alternative to him would be worse. In fact, the alternative—Boris Yeltsin—may turn out to be better.

History will view Gorbachev as a transitional figure, a bridge between a system based on communism and one based on freedom. He was too closely associated with yesterday's tyranny and today's disorder to lead tomorrow's reforms. While he took the crucial first steps down the road toward peaceful change, the people will make the rest of the journey without him. As a reforming Communist, Gorbachev followed Bismarck's maxim, "If there is a revolution, we would rather make it than suffer it." For seventy-five years, Gorbachev's party made a Communist revolution, while the people suffered it. In August 1991, the people made their own democratic revolution. And now Gorbachev must suffer it.

While the upheaval in the Soviet Union swept the old regime away, no revolution can wipe the slate of history clean. Vestiges of the past stand alongside opportunities for the future. All-too-familiar problems confront the new noncommunist leaders: the deepening economic crisis, the redefinition of relationships among the elements of the former Soviet Union, and the construction of a viable postcommunist political system. Toppling a corrupt old regime was far easier than erecting a just new order. In the euphoria of the moment, we must not forget that along with great opportunities, Soviet reformers now face profound dangers.

In any revolution, two battles must be fought, one over ideology and one over control of the state. The democratic forces have won the first and prevailed in the first major clash of the second. The looser restrictions on the Soviet press had made the Soviet Union, as one hard-liner acidly remarked, "the most anticommunist country in the world." But the victory of freedom will not be secure until new democratic institutions are firmly in place. Events will take many different turns. Since our interests will be profoundly affected by how they play themselves out, we cannot afford a policy of passively wishing the reformers well from the sidelines.

All former Soviet republics have claimed sovereignty and asserted the supremacy of their laws over Moscow's. It is inevitable that virtually all will follow up with full declarations of independence. Managing economic ties forged during seventy-five years of union, such as electrical power grids and natural gas pipelines, will require some kind of mechanism until the republics get on their own feet economically. Kremlin leaders will probably rule neither a federation nor a confederation but rather will oversee a loose economic commonwealth. The center will coordinate, not govern, the actions of republics. While it may control defense and foreign policies initially, the republics will take over even these tasks as they acquire the necessary capabilities. As they do so, the Soviet Union will complete an evolution from an evil empire to a voluntary commonwealth of free and equal nations.

Another potential course of events leads toward a more troubling destination: the eventual rise of a new imperial center based not on communism but on Russian nationalism. History offers few examples of one-round victories even for causes as noble as the August 1991 revolution. The situation in the Soviet Union is unstable and the ultimate outcome unpredictable. The Soviet scene is strewn with political tinder that could ignite into a conflagration. A Russian imperial tradition stretching back four centuries, a cadre of more than 15 million defrocked but unrepentant hard-line Communist bureaucrats still in positions of power, a Russian republic dominant in resources and military might, a national mosaic that scattered tens of millions of ethnic minorities in the newly independent and often highly nationalistic republics, a people increasingly desperate as the economy plunges into a deep depression—all these could spawn a variety of deadly scenarios. While these threats appear distant as we savor the victory over communism, the difficulties in achieving economic recovery could bring them closer.

The initial steps taken by Gorbachev and Yeltsin in the aftermath of the coup have directed events along the path toward some kind of commonwealth. The replacement of the Communist-dominated Congress of People's Deputies with a new republic-appointed interim Supreme Soviet and Moscow's acceptance of all republic declarations of independence and sovereignty in September 1991, including freeing the Baltic states after fifty-one years of Soviet domination, laid the cornerstone of the new order. With the center conceding its primacy, the focus of politics has shifted from the halls of the Kremlin to the capitals of the republics. Moreover, as long as Yeltsin remains committed to establishing democracy in Russia and the legendary capacity of the Russian people to endure difficult times is not exhausted, the temptations inherent in the Russian imperial tradition or other forms of political extremism will be kept in check.

But the current situation is replete with potential dangers. Leaders other than Yeltsin might tap into a vein of political radicalism at some point. The people might not continue to support moderates such as Yeltsin if economic conditions fail to turn around in the near future. Four other factors could also turn events down a darker path:

—A dangerous logic supports an eventual alliance between the remnants of the Communist party and extreme Russian nationalists. Because both suffered severe reverses after the

August 1991 revolution—the dissolution of the party and the breakup of the traditional Russian empire—they are natural allies against the new noncommunist leaders. An obvious strategy would be to portray the democrats as leaders who "stabbed Russia in the back" and to seek a resurrection of the center's power as a means to restore Great Russia and to provide a new mission for the country.

—In addition to their overwhelming support for democracy, the Soviet people harbor a traditional desire for order imposed from above. This impulse continues to insinuate itself into popular thought even today. Opinion polls indicated many Soviet citizens had disdain for Gorbachev's inability and unwillingness to govern with what they called "the strong hand." Many wanted him not only to take decisive action but also to crack heads to make his policies stick.

—Interethnic tensions that crosscut every corner of the former Soviet Union represent an explosive source of conflict. The potential battle lines are drawn not only between the Russians and the non-Russians but also among the non-Russians. Gagauzi are pitted against Moldavians; Armenians against Azerbaijanis; Abkhasians, Ossetians, Adzhars, and Meshketi Turks against Georgians; Kazakhs against Uzbeks and Turkomans; Tadzhiks against the Uzbeks; and scores of other smaller ethnic groups in each former republic against those in the majority. Over the past five years, these conflicts sometimes turned into violent clashes that killed 1,000 people, injured 8,500, and sent 700,000 fleeing their homes. More such violence—particularly if directed at ethnic Russian minorities—could easily feed the rise of extremism and provide an ideal pretext for intervention by a newly assertive imperial center.

—Despite their victory in the August 1991 revolution, the reformers are not an invincible movement. They lack political unity and administrative talent. Some analysts estimate that more than three hundred new anticommunist parties and groups—such as the Democratic Union, the Popular Front, Constitutional Democrats, Social Democrats, Movement for Democratic Reforms, the Russian Democratic party, the Democratic party of Russian Communists, and the Republican party of Russia—have sprung up nationwide. Their administrative weakness undermines their ability to take over the vast bureaucratic empire of the state and leaves them vulnerable to more organized and better marshaled political forces. The fragmentation of empire has been followed by the fragmentation of parties.

Perilous historical analogies can be drawn to the tumultuous change sweeping the former Soviet Union. We could see a replay of the Bolshevik Revolution, with a fragile democratic order crushed by a reactionary coup. We could see a reprise of the fall of the Weimar Republic, with an economically wounded democratic government gradually eclipsed by ultranationalists promising renewed glory. We could see a variation on the toppling of the Fourth Republic in France, with colonists under siege in a distant outpost conspiring in a coup with imperial hard-liners at the center. The restoration of Communist rule in the republic of Tadzhikistan through a coup is a sign of the kinds of dangers that could lie ahead.

These are not grounds for panic, but they are powerful arguments against complacency. In fact, though the most likely outcome in the short term is a new commonwealth, the rise of a new imperial center will remain an ominous outlying possibility in the longer term.

Promoting the principle of democratic self-determination should be the hallmark of our policy. For a multinational state ruled by a dominant nation with long-standing imperial traditions, a direct contradiction exists between democracy and unity. In the wake of democratic reform, smaller nations will inevitably exploit democracy to free themselves from the unity imposed by the center. And if the center insists on political unity, it will be inexorably driven to dismantle democracy. We must recognize that the defeat of Moscow's imperial rule was an indispensable precondition for securing the triumph of freedom and democracy.

Democratic self-determination involves two elements. First, nations must be allowed to exercise their right to choose their own destinies through democratic means. To reject this right *a priori* would deny our own heritage. Second, nations that exercise that right must uphold democratic values—especially in terms of respect for the rights of minorities—in their own societies. To insist on the first but overlook the second would open the door to new tyrannies at the republic level. While it involves close case-by-case judgment calls, promoting democratic self-determination is the only approach to the Soviet political crisis consistent with our fundamental values.

Today, the worst mistake we could make would be to build up the power of the center. Those who want to prop up Gorbachev in order to avoid the dangers of "instability" misunderstand the situation. There are two kinds of stability—the dynamic stability of a system based on consent and the rigid stability of one based on coercion. The history of Moscow's domination of the republics proved that rulers can maintain stability through force. But the lesson of Gorbachev's limited reforms is that the system could not survive after the screws of state repression had been loosened. As a result, real and enduring stability for the former Soviet Union lies in a decentralized system based on democratic self-determination. We should not sacrifice democracy or self-determination on the altar of stability. While the risk of some instability is a price worth paying for freedom, stability at the price of freedom is not worth the cost.

Instead of inadvertently helping the antidemocratic forces at the center, we should be guided by a simple principle: if you want reform, help the reformers; if you want democracy, help the democrats. By launching a few key initiatives, we can enhance the prospects for the democratic evolution of the post-Soviet system:

Expand contacts with democratic republic governments. We should extend a hand of cooperation—and when appropriate, diplomatic recognition—to those who respect democratic values. By associating ourselves with democratic nationalists and distancing ourselves from undemocratic leaders, we can exercise a subtle but constructive influence over the political evolution of the republics. As democrats take power, U.S. policymakers should meet with them, not just for photo opportunities, but also for substantive discussions to hammer out agendas for mutual cooperation.

We should give a cold shoulder to undemocratic republic leaders, especially those that tolerate or encourage persecution of ethnic minorities. Some ethnic tensions and violence are inevitable. Moscow's henchmen in the republics have stoked these passions for decades as part of their divide-and-rule strategy. Moreover, during the decades of totalitarian repression, these nations lacked the opportunity to work out their differences through mutual accommodation. Our policies should reach out to help those leaders who are part of the solution rather than the problem.

Encourage republics to make a clean break with the Communist past. We should remind new democratic leaders of the need to remove systematically Communists who still hold positions of power. As Franz Kafka warned, "Every revolution evaporates, leaving behind only the slime of bureaucracy." Before reform can succeed, Soviet society must be cleansed of the slime of seven decades of communism. For the most part, the Soviet people know this lesson better than we do. They know that communism pervades virtually every level of society through ubiquitous party functionaries. They know that ridding the country of its Communist icons—such as statues of Lenin and hammer-and-sickle emblems—is not enough. They know that real reform in the former Soviet Union can only come when holdovers from the old regime are swept out of office.

Those who criticize Yeltsin for supposedly conducting "witch-hunts" against Communists should remember that the world applauded the purge of Nazis in postwar Germany and the war crimes trials at Nuremberg and that peace under Soviet communism killed twice as many people as the wars of German Nazism. Like Nazism, communism is a malignant cancer, and it must be cut out root and branch.

Press nondemocratic republic governments to hold free legislative and presidential elections. Despite the victory of democratic forces in the August 1991 revolution, only a handful of republics of the Soviet Union have governments chosen in free and fair elections. As a result, the United States should not only press for rapid democratic evolution among the former republics but also link the level of our contacts and cooperation to their progress toward democracy. The National Endowment for Democracy, for example, should place top priority on projects enhancing party organization and media diversity in these areas. Because of his legitimacy as the elected president of Russia, Yeltsin dictated the post-coup agenda to Gorbachev, thereby forcing the Soviet president to move decisively toward democratic reform. If other republic leaders follow in Yeltsin's footsteps in facing the voters, together they could form a united front that could win any battle over the shape of the new Soviet commonwealth.

Expand educational and cultural exchange programs with the former Soviet republics. Throughout the former Soviet Union, a desperate desire exists for contact with the West and particularly the United States. In light of this democratic revolution, we should aggressively advance people-to-people exchanges, placing special emphasis on developing a program that sends U.S. teachers to work in schools and universities in the former Soviet republics. We should work to distribute books about democratic government and market economics. Most important, instead of phasing out Radio Liberty, we should increase its broadcasts, dedicating much of the additional time to teaching actual skills—such as accounting—that will be needed in a market economy.

Channel humanitarian aid through international relief organizations or democratic republic governments. The United States should never send humanitarian aid through the central government. Much of the assistance sent to the victims of the Armenian earthquake and the Chernobyl disaster never reached the intended recipients but got lost in a maze of bureaucratic red tape. Even worse, recent Western grants of food assistance have been distributed through the KGB, which exploited them for political purposes. In the future, if we want our help to reach the most needy, we need to work with those in the republics who share our values.

How we pursue these policies will be shaped by how we handle the two top leaders of the former Soviet Union. Gorbachev and Yeltsin are the odd couple. They do not like each other. In part, this is because of style. Both were born peasants. Gorbachev became an aristocrat, while Yeltsin remained a peasant. Gorbachev is a man of the world, while Yeltsin is a man of the people. Their dislike for each other also stems in part from substance. They started together as Communists, but they now have profoundly different beliefs. Gorbachev remains a Communist, while Yeltsin turned in his membership card almost two years ago.

Within the foreign policy establishment, a great debate rages about which leader—Gorbachev or Yeltsin—America should deal with. That controversy is naive and parochial. The Soviet people, not the foreign service officers in Western capitals, will make that decision. Ultimately, we will have to deal with the one who has more power, not the one we like the best or with whom we are more comfortable.

Officials in the Bush administration have left no doubt that they would prefer to deal with Gorbachev. This is understandable. They have a good personal relationship with him. They respect him as a world-class leader and credit him for taming Soviet foreign policy. They appreciate all that he has done in initiating the reforms that made the new Soviet revolution possible. But for some, their approach also involves a measure of petty ego. Most of the foreign policy establishment bet on Gorbachev. And there is nothing that an intellectual hates more than to have to admit that he was wrong.

The stakes are too high to allow these personal factors to affect the decision about whom we should deal with. Only two questions are relevant: Who has the most power, and who most shares our values? On both counts, the answer has to be Boris Yeltsin.

Gorbachev still heads the center. But today the center exists at the sufferance of the republics, not the other way around. Under Gorbachev's nine-plus-one formula—the new union treaty that was overtaken by the August 1991 revolution—the center delegated power to the republics. Now, the republics will delegate power to the center—and what they give, they can take away.

While all of the newly independent republics should be

treated with equal respect, the fact is that the Russian republic is overwhelmingly the first among equals. It has 51 percent of the population, 60 percent of industrial production, 76 percent of the territory, and will likely have all of the nuclear weapons of the former Soviet Union. Russia also produces 90 percent of the oil and timber, 76 percent of the natural gas, and 80 percent of the hard currency of the USSR. Even the Ukraine, whose population and resources put it on par with France, Britain, and Italy, places a distant second among the former Soviet republics. Whether we liked the way Yeltsin threw his weight around after the coup or not, we have to face up to the fact that Russia's power gives him a veto over the center and over the other republics in any future commonwealth. As Russia goes, so will go the other republics. If reform fails there, it will fail everywhere. If it succeeds there, others will follow.

That is why the bashing of Yeltsin has been not only petty but counterproductive. Even if he were an intellectual lightweight and an opportunistic demagogue intent only on gaining power for himself, he is the indispensable man in the former Soviet Union today. The fact that Yeltsin has more power does not mean that we should not continue to treat Gorbachev with the respect he has earned. It does mean that in trying to build Gorbachev up, we should not tear Yeltsin down. Gorbachev is a man of the past. Yeltsin is the man of the future.

Despite their dislike for each other, Gorbachev and Yeltsin need each other. Gorbachev's political reforms made Yeltsin's election as president of the Russian republic possible. Yeltsin's courageous leadership of the resistance to the August coup made it possible for Gorbachev to return to his Kremlin office rather than to spend a comfortable retirement in his dacha in the Crimea. In light of the enormous difficulties that still face the former Soviet Union, both men will need each other in the future as well.

Our diplomats must therefore deal with Yeltsin. Our ambassador to the new Russian republic will have an incredible opportunity. He will hold the most important diplomatic post in the world. If he treats Yeltsin with the respect due the elected leader of a major nation and the key historical figure in the new Soviet revolution, he will have the opportunity to shape not only Yeltsin's thinking but also the Soviet future. Yeltsin may not know which fork to use at a state dinner, but he has a sharper knife than any other Soviet leader. And without him, the high hopes of the second Russian revolution will be dashed.

The new power of Russia and the other republics may become an inconvenience to those in the West accustomed to hearing the Soviet Union speak with the voice of a single superpower. But we must reconfigure our diplomatic channels. While democratic unity is a strength, Communist unity was a prison. We should not complain about having to interact with many governments instead of one. We will have to recognize these realities and appoint as many as fifteen ambassadors to the newly independent republics of the former Soviet Union. However annoying these developments might be for our diplomats, we should keep in mind that the Soviet nations have waited seventy-five years to speak with their own voices.

The transition from communism to free-market democracy will be a tortuous process. When the newly independent republics stumble, voices will arise in the West claiming that we should have done more to support the center. That view is wrong. Even the most mature democracies in the West experience boom and bust economic times and have difficulty making hard economic choices. What is good politics in a democracy often proves to be bad economics. This will be true ten-fold in the new democracies in the former Soviet Union and Eastern Europe. We must not throw up our hands and give up on these nations when they hit the rough spots on the road through the unexplored territory from communism to freedom.

Since the August 1991 revolution, Western observers have reduced the Gorbachev-Yeltsin relationship to that of a horse race, waging daily bets on whether Gorbachev has pulled in front of or dropped behind Yeltsin. That approach sidesteps the strategic issues involved. Our key strategic interest lies not in rescuing the center or Gorbachev politically. Our interest centers on dismantling the vestiges of the Communist system that has oppressed its people for seventy-five years, that has engaged in unremitting expansionism against the free world, and that could someday spawn the rise of a new imperialism. Western policies should help those who strive to build genuine democracy, who accept the need for a rapid transition to market economics, and who believe in democratic self-determination for the Russian and non-Russian nations.

If the new leaders in Moscow and the former Soviet republics take the path toward a new commonwealth, we can open up a new agenda of positive cooperation. The first item must be to dispose of old business left over from the cold war on the basis of our new common values. The second will be to chart a broad program of cooperative relations, particularly in terms of U.S. support and assistance for republics undertaking the painful process of erecting market economies on the ruins of the Soviet command economy.

In my March 1991 meeting with the foreign minister of the Russian republic, Andrei Kozyrev, he said that the West was exaggerating the apparent revolution in Soviet foreign policy under Gorbachev. He stated emphatically that Gorbachev had simply bowed to the inevitable when he accepted the demise of Moscow's satellite regimes in Eastern Europe and that the hard-liners advising him would fight to the last to prevent further "retreats" in the underdeveloped world or concessions on arms control. He warned that the problem was larger than Gorbachev, arguing, "The Communist system itself is inherently expansionist."

Kozyrev was right at that time. But the new democratic revolution in Moscow and the former Soviet republics has put our relations on a new footing. During the cold war, while our two peoples could be friends, our two countries could not. In World War II, Washington and Moscow were not friends but allies. In the postwar period, because of our irreconcilable differences, the U.S. and Soviet governments could never be friends but could not afford to be enemies. Today, with the triumph of democratic values in the Soviet Union, we can reconcile the issues that drove us apart. In the future, we can look forward to being not only allies but also friends.

To resolve the issues left over from the cold war, the new leaders in Moscow must revise their policies in five key areas:

Excessive military spending. Despite the lack of any real threat to justify high military budgets, Gorbachev continued the massive buildup of Soviet capabilities. According to CIA estimates, he increased military spending by 3 to 4 percent annually from 1985 through 1988, resulting in a total rise of 20 to 25 percent. He told a group of factory workers that such spending rose 45 percent over the same period. Even with the major cuts in military forces announced after the August coup, Moscow will spend more on defense under Gorbachev than it did under Brezhnev.

The contrast between the levels of U.S. and Soviet military

spending is stark. While the share of the U.S. GNP allocated to defense peaked at 6.3 percent in 1985, it dropped to 5.5 percent in 1991. Further reductions are projected to move that figure to 3.6 percent in 1996, the lowest level in fifty years. According to the best independent Western estimates, Moscow allocates between 23 and 26 percent of GNP to the armed forces. Former foreign minister Shevardnadze, as well as reform-minded Soviet publications such as *Moscow News,* have in recent months estimated the figure to be no less than 20 percent. In light of the precipitous decline of the Soviet economy, official Soviet statements have estimated that before the recently announced cuts defense spending consumed 34 percent of the GNP. In 1990, for example, the Soviet Union produced twice as many tanks and ten times as many artillery guns as all member countries of NATO combined.

In the early 1980s, the West feared that a strategic "window of vulnerability" had opened as Moscow started deploying the SS-18 model 4, a ten-warhead ICBM capable of destroying targets hardened against nuclear attack. Under Gorbachev, Moscow has initiated deployment of the even more accurate and capable SS-18 model 5 and model 6. He also funded the production of 320 road-mobile SS-25s and 30 rail-mobile and 30 silo-based SS-24s, as well as the first deployments of the SSN-23 sea-launched missile and the AS-16 air-launched cruise missile. In 1990, the Soviet Union completed twelve nuclear submarines compared with nine a year in 1988 and 1989. In 1990, it produced 1,900 antiship cruise missiles, compared with 1,400 in 1988 and 1,600 in 1980. When he won the Nobel Peace Prize in 1990, Gorbachev must simultaneously have been awarding the Lenin Peace Prize to Soviet arms producers.

Like his predecessors Brezhnev, Andropov, and Chernenko, Gorbachev had a hard time saying no to the Soviet military-industrial complex. He has pleaded for Western tolerance of excessive military production, citing the monumental difficulties—particularly massive unemployment—in converting facilities to civilian production. That argument crumbles under scrutiny. Like most government spending, military procurement is nonproductive spending. Because it does not produce any goods that consumers can buy, it acts as a drag on, not a stimulus for, economic growth. Moscow would be better off shutting down defense plants and paying workers *not* to produce tanks and other equipment. Then, the steel, electronics, and other inputs could at least be put to better purposes—such as, for example, alleviating shortages of consumer goods.

Yeltsin and the other democratic leaders should be more willing to phase out excess military production than their hard-line predecessors. We should encourage them not to temporize but rather to follow the pro-fitness slogan of a popular line of athletic shoes: "Just do it."

Obstructing arms control talks. Since any genuine reform of the Soviet economy will require its demilitarization, Gorbachev should have been seeking drastic negotiated arms reductions. But he has not done so. Even Gorbachev's positive response to many of President Bush's arms control proposals in October 1991 fail to rectify the flaws in the CFE and START treaties caused by Soviet obstinacy at the negotiating table.

In implementing the CFE agreement, Gorbachev's defense team engaged in blatant and systematic mendacity to circumvent the limits and verification provisions of the treaty. In doing so, they developed the potential capability to field a massive strategic reserve force that could have been used to tip the continent's balance of power in the future:

—In their most brazen attempt, they sought to violate the

letter of the treaty by excluding more than 5,000 pieces of equipment from agreed-upon limits by reassigning three army motorized rifle divisions to the naval infantry, to civil defense units, and to strategic forces security detachments.

—They also moved 70,000 pieces of treaty-limited equipment to depots east of the Ural Mountains—a redeployment ten times greater than Operation Desert Shield/Storm—in order to avoid counting them against treaty totals. In May 1990, Soviet negotiators indicated that 31,990 tanks, 49,300 armored personnel carriers, 51,000 artillery pieces, 6,490 combat aircraft, and 2,950 attack helicopters would come under CFE provisions. But in late 1990 they presented revised figures of 20,694 tanks, 29,348 APCs, 13,826 artillery pieces, 6,445 combat aircraft, and 1,330 attack helicopters.

—They submitted a list of 895 so-called "objects of verification"—military installations and units where treaty-limited equipment was located—after previously committing themselves informally to a 1,756 total. Meanwhile, NATO estimated 2,661 as the lowest possible count for such objects. This huge discrepancy meant the Soviets could store equipment beyond the prying eyes of CFE on-site verification teams at over a thousand sites.

Even the agreement to resolve the issue of the disputed three divisions fell short of what the West should have demanded. We must insist that the new noncommunist government in Moscow pledge to destroy the mountains of weaponry stashed east of the Urals.

President Bush deserves great credit for seizing the moment to press for major reductions in nuclear weaponry. But as a result of previous Soviet obstinacy, the START treaty—which calls for a 30 percent reduction in U.S. and Soviet strategic forces—is fatally flawed. Despite the additional informal arms control agreements concluded by President Bush and President Gorbachev in the aftermath of the August 1991 revolution, planned reductions will not enhance strategic stability or be fully verifiable. In negotiation with the new leaders in Moscow, we should make the correction of the flaws in START—either through amendments or a quick follow-up accord—a test case in putting cold war issues behind us.

Arms control is part of U.S. defense policy, not vice versa. As long as the knowledge of how to build nuclear weapons exists, we cannot indulge fantasies about eliminating them from the face of the earth. A nuclear-free world would be a world safe for conventional aggression. And it would create irresistible incentives for aggressors to develop a nuclear capability covertly and thereby gain a decisive military advantage.

Our objective must be not disarmament but a stable strategic balance. The START treaty's effect on strategic stability represents the key criterion for evaluating its contribution to our security. The stability of the strategic balance turns on the incentives for each power to use or not use nuclear weapons in a crisis, and the best measure of those incentives is the ratio of first-strike warheads to first-strike targets. To be useful for a first strike, a warhead must be accurate and powerful enough to destroy a target hardened against nuclear attack, such as ICBM silos, command bunkers, or communications systems. First-strike targets are those weapons and facilities essential for launching a retaliatory attack. If Moscow possessed enough first-strike warheads to threaten credibly all first-strike targets in the United States, the Kremlin could have an incentive to threaten or actually to use nuclear weapons in a crisis.

At the same time, unless a START agreement contains airtight verification provisions, the treaty will not serve our interests. In the past, if verification procedures fell short of this standard, we could be sure about two things: the United States would observe the treaty to the letter, and the Soviet Union would violate it to the limit. Since all of the verification issues have relatively easy solutions, we should take the time to resolve them in order to prevent suspicion from arising in the future.

Most of the arms control measures agreed upon since the signing of START affect the least important weapons in terms of the nuclear balance. Ground-based tactical weapons, sea-based cruise missiles, and bomber-borne weapons are irrelevant or peripheral to strategic stability. To enhance stability, the focus of new arms control efforts should be on reducing the number of ICBMs carrying multiple warheads capable of destroying first-strike targets. President Bush's proposal to eliminate such missiles was on the mark, but Gorbachev rejected it. In the absence of such a comprehensive solution, we must insist on rectifying four flaws in START:

First, the permitted number of Soviet heavy ICBMs should be reduced from 154 to 77. When the Reagan administration agreed to the first figure, it assumed that the limits would apply to the SS-18 model 4, the accuracy of which required Moscow to allocate two warheads to each target. But the improved accuracy of the SS-18 model 5, which the Soviets began deploying in 1990, enabled Soviet military planners to employ one-on-one targeting. As a result, the modernized SS-18 gave the Soviet Union the same military capability with half the number of missiles.

Second, the "downloading" of missiles should be banned. In all previous strategic arms control negotiations, the number of warheads attributed to each missile was determined by the maximum number that were deployed or simulated in test flights of that system. Since the Soviet SS-18 and the U.S. MX missiles have been tested with ten warheads, for example, each missile of these types would count for ten warheads against START limits. But both sides have been tempted to permit some systems to be downloaded to carry fewer warheads than their maximum capabilities. The limited downloading permitted under START sets a dangerous precedent. If the practice is expanded in subsequent agreements, it will significantly favor Moscow. Soviet missiles have far greater "throw weight," which means they have the capability of carrying more warheads. If we allow downloading, we will create a situation in which Moscow's strategic forces have the ability to deliver many more warheads than START permits—which, in turn, would mean that the Kremlin could "break out" of the agreement on short notice simply by "uploading" additional warheads.

Third, the permitted number of "nondeployed" missiles should be reduced. Each side produces more missiles than are put on active duty. Most excess systems on the U.S. side are consumed in test flights. But there is substantial evidence, including statements by top Soviet military leaders, that the Soviet Union produces more missiles than needed to fulfill testing requirements. That raises concerns about the possibility of a covert Soviet strategic capability, a danger accentuated with the advent of road and rail-mobile Soviet ICBMs. The only difference between a deployed and nondeployed mobile ICBM is whether it has been loaded onto its trucklike or railcar launchers. Without much tighter limits on nondeployed missiles, START offers no guarantees of enhanced strategic stability.

Fourth, perimeter-portal monitoring should be established around all plants producing first-stage rocket motors for mobile ICBMs. While limits on silo-based ICBMs can be verified with a high degree of confidence through satellite reconnaissance, monitoring mobile ICBMs represents a very difficult challenge. The only way to be confident about the estimated number of such systems, both deployed and nondeployed, is to monitor at the factory gate the total output of first-stage rockets, which are the critical component that gives the missiles an intercontinental range. Moscow rejected perimeter-portal monitoring of those facilities, and the United States erred by accepting such verification only at mobile-missile final-assembly plants. But the Soviet military can—and has in the past—married the first-stage rockets to the other missile components at locations other than the assembly plants.

Until stable democracies emerge in the former Soviet Union, deterrence and strategic stability will remain critical priorities. Unless the two sides adjust the START agreement's terms on Soviet heavy ICBMs, downloading of warheads, nondeployed missiles, and perimeter-portal monitoring, it will exacerbate, not diminish, our vulnerability. In addition, if we do not strengthen these key provisions, the START limits on mobile Soviet ICBMs will become unverifiable.

As we look beyond START, we must also address the issue of the role of strategic defenses. In 1972, I signed the Anti-Ballistic Missile Treaty, which sharply restricted the deployment of ground-based and banned space-based defenses against ballistic missiles. While the agreement suited our interests at the time, it is time to renegotiate its terms. With today's technologies, a combination of limited space-based and wider ground-based defenses would enhance, not erode, strategic stability and mutual security. A comprehensive nationwide defense against nuclear attack remains unfeasible. But a limited defense of our command and control systems and nuclear forces—such as President Bush's proposed

Global Protection Against Limited Strikes system—would significantly strengthen strategic stability. Moreover, the United States could offer eventually to extend these defenses to protect all nations—including the republics of the former Soviet Union—from limited ballistic missile attacks.

In addition, as more third world states acquire ballistic missile capabilities, the United States cannot afford to remain defenseless against them. Today, fifteen developing nations have such capability, with three more expected to join the club before the year 2000. It is only a matter of time before rogue states such as Iraq or Libya acquire missiles with intercontinental ranges. Iraq has already developed a ballistic missile with a range of 1,250 miles—enough to reach Stavropol, Gorbachev's original Communist party base. While Gorbachev has shown some signs of flexibility on renegotiating the ABM Treaty, the new government in Moscow might be more interested, especially since those countries technologically closest to acquiring nuclear weapons and ballistic missiles are geographically closer to the Soviet Union than to the United States.

Some observers contend that because of the democratic revolution in the Soviet Union, arms control has become passé. After all, they argue, democratic nations have seldom waged aggressive wars. While we welcome the democratic revolution in the former Soviet Union, we must recognize that its success has been partial and its longevity is far from certain. We must base our defense policies on a potential adversary's capabilities, not his presumed intentions. We have had an era of new thinking in military policy under Gorbachev. We now need an era of new actions in defense policy under the new noncommunist leadership.

We must seize the moment to reduce the burden of arms in a way that will serve the interests of the newly independent

Soviet republics as well as ours. It is obscene that the former Soviet Union should be spending so much on arms even when it faces absolutely no threat from a major power abroad.

Bludgeoning Eastern Europe's economies. Since the anti-communist revolutions of 1989, Gorbachev has retaliated by waging economic war against the new Eastern European democracies. He has orchestrated a two-pronged assault—extorting high prices for Soviet raw materials and shutting off Soviet markets to East European exports. He inflicted more damage through his policies than we could offset through our aid programs. With the new leadership in Moscow and the former Soviet republics, we should find ways to reverse this process, increasing trade and stimulating both economies.

During its forty-five years of domination, Moscow made Eastern Europe dependent on Soviet raw materials, particularly energy. In 1988, Poland bought 80 percent of its energy resources from Moscow, while Czechoslovakia imported 95 percent and Hungary 90 percent. These imports were purchased at negotiated prices well below world market levels and paid for in the soft currencies of the Soviet bloc. When the East Europeans won independence, that changed. Gorbachev demanded payment in hard currencies for goods, thereby adding $20 billion to Eastern Europe's energy bill overnight, an increase four times greater than the one the United States experienced in the 1973 oil shock.

At the same time, the Soviet Union canceled thousands of orders for East European goods as economic retaliation for the political break with Moscow. Since the Kremlin had forced the East Europeans to meet its requirements since World War II, all were acutely dependent on Soviet markets. After the revolutions in 1989, Soviet trade officials made the rounds of Eastern European capitals canceling long-standing

export orders, unceremoniously telling the Czechoslova-
kians, for example, that Moscow no longer wanted any more
of "your damn tram cars." Gorbachev's overnight cancellations and refusal to pay for goods under contract—causing
East European exports to fall to one-quarter of their previous
level—severely undercut their ability to earn the funds
needed to purchase raw materials, as well as triggering massive unemployment in districts geared for production for the
Soviet Union.

Backing third world totalitarian regimes. Before we consider helping the former Soviet Union, its leaders should help
themselves by terminating their aid to their brutal client regimes abroad. In 1990, Gorbachev budgeted $6 billion for
Cuba, $2.5 billion for Vietnam, $3.5 billion for Afghanistan,
$1.5 billion for Syria, $1 billion each for North Korea, Angola, and Libya, $500 million for Ethiopia, and $50 million
for the Sandinistas in Nicaragua—a total of over $17 billion,
which could have bought 22 million tons of grain or re-
trained 11 million workers with skills needed in a market
economy.

The case of Afghanistan is particularly galling. For thirteen
years, the Kremlin has propped up the cruelest tin-pot totalitarians in the third world. When Gorbachev came to power
in 1985, he authorized an escalation of the brutality of the
Soviet military campaign in Afghanistan and gave the go-
ahead for a terrorist campaign in Pakistan, which eventually
killed 5,000 civilians in 4,500 bombings. In addition, strong
circumstantial evidence implicated Moscow in the August
1988 assassination of Pakistani president Zia ul-Haq.

In a desperate effort to find a winning formula, Moscow
had traded one Afghan ruler for another until choosing President Najibullah, who earned his stripes as head of the
KhAD, the Afghan KGB, where he personally oversaw tor-

ture and mass execution of suspected opponents. It is ironic to note that when I visited Moscow in March 1991, KGB chairman Kryuchkov brazenly described the Kremlin's designated killer as "being too humanitarian." Incredibly, some U.S. journalists subsequently swallowed this propaganda line in referring to Najibullah as a "moderate."

The new governments in Moscow and the former Soviet republics should take decisive action. Since the Soviet withdrawal in early 1989, Gorbachev has obstructed U.S.-Soviet talks to devise a just political settlement of the conflict, while keeping Najibullah's government alive through $300 million in aid each month and thousands of Soviet advisers who not only provide the regime's backbone but also man the SCUD missile bases around Kabul. The U.S.-Soviet agreement to cut off military aid to both the Kabul regime and the resistance and to hold U.N.-supervised elections is flawed. Kabul has stockpiled at least two years of arms and ammunition, while the resistance scrapes by from day to day. A just settlement can only be assured if the elections are preceded by the removal of Najibullah from power and the creation of a neutral transition regime, headed by the former king of Afghanistan, Zahir Shah, that would take full control of the state—including the armed forces and security services—and that would conduct the elections for the new government.

The new leaders of the former Soviet Union—particularly in the republics—should have a natural sympathy for the plight of the Afghan people. The courage of the Afghan resistance was a major factor in precipitating the collapse of the Soviet empire in Eastern Europe. When the Soviet army failed to win decisively in Afghanistan, the peoples of satellite states recognized that their historic opportunity had arrived —that the Kremlin lacked the will to pay the price of empire. Within two years, Soviet democrats had won the same battle.

As a spark that started the process, the cause of the Afghan people should receive top priority in our new relationship.

As Yeltsin put it, "Moscow can't afford foreign charity." The recently announced pullout of military and intelligence personnel from Cuba and cutoff of economic and military aid does not go far enough. Much of Moscow's assistance to Castro has come not through grants but subsidized trade deals in which, for example, the Soviet Union purchases Cuban commodities at prices far above the free-market levels. It is time to let Castro sink or swim—something which thousands of Cubans trying to escape from the last bastion of communism in the western hemisphere have tragically been forced to do.

Escalating espionage and active measures. If the cold war has ended, Gorbachev never got the message to the KGB under Kryuchkov. The carefully cultivated international image of a kinder, gentler Soviet Union is starkly contradicted by the escalation of hostile intelligence activities directed at the United States and our allies in recent years. Every great power needs an intelligence service capable of clandestine collection of information about actual and potential threats to its security, but the KGB's activities—both in scale and type—extended far beyond the legitimate requirements of a normal country.

Like the Soviet military, the KGB appears to operate outside any budget constraint. The entire U.S. intelligence community—which includes not only the CIA but also the Defense Intelligence Agency, the National Security Agency, parts of the Federal Bureau of Investigation, and other agencies—employs approximately 35,000 people. The ranks of the KGB and the GRU, the Soviet military intelligence service, number over 900,000. Moreover, according to Western intelligence services, the level of Soviet espionage activity has gone up, not down, in the Gorbachev years, despite the reduction in international tensions.

A key focus of Soviet espionage has been the theft of Western technologies. In the 1930s, the Kremlin sought to boost the Soviet economy by stealing scientific knowledge and technologies—from basic research to blueprints for turnkey factories—through spies. In the 1970s and 1980s, the Soviet intelligence services returned to this practice with a vengeance, targeting not only military and dual-use but also nonmilitary technologies. The CIA reported that in the early 1980s Soviet intelligence services targeted 3,500 items annually. The KGB's Directorate T, which specializes in acquiring scientific and technological data, orchestrated efforts that secured about one-third of these items every year. In the Gorbachev era, intelligence officers in Directorate T have not been furloughed but rather have been working overtime.

In addition, the former Gorbachev government continued a vigorous program of so-called "active measures," covert political activities such as disinformation designed to advance Soviet foreign policy. The KGB has become expert in the use of forgeries to discredit Western governments and in planting false stories in the world's newspapers. One current line of disinformation, which has surfaced in the news media throughout the third world, claims that the AIDS epidemic started after the virus was created by Pentagon experiments to develop new biological weapons. Another widely disseminated KGB fabrication asserted that the United States systematically buys Latin American babies for use in medical experiments and for organ transplants. Though Kremlin officials claim to have curtailed such active measures, their statements so far represent just one more case of disinformation.

Vadim Bakatin, the new chairman of the KGB, has pledged

to reform it. Before we enter a more cooperative relationship with Moscow, we must insist that he does so thoroughly. Replacing the top leadership will not suffice. New military and security structures—committed to upholding rather than subverting democracy—are needed with new personnel from top to bottom.

All of these practices must stop before we can forge ahead in a wider cooperative relationship with the new leaders in Moscow and the former Soviet republics. Yeltsin and the democrats around him will not need a hard sell. But Gorbachev and the holdovers in the apparatus will not be so easily swayed. We should not provide any economic assistance until Moscow's foreign policy has made an irreversible break with the past. Unless the Kremlin revises these policies voluntarily, it would not be in our interest to help its leaders out of their crisis.

Once the problems of the past are cleared from the agenda, we can turn to the opportunities for wider cooperation for the future. In light of the dire crisis in the former Soviet Union, Western assistance to the newly independent republics must be the initial focus of our partnership.

We must understand when such aid would help and when it would hurt. Under Gorbachev's previous government, Western aid would have undercut, not bolstered, the prospects for reform. Western proposals for unconditional aid or for incremental assistance linked to step-by-step reforms are totally counterproductive, encouraging Soviet policymakers to lobby Western leaders rather than get on with the business of reforming their own economy.

In my conversation with Gorbachev in 1991, I discovered that he retained his steadfast faith in the flawed tenets of

Marxism-Leninism. I had noted his observation in *Time* magazine in May 1990 that "as we dismantle the Stalinist system, we are not retreating from socialism, but we are moving toward it." I had assumed, however, that his thinking had grown as the Soviet economy had shrunk. I was thus surprised by how adamantly he defended the Soviet Union's socialist system. He argued that Soviet society was profoundly "different" from those in the West and that the tradition of "communes" in rural Russia had created a setting conducive to state-directed economic life. He made no bones about his intention to hew to the straight-and-narrow path of socialism. The sad truth is that a college freshman who passed Economics 101 knows more about the workings of the market than the president of the Soviet Union. While Gorbachev is a brilliant politician, he knows very little about economics—and what he does know is wrong.

His economic mismanagement has brought catastrophic consequences upon the Soviet people. Industrial production fell by 20 percent in 1990 and an estimated 40 percent in 1991. Total GNP declined approximately 15 percent in 1991 —worse than that of the Great Depression in the United States. Inflation, which exceeded 20 percent in 1990, soared to over 100 percent in 1991 on the heels of a 300 percent increase in the money supply. The 71 million Soviet citizens who lived on $15 per month or less were pushed to the edge of destitution. The monetary "overhang"—the pool of pent-up buying power spawned by inflated wages and the absence of goods to purchase—mounted to an estimated 450 billion rubles. The red ink of the state budget ballooned to 10 percent of GNP in 1990, more than double the level of the U.S. federal deficit. Over 50 percent of record Soviet food harvests were wasted, either rotting in the fields and in transport or stolen outright.

The reason for the failure of Gorbachev's economic reforms can be summarized in two words: half measures. For seven years, he has futilely searched for a workable halfway house between the free market and state socialism. No one can fault him for a lack of ingenuity. On twelve occasions—nine during the last two years alone—Gorbachev and his advisers tabled a new proposed economic plan to rescue the Soviet system. But Gorbachev was tilting at windmills. He was trying to revive an economic system that was dead beyond resurrection. Rapid and self-sustaining economic growth has occurred only in countries that respect the right of individuals to own private property. Yet as late as mid-1991, he continued to denounce private property, remarking in an interview, "People do not want to work in the factory whose owner has accumulated money in some unknown way. Small private property might be allowed in trade."

In working with the new noncommunist leaders in Moscow and the former Soviet republics, we should not allow the euphoria of their political victory to cloud our judgment on the issue of economic reform. Along with Western Europe and Japan, the United States should provide economic aid once needed reforms are in place. But we should stipulate clear conditions that must be met before major aid could be considered, both for our sake and for that of the reformers in the former Soviet Union. A banker does a borrower no favor by making him a bad loan.

Without the root-and-branch dismantling of the socialist system, any Western aid to Moscow would be wasted. With its estimated GNP of $1,900 billion—the equivalent of the U.S. economy in 1977—the former Soviet Union's fundamental economic problem cannot be a lack of resources. Instead, it is a misapplication of those resources and the absence of proper economic incentives for individuals and enterprises. Until the new noncommunist leadership tackles those issues, no amount of Western aid will bring the economy out of its present nosedive.

Those in the West who favor aid schemes often oversimplify matters by calling for a Marshall Plan for the former Soviet Union. No legitimate parallel exists between the postwar reconstruction of Europe and Japan and the post-cold-war requirements of the former Soviet Union. The Marshall Plan—which provided $13.3 billion in aid over five years—simply jump-started the world's war-battered free-market economies. While they needed new infrastructure and new investment capital, they already had the basic market institutions and centuries of entrepreneurial experience. In the Soviet case, markets must be invented. Private property, free prices, capital markets, experienced business managers, even personal checkbooks—none of these existed in the Soviet system. Providing economic aid before Moscow and the former Soviet republics revamp their primitive economic institutions would be like pouring water into a leaky bucket.

Even the most enlightened reformers are daunted by the obstacles to overhauling their economy. First, no country has ever undergone a transformation from a command to a market-based economy. The trillions of economic decisions made daily in a market economy had been senselessly concentrated in the endless gray buildings of the Moscow bureaucracy. Untying the proverbial Gordian knot is simple compared to the task of decentralizing the Soviet economy without triggering total chaos.

Second, powerful vested interests—the Communist party apparatus and the central bureaucracy—are not only certain to oppose radical reform but are also fully capable of sabotaging its implementation. After the August 1991 revolution, the commanding heights of the Soviet economy were conquered by the reformers. But much of the battlefield, from ministries through enterprises, still remains under the control of the economic shock troops of communism. Those who had spent their lives shaking down the system will not take kindly to those who seek to shake it up. Communists in the apparatus are on the defensive. But if they close ranks, they could paralyze even the best reform program.

Third, seventy-five years of communism have instilled a pervasive egalitarian ethic and a resistance to change in the average Soviet worker. He came to believe that each should be rewarded equally regardless of his productivity. In contrast to Deng's economic reforms in China, which gave millions of Chinese an equal opportunity to work their way out of poverty, too many people in the Soviet Union prefer a system that guarantees them an equal share of poverty. As one of Gorbachev's former top economic advisers put it, "Ideology has become psychology."

While the new noncommunist leadership deserves our help in crafting a coherent reform program, we must recognize that the West cannot save the Soviet economy. Only the nations of the former Soviet Union can save themselves. The Soviet system was bankrupt, and many of the new postcommunist leaders understand the need to place it in voluntary receivership. While the reform process will involve wrenching economic dislocations, the Soviet republics must adopt the reforms that will provide the incentives for the people to work their way out of bankruptcy. We should provide whatever help they need to steel themselves for this challenge but should refrain from any assistance that would make them back away from it.

Those who patronizingly claim that nothing short of a Western bailout can save the nations of the former Soviet Union are wrong. The Soviet Union was not a nuclear-armed

Bangladesh. Its natural resources, while increasingly expensive to develop, remained abundant. Its labor force, despite its poor work ethic, was highly skilled and would have responded to proper incentives. Its scientists were recognized internationally. If the new noncommunist leadership adopts the right reforms, the accomplishments of the nations of the former Soviet Union will astonish the world.

While there are scores of needed economic reforms—free prices, private property, capital markets, and others—there are two fundamental political requirements: painful honesty and strong leadership.

Yeltsin can be legitimately faulted for not fully facing up to the sacrifices that his market-oriented program will require from the Soviet people. He is not ignorant of the difficulties and suffering inherent in the transition. But his rhetoric on the free market—not unlike Gorbachev's on *perestroika* in his early years in power—will foster unrealistic expectations of instant prosperity. Like most revolutionaries, he has been more effective in destroying the old than in building the new.

It is absolutely imperative that Yeltsin bite the bullet and explain to the people the sacrifices that will be necessary to transform the system—sacrifices that will stretch out over a generation. If he does so, he will increase the reserves of political capital he will need to buy time for the reforms to work. As they demonstrated in World War II, the Russian people are capable of great sacrifice and will endure great suffering if they believe in their cause. In the current economic crisis, they can only understand their cause if their new noncommunist leaders explain it to them with no holds barred.

There is a natural fear among democratic politicians to engage in such frank talk. Even when I visited the Soviet

Union in March 1991, I found that ironically the greatest danger they faced was not winning elections but governing after they won. At that time, democrats who came to office at the local and republic level were rendered totally impotent by the Communist-dominated bureaucracy, which controlled virtually all factories, distribution networks, and financial resources. Those who took office did not necessarily take power. While the Soviet people understood the constraints under which democratic officials operated, their patience was beginning to fray. Today, with the leverage of the reformers increased by the August 1991 revolution, the people will set a higher standard: they expect their leaders to deliver on their promises of a better life. Only if the new noncommunist leaders level with the Soviet people will their policies be given enough time to work before a political backlash sets in.

Yeltsin's critics have wrongly faulted him for exploiting his political advantage immediately after the coup to strong-arm Gorbachev into adopting a more radical course. But strong leadership sometimes involves arm-twisting. On the difficult road to economic recovery, the nations of the former Soviet Union do not need leadership by committee, which is no leadership at all. Instead, they need leaders who will take decisive action to break the back of the old system and lay the foundation of the new system as quickly as possible. Those who urge gradualism warn that rapid change will create economic chaos. But in the former Soviet Union, economic calamity has already arrived. A course of gradual change will allow the economic hemorrhage to continue, while an accelerated program will cauterize the wound as quickly as possible.

After a visit to the Soviet Union in 1919, Lincoln Steffens, a liberal American journalist, wrote, ecstatically, "I have been over into the future and it works." Now, millions of people in the Soviet Union have experienced that future, and they know that it does not work. While they have turned away from communism and toward the free market, what course they will ultimately settle upon remains very much in doubt.

In this respect, the greatest contribution the United States could make is not financial but ideological. It would be a great tragedy if the newly liberated nations of the former Soviet Union gave up on freedom and turned toward democratic socialism. Soviet communism was an unmitigated evil. Democratic socialism is a fashionable fraud. The only economic success stories in the developing world have come in countries whose leaders rejected the siren call of socialism tempting them to sacrifice opportunity and progress on the altar of equality.

We must seize this historic moment—when we celebrate the defeat of communism—to develop a strategy for the victory of freedom among the nations of the former Soviet Union. The stakes could not be higher. These nations know that communism does not work. They have great expectations that the free market will work in their countries as well as it has in the West and in much of East Asia. They have rebelled against the failed policies of communism. But if freedom fails, they will rebel against it as well.

They will not return to communism, but communism is only the most advanced form of socialism. A return to socialism of any kind—even the democratic variety so popular in Western intellectual circles—would be a tragedy for the peoples of the former Soviet Union. It would condemn them permanently to the backwaters of third world economic stagnation. The battle in the West between those who favor progressive democratic capitalism and those who favor benign democratic socialism predated the cold war and will endure after the cold war. We have won that battle in Western Europe and noncommunist East Asia. The West must now win it in the East.

Our strategy should focus on winning over the new leaders in the republics. No aid should be provided to the center, which will always be dominated by those who carry the baggage of the Communist past. Instead, we should institute direct ties with the republics and help them establish the institutions needed to make the free market work. The United States should extend a helping hand to all republics that move toward a free-market system. But we should embrace only those who explicitly denounce the deadly danger of democratic socialism and formulate programs to move aggressively toward the free market. The essence of our strategy should be to differentiate among the republics, providing greater assistance to those who make the most decisive break with the past.

We must accept the fact that the first generation of Soviet revolutionaries might fail in this respect. Boris Yeltsin, for example, has said, "If from the entire spectrum of parties internationally I were to choose one, I would choose the position of a social democrat." As a fast learner, Yeltsin may move away from this position just as he abandoned communism. He should recognize the electoral defeat of the social democrats in Sweden as a warning against the dangers of taking the socialist path. But if he does not, the West should not subsidize the failed economic theories of socialism any more than it should have funded the failed political theories of communism.

The true debate can now begin. Liberals who wanted the state to mandate economic equality tended to see the Soviet system as a model they had to defend. They no longer have to serve as apologists for the repression and aggression of the

Soviet Union. Conservatives who wanted markets to generate economic opportunity were preoccupied with attacking the brutal excesses of communism. They can now direct their fire on the failure of democratic socialism. For seventy-five years, communism has distorted the battle between those who stood for capitalism and those who stood for socialism, between those who favored free markets and those who favored state-controlled markets, between those who exalted individual rights and those who put highest priority on group rights.

A century of prosperity in the capitalist West is an irrefutable argument that equality at the cost of freedom and opportunity is too high a price to pay. Today, as we join this great debate, we must do whatever is necessary and feasible to convert the newly independent nations of the former Soviet Union to our cause.

The starkest contrast between my impressions of the Soviet Union in 1959 and 1991 was in the spirit of the people. When I stopped by a public market in 1959, I could see that while Soviet citizens were obviously poor in goods, they were rich in spirit. They believed that they were on the right side, that the promises of a better life would come true, and that their system would triumph in the future. When I visited another market in Moscow in 1991, I found the people better off materially but depressed spiritually. Not angry or hostile, they instead seemed resigned to the fact that nothing worked and that their living conditions would only get worse. Sadly, they had given up not only on communism but also on themselves.

The people had invested great hopes in Mikhail Gorbachev. But he had failed to live up to them. In my meetings with the reformers, few had kind words for Gorbachev, whom they chastised for failing to go the final mile. One called him "indecisive." Others viewed him as "ruthless" and "an opportunistic party-man." Another characterized him as "a talker, not a doer." In reference to the January 1991 killings in the Baltic states, still another reformer even called him "a brutal wimp." After strongly criticizing Gorbachev's timid economic reforms, Boris Yeltsin bluntly told me, "He is a weak man."

Who is the real Gorbachev? He is still a Communist. He is an atheist. He is a Russian nationalist who, to borrow from Churchill, desperately wants to avoid presiding over the dismemberment of the Soviet empire. He is a shrewd politician who knows how to survive. He is a highly intelligent, sophisticated, and supremely self-confident leader with the great ego characteristic of most successful statesmen.

In the period between our meetings in 1986 and 1991, Gorbachev had changed profoundly. Though he was still at the top of his game intellectually in both encounters—addressing complex issues as effortlessly as Ozzie Smith fields grounders for the St. Louis Cardinals—those five years in power seemed to have added ten years to his age. His self-confidence remained unshaken, but his characteristic optimism had waned. While spirited in conversation, his iron emotional control, which I had previously observed, had also frayed with time.

When I first met him in 1986, Gorbachev had been in the vanguard of reformers, pressing the party apparatus through the pressure of *glasnost* and limited democratization. By 1991, however, he had become the point man for the reactionaries, fighting to keep democratic and nationalist forces at bay. His fatal flaw throughout his journey was his unwillingness to accept the fact that a socialist economy could not work and that a centralized empire could not survive in an age of nationalism. The intended purpose of *glasnost* was to open up the system so that the people would support reforms to strengthen the Communist system. Instead, it opened the system up to self-destruction.

His greatest strength—his unswerving belief in his ideals—was also his greatest weakness. His commitment to his ideals was admirable, but his choice of ideals was deplorable. A devoted Communist, he neither trusted the will of the Soviet people nor understood the fundamentals of market economics. He resigned from the leadership of the party but could not abandon his faith in the party. A proud Russian nationalist, he viewed the Soviet state as a great historical achievement and could not comprehend the nationalists in the republics who borrowed from Lenin in dubbing it "a jailhouse of nations." As President Zia ul-Haq of Pakistan observed shortly after meeting the new Soviet leader in 1985, "Gorbachev is a product of the system. He will try to improve it, but he will not abandon it."

Like other major historical figures before him, he has found that those who plant the seeds of reform seldom reap the harvest. He missed his historical moment in 1986. At that time, he could probably have won a popular election. But he chose not to face the people. Today, he probably could not even poll the 25 percent that Lenin's Bolshevik party received in the free elections for the Constituent Assembly in 1917. In fact, the only way Gorbachev could win the union presidency would be if its powers were so weakened that he would pose no threat to the progress of democratic and free-market reform. He has learned the hard lesson that his early popularity had derived not from his personal leadership but from the hopes of the people for progress. He brilliantly adopted the rhetoric of reform. The people liked what they heard but did not like what he did. When he reversed field, the people backed others who remained true to those ideals. He thought the Soviet people wanted a re-forming Communist, but what they really wanted was re-form without communism.

When Gorbachev returned to Moscow after the failed coup, many of his loyal friends in the West insisted that he had "not been diminished." This was wishful thinking. He is a resilient fighter who will not just fade away as do most politicians after suffering a defeat. But he will not regain the power he tried so hard to get and keep. The August revolu-tion not only swept away communism but also took away the enormous powers Gorbachev had previously concen-trated in his hands.

To save his nominal power, he gave up his leadership of the party, acquiesced to freedom for the Baltics, and jetti-soned central control in accepting an interim confederal ar-rangement among the republics—the Union of Sovereign States. But this may turn out to be a tactical pause. He may hope that when the republics experience the hardships of independence, they will be forced to return to the center—and to him—for new leadership. While Gorbachev is fighting for his political survival, this desperate gambit demonstrates that he is being pushed by the gusts of the democratic revo-lution, not leading it.

In order to confirm their past paeans to Gorbachev, the instant historians have judged his actions during the coup too glowingly. Eduard Shevardnadze, Gorbachev's former foreign minister and close personal friend, has been a more objective observer. When I met with him in 1991, he pro-vided a critical but guardedly optimistic evaluation of his former boss, chastising the Soviet president for toying with the danger of dictatorship but predicting he would soon "cross the Rubicon" on important economic reforms. After the coup, however, Shevardnadze wrote a brutally frank assessment and perhaps a fitting epitaph of Gorbachev, observing, "Now I am convinced that none other than Gorbachev himself had been spoon-feeding the junta with his indecisiveness, his inclination to back and fill, his fellow-traveling, his poor judgment of people, his indifference toward his true comrades, his distrust of the democratic forces and his disbelief in the bulwark whose name is the people, the very same people who had become different thanks to the *perestroika* he had begun."

Gorbachev positioned himself in the middle and as a result lost both the right and the left. In attempting to please all, he ended up pleasing none. Reformers could not trust him, and reactionaries dropped him when they could no longer use him. Was he then one of those tragic failures brought down by good intentions? No. History will judge that he met the test of greatness: he made a difference. He opened the eyes of the Soviet people to the fatal flaws of the Communist system. While he erred in believing that it could be reformed, his reforms took on a momentum of their own and revolutionized his country and changed the world. Regardless of what happens to him now, he has earned his place in history as one of the great leaders of the twentieth century.

As a dedicated Marxist, Gorbachev would have been wiser if he had studied one of Marx's ironically prescient observations: "Russia has only one opponent: the explosive power of democratic ideas, that inborn urge of the human race in the direction of freedom." Marx could never have suspected that an idea he captured in one sentence would bring down a Soviet state erected upon the ideology he expounded in multiple volumes. Yet we have witnessed the full flowering of that basic inborn human urge for freedom in the former Soviet Union.

Without radical reform, this opportunity will quickly fade away. What was once known as the Union of Soviet Socialist Republics is not a union, not Soviet, and not socialist. If the new leaders in Moscow and the former Soviet republics hesitate, their people will be doomed to the sidelines of history. They would be forced to live in the past, barred from receiving the rewards of the great revolution in human freedom now sweeping the world.

The conflict between the center and the republics—one seeking to rule from the top down and the other from the bottom up—is irreconcilable. After the failed coup, the center ultimately will not hold. The centralized command structure will give way to a decentralized commonwealth based on democratic self-determination and free-market economics. As the world's only superpower, America must take the lead in adjusting to these new realities. As the center grows weaker and the republics grow stronger, we should focus on advancing peace and freedom at both levels and through all channels.

By encouraging institutions pressing for political pluralism and market economics, we can help accelerate the demise of communism and the advent of liberty. Each of the nations of the former Soviet Union has rediscovered its identity, its heritage, and its freedom. These nations have spoken out for the first time since they were silenced by the armies of empire. After the long winter of Communist tyranny, it is now a springtime of nations.

The ideals of communism fed a spiritual hunger for creating a perfect society. In the wake of their demise are a broken ideology, a broken dream, and millions of broken lives. The new revolution of freedom does not promise a new utopia. Instead of a perfect society, the democratic revolution promises only a government as good as its people. The nations of the former Soviet Union have earned their freedom. Now they must learn how to reap the boundless rewards of freedom. The promise is within reach. It is up to the Soviet people to realize that promise.

The peaceful revolution in the Soviet Union has dramatically changed the world. It has a special meaning for the people of the Soviet Union, the United States, and the world. For the peoples of the Soviet Union, seventy-five years of bondage have ended. They are now free and can join the family of free nations.

For the United States, the great ideological and geopolitical rivalry with the Soviet Union has ended. The only power able to destroy the United States is now in the midst of a sweeping democratic revolution. We can now work with our former rival to eliminate the fear of war and reduce the burden of arms.

For the world, the superpower that has been the principal source of aggression for most of this century can now become a force for peace. The awesome power to destroy the world is in the hands not of Stalin or Andropov but of the Soviet people. It is now in good hands.

As a result of the new Soviet revolution, the world stands on the eve of an era of unprecedented opportunities for peace and progress. We must remember, however, that democracy is like a fragile plant. If it is not nurtured and cared for, it will wither and die. But once it sinks its roots, people will care for it. They will not fight to extend it, but they will fight to defend it.

In my meeting with Mao Zedong in 1976, the last time I would see him, he asked a profound question: "Is peace America's only goal?" I responded that our goal was peace but a peace that was more than the absence of war—"a peace with justice." Today, we need to ask ourselves a similarly profound question: Is stability our only goal? Our goal should be more than a new world order. Order can keep the peace, but peace is not the ultimate end, only the necessary beginning. Peace should be the means to a higher end—a new world in which all people can enjoy the blessings of freedom, justice, and progress.

With the collapse of the Communist Soviet empire, we should no longer view Moscow or the former Soviet republics as permanent adversaries. Bitter competition during the cold war can be transformed into allied cooperation in a warm peace. Over a century and a half ago, Tocqueville made a remarkably prescient observation about America and Russia: "There are at the present time two great nations in the world, which started from different points, but seem to tend toward the same end. . . . The principal instrument of the former is freedom; of the latter, servitude. Their starting-point is different and their courses are not the same; yet each of them seems marked out by the will of Heaven to sway the destinies of half the globe." History has advanced beyond even Tocqueville's prescience. Today, a democratic Russia working with a democratic America can sway the destinies of not just half but all the globe.

Thirty-two years ago in Moscow, Khrushchev arrogantly predicted to me, "Your grandchildren will live under communism." I responded, "Your grandchildren will live in freedom." At the time, I was sure he was wrong, but I was not sure I was right. As a result of the new Soviet revolution, I proved to be right. Khrushchev's grandchildren now live in freedom.

3

THE COMMON
TRANSATLANTIC
HOME

SIX YEARS AGO, Mikhail Gorbachev unveiled his vision
of the future of Europe: a "common European home" from
the Atlantic to the Urals. Founded in a "common cultural
and historical heritage," this new Europe would integrate its

---

economies and cooperate to guarantee peace and security and would unite a continent divided by fifty years of cold war tensions. Yet as attractive as many observers found his proposal, it was significant less for what it included than for what it omitted: a major role for the United States. By drawing the boundaries of the common European home at the eastern shores of the Atlantic, Gorbachev implicitly excluded America from the continent's future.

In reality, the idea of a common European home was simply an updated version of Moscow's traditional policy of seeking to divide the United States from its European allies. Though he claimed to have no such ulterior motive, Gorbachev clearly sought to achieve through diplomacy and propaganda what his predecessors since Stalin had failed to achieve through missile flexing and intimidation. In doing so, he casually overlooked the fact that the real bonds of culture and history extend from Europe to America, not from Sverdlovsk to Brittany. The values of the Western tradition, the steadfast adherence to democratic principles, and the belief in the fundamental dignity of the individual create philosophical ties that bind more strongly than the happenstance of the continent's geography.

The West, however, cannot afford to dismiss Gorbachev's gambit as empty rhetoric. His vision appealed to many because new realities in Europe demand new approaches to the problems of Europe. A liberated Eastern Europe and a vastly diminished threat from the Soviet Union doom to failure policies based on the cold war status quo. This does not mean the United States should declare victory and disengage from Europe. It does mean that U.S. policymakers must articulate a new vision for Europe and recast America's role to meet today's problems.

The Soviet Union has lost the cold war in Europe. But this

does not yet mean that the West has won it. We must still consolidate the victory. The countries of Eastern Europe lack a security structure. Massive economic problems threaten their fragile new democratic systems. Germany, uncertain of its proper role, has drifted from its geopolitical moorings. With new noncommunist governments in Moscow and in many former Soviet republics, the rationale for a strong NATO with a major U.S. military presence has eroded. To cope with these new conditions, we need policies that renew existing transatlantic institutions such as NATO and that build bridges to integrate Eastern Europe into the West. While Gorbachev spoke of a common European home, we should dedicate ourselves to building a common transatlantic home.

Since World War II, U.S. policy in Europe has been based on four fundamental geopolitical facts:

Soviet military presence in the heart of Europe. World War II brought Soviet troops to the banks of the Elbe. On June 4, 1945, Winston Churchill sent an urgent message to Harry Truman, the new President of the United States. He warned, "An iron curtain is coming down on their front. We do not know what lies behind it. It is vital that we have an understanding with the Russians now, before our armies are mortally weakened, and before we withdraw to our zones of occupation." Unfortunately, his advice was ignored. When the United States reduced its armed forces from 12 million to 1.6 million troops by 1947, the West accepted Soviet conventional superiority and thereby lost its leverage to force a Soviet pullback. After Moscow neutralized the U.S. nuclear advantage by developing its own atomic weapons in 1949, the East-West standoff in Central Europe was frozen into place. With 380,000 crack Soviet troops in East Germany alone, deterring further Soviet aggression or intimidation became the central U.S. preoccupation in Europe for half a century.

Soviet imperial domination over Eastern Europe. Within three years of the end of World War II, Stalin had installed puppet regimes in every East European country. Moscow exercised ironclad control over their Communist leaders. When the Kremlin told them to jump, they only asked how high. These countries were dominated militarily and geopolitically by the Moscow-controlled Warsaw Pact, which sanctioned the presence of as many as 800,000 Soviet troops on East European soil, and economically by the so-called Council of Mutual Economic Assistance. When Hungary and Czechoslovakia stepped out of line in 1956 and 1968, the Kremlin brought the full weight of the Red Army upon them, providing an object lesson of the consequences of the expansion of Soviet domination westward.

Soviet-imposed division of Germany. In the immediate postwar years, Germany lay in ruins, its territory divided between Western and Soviet occupation forces, its industrial infrastructure in shambles, and its population decimated by the wartime loss of 6 million people. But free-market economics and democratic politics—both made possible by NATO's protective shield and by the Marshall Plan's economic aid—produced the "German miracle." After forty-six years apart, the 62 million people in West Germany enjoyed a per capita income of $20,440, while the 16 million in East Germany languished with one of less than $5,000. Yet a profound tension remained. The unnatural division of Germany highlighted the unnatural division of Europe. Bonn's dependence on NATO for security pulled it toward the West. But Moscow continually exploited its control over East Germany to try to pull West Germany to the East.

Fragmented and vulnerable Western Europe. The end of

World War II left Western Europe politically and militarily vulnerable. The nations of Western Europe had common interests and values, but no common political structures. Divided by traditional rivalries and preoccupied with rebuilding their economies, these countries needed the United States to forge a common Western strategy to cope with the Soviet threat. Only the United States had the economic and military power to advance Western security through NATO and to push Western Europe to take the first timid steps toward unity through the European Economic Community. Europe's great powers had become medium powers, relegated to the second tier of states by their size, their dependence on the U.S. nuclear guarantee, and their inability to coordinate their defense and foreign policies.

None of those conditions is valid today. Yet U.S. policies are to a great extent still premised on them. The deployment of over 300,000 U.S. troops in Western Europe, the expenditure of $180 billion per year on European defense, the reluctance to provoke Moscow by developing security ties with Eastern Europe, and the advocacy of European economic integration even at the price of accepting protectionism all were policies well suited to coping with the challenges of the past. But today they are as obsolete as a Model T Ford.

As we revise our policy toward Europe, we must address five new realities:

Security vacuum in Eastern Europe and the former Soviet Union. The termination of the Warsaw Pact in March 1991 and the disintegration of the Soviet Union in August 1991 have left half of Europe without even a shadow of a security structure. These changes, though overwhelmingly positive, have created two new challenges. The first is the vacuum of power created in Eastern Europe and the former Soviet Union. The fact that during the postwar period virtually all European states were members of NATO or the Warsaw Pact created a certain geopolitical stability. While acute tensions divided the two sides, the lines between the blocs were clearly drawn, thereby decreasing the risks of adventurism and reducing the chances of a miscalculation leading to war. Today, however, Eastern Europe faces a period of unprecedented instability without any functioning security organization.

This would not matter if the East European states and the western former republics of the Soviet Union were strategically insignificant or had strong, stable governments. But neither is the case. Eastern Central Europe has been the focal point of the continent's political struggles for two hundred years. Both world wars were triggered in the region, and the four partitions of Poland between Germany and Russia attest to its geopolitical importance. The new East European democracies are weakened by ethnic divisions, hobbled by economic chaos, and unpracticed in the art of self-government. Moreover, compared to the newly independent republics of the Soviet Union, Eastern Europe is a pillar of geopolitical stability.

The second challenge strikes at the heart of NATO and the U.S. presence in Europe. Many believe that with the dissolution of the Warsaw Pact and the collapse of the Soviet Union, no compelling reason exists for the deployment of U.S. troops in Europe. Even though informal agreements will reduce U.S. forces to approximately 150,000, pressure will grow from West Europeans to phase out our forces totally and particularly our nuclear weapons. Among Americans across the political spectrum, budgetary pressures will focus increasing attention on slashing the amount spent annually on European defense, especially as our NATO allies trim back their own military expenditures. Without a renewed mission, the most successful alliance in history will become a footnote in history.

Fragile new democracies in Eastern Europe. Since their liberation from Soviet domination, the people of Eastern Europe have learned a chastening lesson: tearing down a corrupt old regime has always been easier than building a just new order. As Tocqueville observed, democratic government does not ensure good government. While no one would suggest turning back the clock, the central issue in Europe today is whether the new East European democracies will have enough time to implement reform before their economic problems overwhelm them.

The euphoria of revolution has been dampened by the hard realities of government. The economic and political transformation these countries must attempt is unprecedented. Handicapped with suffocating bureaucracies, worthless currencies, obsolete technology, globally uncompetitive goods, inefficient state-owned industries, and unproductive workers, even radical reforms will not remake their economies with the wave of a wand. Moreover, despite already low standards of living, conditions will inevitably get worse before they get better. Politically, the lack of tested leaders, established parties, and democratic traditions combined with potential ethnic rivalries and deepening economic chaos create fertile ground for demagogues. No democratic regime in history has ever weathered a storm of such overwhelming magnitude.

Unified but drifting Germany. Unification has put Germany at the pinnacle of its potential political and economic power in Europe. With 78 million people, it is the most populous country in Europe. If workers in east Germany were to match the productivity of those in the west—which is inevitable over time—the united country's GNP would today total at least $1.5 trillion, almost double its closest European rival. Though their size will be reduced, the current unified German armed forces number 590,000 troops, twice the size of Britain's and the largest military establishment in Central Europe except Moscow's. With its geopolitical weight, Germany potentially can dominate not only European economic institutions but also its political and security structures.

None of these facts has been lost on Germany's neighbors. The fall of the Berlin Wall did not sound the death knell of traditional anxieties about Germany. France and Britain were profoundly ambivalent about unification. Other members of the European Community voiced concerns about Germany's inevitable preeminence in the region. Poland, embroiled by Bonn in an unnecessary dispute over ratification of their common postwar border, feared German revanchism. East European governments implored U.S. firms to invest on their territory in order to avoid German economic domination. For many Europeans, the unification of Germany harkens back to a time fifty years ago when Germans rode through European capitals not in Mercedes limousines but in Tiger tanks, expanding influence not through economic cooperation but through military domination and terror.

While Germany's power will inevitably grow, the key question is how it will be used. Germany is not a potential rogue state or threat to its neighbors. The changes wrought by forty years of democracy and close association with Western institutions have transformed its society. But Germany must undergo a profound adjustment. During the cold war, free Germany lacked the power and confidence to chart an independent foreign policy and felt compelled to maintain a tight alliance with the West. With the waning of the cold war, that has changed. While still limited by the legacies of World War II, Germany is now tentatively staking out its new European and global roles. Our challenge lies in helping the Germans define constructive ways to use their new power.

There are two key concerns. The first centers on the re-emergence of Germany's geopolitical tradition of keeping one foot in the East and one in the West. The cooperation between Imperial Germany and Tsarist Russia, the covert rearming of Germany after World War I, Germany's role in the industrialization of Soviet Russia under the Rapallo Treaty, and the division of Eastern Europe between Hitler and Stalin marked the darkest chapters of that tradition.

In the Gorbachev era, signs of an emerging special German-Soviet relationship were troubling. German leaders fell victim to the myth that close economic ties would inevitably lead to amicable political relations. In October 1990, Chancellor Kohl stated in a major speech, "The extensive development of German-Soviet relations plays a key role in pan-European responsibility. It must be borne in mind that the united Germany lies at the heart of a no longer divided but merging Europe. This bridging function will obviously yield tangible economic benefits for us and our partners."

Although he played a courageous and historic role in achieving German unity, Kohl's policy of pandering to Gorbachev was wrong. Germany has given or promised to give $35 billion in government aid to the Kremlin in the period from 1989 to the August 1991 coup. This was at a time when Moscow's ability to service its foreign debt had become doubtful at best and when Gorbachev not only continued to challenge Western interests but had also entered a tight alliance with Communist hard-liners. Unless targeted to help legitimate nationalist and democratic forces in the republics rather than the discredited structures of the center, German aid could prop up a dying system and seriously undermine Western interests.

The second concern about Germany focuses on its blatantly irresponsible technology-export policies. Because of its constricted political role during the cold war, Germany threw its national energies into the economic sphere, particularly world trade. This evolved into a practice of selling anything to anyone who had the money, regardless of the potential political or military consequences. German firms designed and built the plant in Rabta, Libya, that has given Libyan dictator Muammar Qaddafi the capability to build chemical weapons. They were the principal contractors for Saddam Hussein's network of hardened command bunkers. Apart from Jordan, more firms from Germany sought to break the U.N.-sanctioned blockade of Iraq than from any other country. In the area of technology transfers, rising German power needs to be matched with a greater sense of strategic responsibility.

Gradually unifying but protectionist Western Europe. After World War II, many observers remarked that the best Europeans were Americans. U.S. enthusiasm for achieving West European unity, expressed through the Marshall Plan and its advocacy of the European Economic Community, exceeded that of all our major allies except Italy. The breakthrough came with the signing of the Single European Act by the original twelve EC members in 1986. Economic integration is to take place in 1992, with a common currency to be introduced in the late 1990s. By shifting so many economic policy issues to Brussels, the influence of European political institutions has grown. And the desire to carve out a world role for Europe has increasingly led to coordination of foreign and defense policies.

A united Europe has not only advantages but also disadvantages for the United States. We clearly benefit from the rise of a stronger and more cohesive political unit to balance Moscow, thereby permitting a reduction in our military role in Europe. We will also gain from having more active partners in Europe to grapple with regional crises around the world. But unfortunately, a united Europe, with a greater GNP than that of the United States, is becoming a "fortress Europe."

The closer post-1992 Europe comes, the more protectionist the European Community becomes. European companies received an average of $115 billion a year in state subsidies during the 1980s, a practice that shows no signs of abating. Today, the annual subsidy for state-owned steel companies is $225 million. If a ship is built with subsidized steel, the builder can get an additional 13 percent in shipbuilding subsidies from the community. Airbus, the European aerospace consortium, receives an estimated $20 billion in subsidies, while Air France raked in $400 million and the Belgian airline Sabena requested $1 billion. Unless the European Community starts to open its domestic markets, it is inevitable that the rest of the world will close theirs.

Some observers have questioned whether European economic integration has become incompatible with U.S. interests. On the whole, the strategic benefits continue to outweigh the economic costs of rising protectionism. But as European security concerns are reduced and as economic issues assume greater relative importance, the United States can no longer automatically support unity at any price.

Collapse of Soviet communism. The August 1991 revolution has created an unprecedented opportunity to base peace not on the balance of military power but on the foundation of common Western values.

Since the end of World War II, all Communist Soviet leaders consistently pursued four objectives in Europe. They wanted the United States out of Europe. They wanted a denuclearized Europe. They wanted NATO dissolved. And they wanted a neutral Germany. It is ironic that despite the Soviet defeat in the cold war, Gorbachev came closer to achieving these objectives than at any point during the cold war. While Americans love checkers, Gorbachev knew chess and played to win. In the new Europe, he played for position, thinking ahead ten moves in the hope of boxing us into moves that would inevitably have led to a Soviet checkmate.

In the Gorbachev period, the Soviet Union tried to seduce Germany into a middle ground between East and West and hoped that the United States—unsure of its security mission in a Europe that no longer recognizes a Soviet threat—would lack the domestic support for spending tens of billions of dollars on Europe's defense. A gradual U.S. disengagement would have opened the path for the Soviet Union—the strongest conventional power and the only nuclear superpower in Europe—to dominate the continent. Moscow would not have attacked the countries of Western Europe militarily but would have exercised a silent veto over their security policies and could have used its military dominance to extract economic assistance from them as tribute.

Today, the question is not whether but how much the Soviet Union has changed. In the past, Russian and Soviet tsars sought to borrow ideas from Europe in order to try to acquire the power to dominate Europe. The new Soviet revolution represents a historic opportunity to break with that imperial tradition. The new governments in Moscow and the former Soviet republics can now borrow from Europe's free-market and democratic traditions in order to become part of Europe philosophically, as well as geographically.

With the collapse of the Soviet Union, the traditional rationale for the U.S. role in Europe has been dealt a fatal blow. In 1971, the Mansfield amendment—which would have halved the U.S. military presence in Europe—was defeated by only one vote in the Senate. It is only a matter of time before a modern-day Mansfield amendment calling for a total withdrawal is introduced in Congress. Some on the American left argue that our new emphasis should be on domestic issues and that our victory in the cold war allows us to shake off old commitments. Others on the American right argue that a Europe fully recovered from World War II should not need the assistance of the United States and should pay the bills for its own defense. Many Europeans, tired of NATO low-altitude training flights and exhausted by forty years of brinkmanship, simply want the Americans to pack up and go home.

All of these arguments are flawed. First, two world wars have proved that the United States ignores events in Europe at its own peril. Had we been engaged in Europe, rather than sulking in isolation after World War I, we could have tipped the balance of power against the aggressors, possibly deterring rather than fighting World War II. Despite the waning of the cold war, the United States has major political and economic interests in Europe. Our commitment to Europe is based not on philanthropy but on interests. The U.S. role in NATO is not only needed on its merits but also gives us significant indirect leverage in addressing such issues as the Persian Gulf crisis and trade disputes. Without a military presence in Europe, we will have no voice in Europe.

In a historical perspective, Europe has been an even less stable place than the Middle East. The rigid stability of a Europe divided into two cold war camps has been the exception for a continent buffeted by centuries of war and instability. With the end of the cold war, Europe will not descend into fratricidal war, but the possibility for conflict and armed clashes will persist and even increase. Yugoslavia's civil war is a case in point. It is astonishing that the return of open warfare in Europe has not set off alarm bells in every European capital. The intermingling of scores of ethnic groups and the myriad competing territorial claims throughout the continent create endless possibilities for conflict and particularly as the relationships among the newly independent Soviet republics are sorted out. We have a profound stake in preventing the return of armed conflict to Europe. If we abandon our major role in Europe, we will relegate ourselves to the position of supporting cast, effectively writing ourselves out of any significant part in Europe's new geopolitical script.

Second, though more self-reliant, Europeans still need a security relationship with the United States. The two major reasons for the creation of NATO forty-four years ago were to deter Soviet aggression and to provide a secure home for the Germans. Those reasons are still valid today. While the threat of aggression by an increasingly democratic Soviet Union is now minimal, the idea that four centuries of Russian and Soviet expansionist tradition will instantly evaporate might be comforting but cannot be counted upon. Moscow still has thousands of strategic nuclear warheads targeted on the United States, the most powerful conventional army in Europe, and a modern blue-water navy. Gorbachev and Yeltsin have already made some welcome changes in Moscow's foreign policy. But Russia is a major world power, and the

Russians are a proud people. We should not automatically assume that a democratic Russia will be an international pussycat.

Europe needs a security structure. A NATO with a major U.S. leadership role has played an indispensable role not only in shielding Western Europe during the cold war but also as an example to the nations of Eastern Europe and the Soviet Union. Today, no alternative security structure exists. Until a viable substitute evolves and proves itself, we would be making an irrevocable error in dismantling NATO or disengaging from NATO. In a period of massive instability in Eastern Europe and the Soviet Union, we should be exploring ways to preserve NATO rather than looking for ways to eliminate it.

Some observers argue that a post-1992 superstate can unify the cacophony of European views and speak with one voice in addressing all these concerns. But that vision has become a pipe dream. Concrete national differences over policy, not petty parochial disputes over procedure, have kept Europeans divided. And they will continue to do so. In the Persian Gulf crisis, our European allies scattered like a flock of quail. A few, particularly Britain and France, fought side by side with our troops in the Kuwaiti deserts. But most, especially Germany, stuck their heads in the sand. In Yugoslavia's internal crisis, mediators from the European Community responded like Keystone Kops. During the initial phases of the crisis, European powers split over whether to support the Communist Serbian and central government or the democratic secessionist republics of Slovenia and Croatia. The community sent teams to act as ceasefire observers but did not marshal its massive political and economic leverage to demand a nonviolent resolution based on democratic self-determination. In its first major political play in the post-cold-war period, Europe fumbled the ball.

No single locus of decision-making exists among our European allies. Aristotle was profoundly perceptive when he wrote that government by the many or government by the few cannot act as efficiently as government by one. In foreign policy, a single point of executive authority is indispensable for decisive action. The premise of those who foresaw the emergence of a European superstate was that Germany would become its natural leader. But the Germans, hamstrung by pacifist tendencies during the Gulf crisis and preoccupied with the costs of unification, forfeited the role. In the meantime, the rest of Europe no longer views German leadership as the answer. Britain and France—who performed decisively in the Gulf—do not wish to defer to Berlin. And the rise of a unified Germany, which dwarfs all other European countries in size, has prompted fears that German leadership will inevitably mean German domination.

The question is not whether but how the United States should maintain its presence in Europe. If we seek to build a common transatlantic home, we must find ways to include those nations in Eastern Europe and among the newly independent republics of the Soviet Union who accept our democratic values. We must also define common purposes and missions with our traditional allies that will give direction to our partnership. While much will depend on the direction of change in the former Soviet republics, a common transatlantic home should be built on five pillars:

1. NATO guarantees for Eastern Europe. Soon after their liberation, the East European democracies began casting about for new security arrangements. At first, they sought to elevate the Conference on Security and Cooperation in Europe (CSCE) into a new all-European collective security arrangement. Then, Poland, Czechoslovakia, and Hungary discussed the formation of a trilateral partnership of their own. Later, all three began floating the idea of creating some kind of "associate status" with the NATO alliance. While NATO has welcomed observers from the new democracies at its headquarters, no concrete security commitment has been expressed or implied. A common transatlantic home requires us to be more responsive to East European security needs.

Collective security through the CSCE is a nonstarter. It has thirty-five diverse members even before the newly independent republics of the Soviet Union are added to its ranks. Its rules requiring unanimity for action create insurmountable hurdles for collective defense. It would recreate the days of the League of Nations, when aggressors could veto collective actions designed to stop them. Moreover, the Conference on Security and Cooperation in Europe is just that: a conference, a diplomatic process, not a real bricks-and-mortar institution. It cannot provide tangible security arrangements, such as the integrated military structure of NATO. Unless institutionalized and bolstered with well-trained and well-equipped forces, the CSCE can never contribute more than added confidence-building measures and a forum for discussion. In a major crisis, it will never be capable of doing more than adopting nonenforceable, wrist-slapping resolutions.

While we should encourage the creation of a trilateral security organization linking Poland, Hungary, and Czechoslovakia, we must not delude ourselves into thinking that alone such action suffices. It is tempting to assume that the defeat of communism will leave peace in its wake and allow all the nations of Europe to focus on economic development. With the profound political instability and dire economic situation in Eastern Europe and the former Soviet Union, the region could still become a geopolitical demolition derby. In any wrenching economic crisis, the potential exists for the rise of demagogues, who might play not only on the pain of the transition to the free market but also on virulent nationalism. In Yugoslavia, Serbian Communists have traded on ultra-nationalism both to keep power and to launch a civil war. While current Russian leaders have combined their nationalism with democracy, we cannot exclude the possibility that others might later emerge who might vent its darker side. If concern still exists about Germany, which has had a democratic government for forty years, there will be even more reason for concern about Russia, which has had a democratic government for less than one year. To put the East Europeans up against Russia would be like fielding an Ivy League football team against the Washington Redskins.

As Europe's only time-tested security structure, NATO should seek to find ways to fill the security vacuum in Eastern Europe, particularly over the next decade when the uncertainty centering on instability within the former Soviet Union will run the highest. This does not mean that NATO members should immediately extend its full Article 5 commitment —"an armed attack on one or more of them in Europe or North America shall be considered an attack on all of them" —to the new democracies. But it does mean that we should think in more subtle terms than an all-or-nothing guarantee. NATO, after all, functions at various levels, including political consultation, military cooperation, and participation in its integrated military command. Because they share our values and because the current vacuum creates an incentive for adventurism, the East European democracies must be brought into NATO's security sphere without granting them immediate full partnership.

In the short term, while Soviet troops complete their pullout from Eastern Europe, NATO should foster political ties with Poland, Czechoslovakia, and Hungary, the only former satellites that have become full-fledged democracies. The

United States and its Western European allies should unambiguously declare that NATO has a critical interest in the survival and security of these new democracies. With the collapse of Soviet communism, there is no reason to withhold such a commitment. While the June 1991 NATO statement of concern for Eastern Europe's security was an excellent beginning, we must go further, putting down a marker that no potential aggressor could ignore. By linking our commitment to democratic rule in East European countries, it will give added incentive to these nations to avoid a reversion to authoritarianism.

In the longer term, NATO should develop formal security links with the East European democracies. Our goal should be their full integration into NATO. In the interim we should take concrete steps in that direction. Historically, almost no previous alliance comes close to matching the level of cooperation inherent in NATO. Its integrated military command stands as the exception, not the rule. Much can therefore be done to build a security relationship with Eastern Europe without bestowing the full rights of NATO membership. For example, formal ties could be developed between NATO and a new trilateral pact between Poland, Czechoslovakia, and Hungary. In a treaty, the two organizations could agree to respond to threats and attacks on the other, though leaving the choice of specific counteractions to each side's constitutional and alliance procedures. At the same time, cooperative programs could train the new East European officer corps at NATO institutions, as well as seek eventually to achieve a degree of interoperability in military equipment.

A whole range of possibilities exists to fill the security vacuum in Eastern Europe through measured NATO actions. There is no magic to any particular combination of policies. But we will never build a common transatlantic home if

NATO forces the East Europeans to live outside its protective walls.

2. U.S. activism in Eastern Europe. Interests, not altruism, lead states to cooperate. We must recognize that in the coming decades the thrust of our policy in Europe should center on those states that most need the U.S. connection: the new democracies in Eastern Europe. The United States should make its new relationship with Eastern Europe as important as its traditional ties with Western Europe.

With the receding Soviet threat and advancing integration, Western Europe's need for close links with the United States will precipitously diminish. But the countries of Eastern Europe, struggling against enormous economic odds, have a great interest in fostering U.S. ties, especially to help them emerge from the shadow of Western European economic domination. Also, as the European Community grants associate-member status to the East Europeans, a close economic relationship could give the United States a potential back door into an increasingly protectionist post-1992 Europe. Although the Bush administration has sketched a credible blueprint for such a relationship, we need to expand its efforts.

We should urge broader implementation of the Polish "shock therapy" model. A clear bottom line has emerged from the experience of transforming command into market economies: faster is better. Trying to phase in the market or build a halfway house between the two systems produces more problems than it solves. Poland, which adopted key macroeconomic reforms almost overnight, experienced the jolt of 200 percent inflation and a 40 percent drop in real income. Even though the Poles still face a long and difficult road to recovery, the mainsprings of the market—free prices, fiscal- and monetary-policy restraint, and international currency convertibility—have begun to turn the situation around. In Yugoslavia, Hungary, and the Soviet Union, where leaders temporized, a vicious cycle developed. Gradualism, far from easing the transition, created protracted agony. That, in turn, generated political pressure to retreat, thereby compounding economic problems and dislocations. Reform through half measures means all pain and no gain.

After helping achieve macroeconomic stability, we should focus not on big-ticket government-to-government aid but on jump-starting the system at the microeconomic level. Before the East Europeans can set the wheel of capitalism in motion, they have to reinvent it. Private property—the link between work and reward—is the key. While Poland, Czechoslovakia, and Hungary have moved quickly, if haltingly, to develop programs to privatize state-owned enterprises, the United States should help on a parallel track by channeling funds into their private sectors, not only through direct investment, but also through infusions of capital by U.S.-sponsored "enterprise funds." Already operating in Poland and Hungary, the funds train local bankers in sound lending practices and provide them with money for loans to entrepreneurs, which average about $15,000. Unlike the European Bank for Reconstruction and Development—whose bureaucrats seem determined to reproduce clones of West European interventionist economic systems—the enterprise funds will foster competitive market-oriented economies at the grass-roots level.

Though the initial response of Western nations to the needs of Eastern Europe was generous, our financial commitment has yet to match our geopolitical stakes in the success of free-market economics in the nations of the former Soviet bloc. In 1991, for example, the city of Denver paid more money for an expansion baseball team than the United States gave in aid to the people of Poland. This is intolerable. If the Polish people are willing to suffer the transition pains inherent in moving from a command to a free-market economy, we should be willing to invest enough resources to ensure that their cause has the best possible chance of success.

We should help the reformist governments of Eastern Europe to privatize small-scale enterprises. Since 1989, investors have promoted the sale of Eastern Europe's economic dinosaurs—those industrial monoliths representative of prehistoric times in Eastern Europe's development. But while these dinosaurs are becoming extinct, little has been done to stimulate the growth of small firms, already an endangered species in Eastern Europe. To make this process more effective, the privatization of small firms must be accompanied by the privatization of the banking, agricultural, and housing sectors.

We should open American business schools in each East European country to teach skills required to make the nuts and bolts of capitalism work. These nations need not only financial but also human capital. Those who advocate a Marshall Plan for Eastern Europe are totally unrealistic. While the nations of Eastern Europe, like those of Western Europe after World War II, are democracies, they do not have a management class capable of effectively using such aid. Forty-five years of Communist "peace" in Eastern Europe were far more devastating to the management class than were five years of war in Western Europe, despite its enormous casualties.

The nations of Eastern Europe lack the tens of thousands of managers, accountants, and other specialists needed to work the levers of capitalism. The U.S. schools would focus not on the esoterics of econometrics but on teaching basic skills on a massive scale. In view of the modest facilities required—just classrooms and books—these institutions could be established quickly and cheaply. In addition, we should not ignore the need to train government regulators, particularly in the banking and antitrust fields. Without strict but sensible regulation, reforms can become a transition not to a market but to anarchy. East Europeans should learn lessons about the S&L disaster from the books rather than from experience.

We should open Western markets to East European exports. Trade represents the major hope for rapid economic development. With Moscow demanding hard-currency payment for its exports, East European energy costs soared by $20 billion in 1991. Foreign debts limit their credit. Because of the current uncompetitive quality of East European goods, the 30 percent of Polish, Czechoslovak, and Hungarian exports that went to the Soviet Union or East Germany—markets now closed or vanished—has few buyers. It is imperative that the European Community grant them associate status as soon as possible and that the United States immediately liberalize trade by increasing the list of imports given duty-free entry. Since sustained economic growth depends not on aid but on trade, the West must lift these counterproductive obstacles.

In order to prevent potential ethnic conflicts, we should work with the continent's leaders to channel the new East European nationalism in constructive directions. Those who look with dismay at nationalism's reemergence should remember that only their sense of distinct identity enabled these peoples to resist and triumph over forty-five years of Soviet indoctrination and repression. Yet, while we should not begrudge natural expressions of nationalism that all Western nations take for granted, we cannot ignore the new potential for ethnic-based conflicts within and among East

European states. National borders do not neatly divide separate nations. Poland, Hungary, Bulgaria, and Romania all have significant national minorities, while Czechoslovakia and Yugoslavia actually are not nation-states but multinational states.

In Yugoslavia, the United States should come down unequivocally in favor of independence for Slovenia and Croatia. Those who contend that they are too small to be independent countries should be reminded that Slovenia, with its two million people, has a larger population than fifty-eight current members of the United Nations. In the year before the current crisis, both republics consistently expressed the willingness to stay within Yugoslavia if its structure was transformed into a confederation. Their calls for reform were rejected out of hand by the Communist leadership of the federal government and the Serbian republic. Tragically, on the eve of the current armed hostilities, officials from the United States and the European Community made ill-advised statements in support of Yugoslavia's central government, thereby appearing to give a green light to the use of force by the Communists. It makes no sense to try to maintain the artificial unity of Yugoslavia. The United States and Western Europe should have backed up their demands for an end to Serbian aggression against Croatia with a resolution in the U.N. Security Council calling for the immediate dispatch of peacekeeping forces to Yugoslavia. In this civil war—the first critical test of the post-cold-war European order—the West has so far earned a failing grade.

In the longer term, we should encourage Europe's leaders —from both west and east—to develop a formal charter of national minority rights. The international community has articulated individual human rights in the U.N. Charter, the Helsinki Final Act, and other documents. But apart from the

Genocide Convention of 1948, it has not stipulated the legitimate rights of national minorities. While the issue arises also outside of Europe—the Kurds and the Tibetans, for example —Europe's democratic consensus might enable its leaders to address the question forthrightly. A new European charter must not shift the basis of law from individual to group rights. But it could set guidelines for guaranteeing legitimate national rights in such areas as language use in education and respect for religious freedom, thereby helping to reduce the danger of civil strife or even war resulting from Eastern Europe's and the former Soviet Union's potentially explosive national mosaic.

All these steps are needed to integrate the new East European democracies into the common transatlantic home. None is a question of charity. Our interests, as well as theirs, will be advanced by making Eastern Europe the focal point of the U.S. political and economic presence in the region.

3. *Close U.S.-German partnership.* While the United States should continue its traditional special relationship with Great Britain based on a common heritage and similar assessments of world problems, we need to develop a close working partnership with Germany because of the scope of our mutual power. Our two countries account for 60 percent of NATO's GNP and its defense spending. Just as Chancellor Kohl and President Bush secured rapid German unification by closely coordinating their actions vis-à-vis Moscow, working together—which will require both sides to compromise—our countries can achieve far more than by working at cross-purposes.

Not only in Europe but also around the world, enduring memories of World War II still limit Germany's ability to play a role commensurate with its economic power and geopolitical importance. In the Persian Gulf crisis, both internal and external anxieties about greater German activism produced a confused and ineffective policy, with Bonn's ultimate military contribution amounting to a paltry 720 troops deployed in the inactive Turkish theater. To allay suspicions about a wider global role for Germany, its leaders must work with the other Western powers, particularly the United States. In view of our mutual interests, we should develop a common agenda, with the United States providing the needed "political cover" for a more active German foreign policy.

At the same time, the United States needs a European partner dedicated to expanding opportunities for world trade. Since Germany's exports account for 35 percent of its GNP —one of the highest totals in the West—Berlin has a profound interest in keeping markets open. We should therefore work in tandem to avoid a post-1992 "fortress Europe," because higher tariffs will lead to a cycle of retaliation. In addition, we must resolve the outstanding disputes in the Uruguay Round of the General Agreement on Trade and Tariffs (GATT) talks. While the West Europeans bicker about retaining $81.6 billion in trade-distorting agricultural subsidies, we risk losing an estimated $5 trillion of additional global economic growth over the next decade that a Uruguay Round agreement would bring. A U.S.-German partnership could not only overcome the pleadings of Europe's and America's special interests, but it could quiet catcalls from pundits on both sides of the Atlantic who support the "go it alone" approach.

In coordinating fiscal and monetary policies among the major industrial democracies, the United States should at times follow Germany's lead. U.S. Presidents have repeatedly tried to "jawbone" the Germans to lower interest rates to stimulate the world economy. But we need to concede the wisdom of Germany's approach. Our looser monetary policies have produced an inflation rate of 6 percent, while Germany's stands at 3 percent. As a result, U.S. interest rates on long-term loans—which are critical for capital development—run significantly higher than those in Germany. We should therefore think twice before pressing the Germans to ease up on the money supply after every momentary blip in the index of leading economic indicators. While their approach might limit growth in the short term, it recognizes the need to eliminate inflationary expectations in order to enhance the prospects of growth in the long term.

Another issue on our mutual agenda should be controlling the transfer of key technologies to the developing world. The activities of German firms in Libya and Iraq have given Berlin a black eye. Germany does not need a reputation for moral indifference or irresponsibility as it tries to reemerge on the world stage. Unless Germany reins in its freewheeling arms exporters and unless the West clamps down on technology exports to rogue states such as Iraq and Syria, we will someday confront a new Saddam Hussein armed not with SCUDs but ICBMs. To create the impression that Germany is a geopolitical chameleon would not only undermine U.S.-German relations but also would reinforce the historical anxieties about a wider German world role.

A U.S.-German partnership does not mean that our interests will always coincide. But our profound stake in such mutual cooperation will override our differences. Working together, President Bush and Chancellor Kohl achieved something Moscow repeatedly vowed it would never accept: a united Germany fully integrated into NATO. While Germany may not be fully comfortable with its growing world role, it is still the undisputed economic heavyweight of Europe. In the future, our partnership should become ever-more pivotal in advancing our common interests and values.

This partnership will take time to develop and will only

work if Germany remains a responsible Western power rather than a country jockeying for position between East and West. At the same time, a special relationship with Germany does not imply the United States putting greater distance between itself and Britain, France, Italy, and other NATO nations. Not only will close relations with our traditional European allies check Germany's drift to the East, but they also make strategic sense. Britain's and France's support, both political and economic, represented a linchpin of success in the Persian Gulf War. Moreover, together they represent a major economic counterweight to Germany within the European Community, as evidenced by the fact that France's advances in integrating communications and computer technologies lead the world.

4. *An open-door policy vis-à-vis the newly independent republics of the Soviet Union.* The purpose of the common transatlantic home is not to exclude any nations but to include those nations committed to free-market and democratic values. Before I met with Khrushchev in 1959, British prime minister Harold Macmillan told me that more than anything else the Soviets wanted to be treated like "members of the club." Now that the nations of the Soviet Union have rejected communism, their credentials for membership are in good order. Before the coup, most of the U.S. foreign policy establishment, in the name of stability, decried nationalist movements that opposed Gorbachev. They were wrong. Stability at the cost of individual freedom and national independence is too high a price to pay. We should not condemn nationalism but only the excesses of extreme nationalists. We must find ways to integrate into the West those former Soviet republics that establish democratic institutions, adopt free-market reforms, and respect the rights of national minorities within their borders.

For most of its history, Russia has been pulled by two

traditions—one to withdraw into an insular existence and the other to join the Western world. The defeat of communism following the August 1991 coup signaled a decisive move away from the tradition of Asiatic despotism that dominated Russian foreign policy for over four hundred years and particularly since the Bolshevik Revolution in 1917. Much remains to be done to undo the legacies of the Russian imperial tradition. But under Yeltsin, Russia has placed its relations with the non-Russian peoples of the former Soviet Union on a new and just footing. If he succeeds in creating a nonimperial, noncommunist Russia, the West should roll out the red carpet of freedom in welcoming his Russia into the common transatlantic home.

5. *Restructuring NATO for new missions.* Alliances are held together by fear, not by love. When fear of a common threat fades, allies tend to drift apart. To paraphrase MacArthur, old alliances never die, they just fade away. Today, NATO must adapt or risk irrelevance. To survive, the alliance must redefine its missions and sense of purpose.

Many observers believe that NATO should become a political rather than a military alliance. In view of the massive changes in Eastern Europe and the Soviet Union, they argue, the focus of NATO should shift from common defense to diplomatic conferences, from force planning to crisis management, from calculating logistics to drafting cables. This view concludes that only by radically overhauling its basic purpose can NATO play a meaningful role in the future.

If adopted, this view would eventually consign NATO to the historical scrap heap. No alliance has ever survived for long after security ceased to be its core function. No political substitute exists for the bonds of collective defense. Moreover, in the hardheaded world of power politics, no diplomatic or political initiative can succeed unless backed by credible military capabilities. This does not mean that NATO cannot add new political missions. But it does mean that we must not confuse NATO's raison d'être—forging a transatlantic security link—with other important but secondary goals. A political function for NATO is useful and even essential. But it cannot replace mutual security as the glue that keeps the alliance together. In this new setting, the key task for the United States is not to disengage from NATO gracefully but for NATO to adapt skillfully.

In the fog of public debate, two options have begun to emerge. The first—the NATO option—centers around a continuing U.S. commitment to a major force presence in Europe. While the numbers of U.S. troops in Europe would substantially decrease, the centrality of our role in the alliance and its integrated military command would remain unchanged. The second—the European Community option—seeks to develop a principally European security structure, though with continued U.S. participation. Ultimately, our allies will coalesce around the latter. While they understand the need for our nuclear guarantee—and accept the voice that gives America in Europe's security decisions—they will object to a U.S. policy that supports European political unity but demands a security relationship in which Washington retains its dominant leadership role.

Our approach should welcome increased West European self-reliance. When we brought our forces to a peak deployment of over four hundred thousand troops in the mid-1950s, I vividly recall a meeting of the National Security Council when President Eisenhower said that he intended this to be only a temporary measure needed until our allies in Europe recovered from the war. We should not allow it to become a permanent crutch. If the Europeans develop the capability of speaking with one voice on political and security matters—which is possible but not inevitable—we should embrace the European Community option.

This does not mean that we should withdraw all of our ground forces from Europe. But it does mean that our function should involve a conventional and nuclear deployment much smaller than today but still large enough to create the essential link of mutual security and to preserve the military infrastructure for any U.S. intervention that might become necessary in a crisis. Forces in Europe are also indispensable for contingencies elsewhere, including the Persian Gulf War. NATO should not cut back on its joint exercises, though their nature and location should take into account sensitivities about disrupting civilian life. Exercises not only iron out glitches in contingency plans but also enhance our ability to work together in areas outside of Europe, such as the Persian Gulf.

NATO must also reevaluate the role of nuclear weapons in its defense plans. Since nuclear artillery and short-range missiles were deployed principally to neutralize massed Soviet armor concentrations in East Germany, we can safely phase them out as President Bush has chosen to do. But as long as nuclear weapons exist, NATO needs a nuclear option based in Europe, though air-based and sea-based missiles should be sufficient to cover all required missions. As a result, we should reject out of hand Gorbachev's proposal to eliminate these systems—a proposal designed to achieve Moscow's traditional objective of a denuclearized and vulnerable Europe.

As NATO finds its footing in the new Europe, it should also expand its mission. In Europe, it should focus not just on common defense but also on pressing for just solutions to such conflicts as the Yugoslav civil war. It must also look beyond Europe. Its creators did not envision that by specifying that the NATO commitment applied to Europe and North America, the alliance would operate only within a strict boundary. Instead, they simply sought to exclude Europe's colonies from security guarantees requiring an automatic response from other members. Today, as demonstrated in the Persian Gulf, challenges to Western interests can arise half a world away. If NATO adheres mindlessly to artificial geographical restrictions, we will simply be shooting ourselves in the foot, compromising our interests to legalism. For example, an effort to cut the oil lifeline of Western Europe is as great a threat to the security of NATO nations as a military attack against a NATO member. While European defense must remain NATO's core mission, so-called "out of area" security cooperation must become its cutting edge. Unless we adopt such a policy, the American people—whose commitment to NATO has depended on the perception of a Soviet threat—will inevitably seek to disengage from Europe as the alliance increasingly speaks of Moscow not as an adversary but as a "partner in security."

While we already cooperate in distant crises, our solutions tend to be ad hoc. To improve NATO's capabilities to cope with out-of-area conflicts, we need to move forward in three areas. First, the European members of NATO should develop a joint rapid deployment force that would function, depending on circumstances, independently or under an integrated command with similar U.S. forces. Second, the United States should welcome European activism in parts of the underdeveloped world where their historical experience exceeds our own. For too long, Americans have assumed that our superior military power gave us superior political wisdom. In addition, because the next crisis will likely take place in the underdeveloped world, the United States should open its overseas bases outside Europe to our NATO allies. Our current policy restricts foreign military powers from using our bases, but we should be more flexible in order to facilitate greater European activism in critical parts of the underdeveloped world. Third, NATO should develop better mechanisms for more coordinated crisis management. Working together, the members of the Atlantic alliance—which control over half of the world economy—wield power that no potential adversary can afford to ignore. In addition, if the Western allies back a common course of action in the U.N. Security Council, potential aggressors will have to take notice.

NATO must loosen, not tighten, its structure. To grow, it needs greater flexibility to be able to respond not only to military but also to political contingencies. This does not mean that either the United States or Western Europe should have a strict veto over the other's actions. Each will have interests that the other will not share. But they must develop ways to arrive at common policies to out-of-area conflicts when possible, as well as equipping the alliance with the needed military, economic, and political instruments to carry them out. Unlike other alliances, which have dissolved as the threat of a common enemy wanes, a renewed NATO can survive the test of victory.

These five pillars provide a framework for a common transatlantic home. The new Europe is not a problem-free Europe, and these objectives cannot be achieved without commitment and resources on both sides of the Atlantic. Yet if we succeed, we will advance Europe's unification, ensure its external security, buttress its internal stability, and protect its key interests around the world.

Europeans need an active U.S. presence. Eurocommunism

has been replaced by Eurocriticism of America's role, but our allies inevitably turn to the United States in any crisis and even count on us to mediate disputes among themselves. The United States has been—and continues to be—the indispensable catalyst for cooperation among Europeans, who often trust us more than they trust each other.

The critical issue for Europe is whether economic unity will produce a parochial or an open Europe. Critics wrongly scorned former prime minister Margaret Thatcher's position on European unification. Her warnings about a unified but inward-looking and protectionist Europe were misinterpreted as opposition to any unity at all. She understood that the rush to create the mechanisms of unity had clouded the need to craft the meaning of unity. In her vision, European economic unification should serve as the necessary precursor to Atlantic economic unification. On the eve of post-1992 Europe, its leaders must understand that unity will serve European interests only if it represents the first step toward moving out into the world and not toward retreating behind the cloistered walls of a fortress Europe.

History's most devastating wars have been fought in Europe. For the past forty-five years, the cold war has ironically kept the peace in Europe. Our challenge is to see that the end of the cold war does not open the door for future hot wars. Beyond that goal, the nations in the common transatlantic home can lead the way to unprecedented economic progress and the victory of freedom throughout the world.

As we build the transatlantic home, the reach of our vision should not stop at the Soviet border. Instead, the doors of a common transatlantic home should be open to newly independent republics of the Soviet Union that meet the economic and political requirements for membership. The former Soviet government—established on Leninist, not democratic, principles—did not measure up to those criteria. But if free-market and democratic reforms continue under the non-communist governments in Moscow and in the newly independent Soviet republics, we should seek their participation in building a common transatlantic home from California to Kamchatka.

4

THE PACIFIC TRIANGLE

MANY OBSERVERS HAVE proclaimed that the world will soon enter "the Pacific century." In their view, Europe dominated the nineteenth century, the United States became preeminent in the twentieth century, and the Pacific rim region will take center stage in the twenty-first century. They foresee this westward shift in history's focal point as the dynamic economies of East Asia become the engine of world economic growth. But a perilous paradox—explosive prosperity combined with political instability—has clouded the region's great potential. Whether the Pacific rim's historical contribution will be greater wealth or greater conflict depends on how the United States manages its relations with the countries of the Pacific triangle: Japan, China, and the Soviet Union.

Enormous geographically, critical strategically, and dynamic economically, the nations of the Pacific rim—with a total population of almost 2 billion—have astonished the world with their recent achievements. Most of the world's successful developing countries are in East Asia. Of the region's twenty-three countries, eight have had average annual economic growth rates of at least 5 percent during the last decade, some of them averaging almost 10 percent. No Western European country experienced such explosive growth. With a total GNP of $4,410 billion, the Pacific rim commands 20 percent of the world economy. In 1989, trade between the United States and East Asia topped $300 billion, outstripping by far the $200 billion in U.S. trade with Western Europe.

Stability, however, has not accompanied prosperity in the Pacific rim. Since 1945, twelve major wars and armed conflicts have taken place in the region. The United States, whose involvement in World War II started and ended in the Pacific, fought two of its three major wars in the postwar period in Korea and Vietnam. Today, 1.5 million troops line both sides of the Korean armistice line, and Indochina remains mired in bloody guerrilla conflicts, while political turbulence plagues the Philippines, Thailand, New Guinea, and others. In addition, deep-rooted suspicions, recriminations, and rivalries pit many East Asian nations against each other.

Because of the lack of a formal security framework like NATO, the balance among the great powers becomes critical in determining the Pacific rim's future. Only the United States possesses sufficient leverage with each of the corners of the Pacific triangle to balance and stabilize the region as each major power seeks to advance its interests:

—Japan, an economic heavyweight but a political and military lightweight, has stumbled as its leaders search for a new role in the world commensurate with its great resources.

—China, a potential economic superpower and a major political player, stands at a crossroads—its people seeking to break with the Communist past but its current leaders unwilling to relinquish their totalitarian control.

—The former Soviet Union, a declining economic power but a towering military power in the Pacific, has the potential to convert its armed might into a greater presence politically and greater access to the region's capital and technology.

The United States interacts with each of the corners of the Pacific triangle—balancing them off each other, stabilizing them as they compete with each other, and at the same time maintaining a distance of peace between them. As a result, the United States has played the major role in securing peace and stability in the Pacific since 1945, thereby creating the indispensable political foundation for its economic prosperity. But traditional ambitions, geopolitical maneuvering, and colliding interests have created a potentially explosive mix. If the United States remains engaged, it will increase the likelihood that a Pacific century will be a pacific century. Without a major U.S. role, it could become a century of conflict.

• • •

Japan has arrived as a world power, but it is still searching for its proper role. Because of the memories of its aggression and brutal occupation policies during World War II, the key to a wider role remains its links with the United States. Yet at a time when our political cooperation could ease Japan's emergence on the world scene, our economic disagreements threaten to break the relationship apart.

In 1990, a headline in a major U.S. newspaper trumpeted, "Japan Takes Lead Role on World Stage." The growth of the Japanese economic powerhouse—whose share of world industrial output increased from 2.5 percent in 1913 to 5 percent in 1938 to 10 percent in 1990—fueled the belief that while Japan lost World War II militarily, it would now prevail over its former foes economically. From 1950 to 1973, Japan's real annual growth rate averaged 10 percent, while the size of its GNP rose from one-twentieth of the U.S. economy in 1950 to over one-half in 1991. Japan has become the second-largest economy in the world, the largest creditor, and the second-largest exporter of manufactured goods. Its per capita income of $25,000 in 1991 was highest among major industrial countries. It has the ten largest banks in the world and spends more on capital investment than America. After the United States, it is the second-largest contributor to the IMF and the U.N. budget. In 1991, Japanese capital financed one-third of the U.S. federal budget deficit. According to some estimates, Japan could exceed the United States in absolute economic output early in the next century.

As the only major country with a stable democratic system along the Pacific rim and as our only major regional ally since the signing of the original U.S.-Japan Mutual Security Treaty in 1951, Japan's importance to the United States extends far beyond simple economic cooperation. The potential achievements of a cooperative relationship are enormous. Together we can use our influence to stem the global tide of protectionism and to keep world markets open. We can also manage refugee flows, curb illegal drug trafficking, and develop programs to address global environmental problems. There is, however, no guarantee of success. Because of our economic tensions, we must renew our relationship or risk losing it.

Since 1945, the United States has dominated its relationship with Japan. Defeated in World War II, occupied until 1952, and dependent on America for security even today, Tokyo played a subordinate role. U.S. officials drafted Japan's constitution, including the clause stipulating that "the Japanese people forever renounce war as a sovereign right of the nation." The war-renunciation clause became the keystone of Japanese strategic planning and forced Tokyo to depend on the United States for its security.

As the Soviet economy and empire collapsed, the foundation of the U.S.-Japanese relationship began to weaken. Many Americans argued that the United States should no longer foot the bill for Japan's defense, especially because this in effect subsidized Tokyo economically. At the same time, many Japanese believed that their need for the U.S. security guarantee had diminished and therefore they no longer needed to exercise restraint in the economic competition between the two countries. Before the waning of the cold war, security concerns tempered this competition. Now, with those restraints weakened, economic concerns have supplanted security issues.

Some U.S. analysts now look at security problems through an economic lens. They argue that the 1 percent of Japan's GNP spent on defense has been totally inadequate and that the United States should lean on Japan to increase sharply its military budget and to assume more of the burden for its own security. They fail to realize, however, that to insist that the Japanese develop military forces beyond those necessary to meet the limited goals of territorial self-defense and sea-lane security is counterproductive strategically and unrealistic politically.

A resurgent Japanese military would cause great regional apprehensions. Historical memories from World War II have not vanished. Despite forty-five years of peaceful policies, the fear in Asia of Japan as a major military power dwarfs European concerns about a united Germany. Any plan for Japan to develop offensive capabilities would meet with strong opposition from Koreans, Chinese, Taiwanese, Malaysians, Filipinos, and Indonesians, all of whom suffered under Japanese occupation during World War II. Instead of enhancing regional security, a Japanese arms buildup would complicate defense cooperation and trigger higher military spending throughout the region.

Internal as well as external fears of Japanese militarism inhibit Japan's defense role. Many Japanese are afraid that the same tendencies that drove Imperial Japan into World War II now lie dormant but could easily be awakened. They fear a replay of the 1930s, when Japan followed up its economic penetration of the region with its military invasion. While they do not believe the Japanese people are innately militaristic, they do fear that a strong military establishment could come to dominate their foreign policy. And they know that their hard-won working relationships with their Asian neighbors would be jeopardized the moment Japan assumed a higher military profile.

Japan's critics overlook the major progress Tokyo has made in providing for its own security. It has increased its support for U.S. forces stationed in Japan to cover 50 percent of their total costs. It has undertaken a sustained military modernization program to develop forces to defend its own territory and to protect one thousand miles of vital sea-lanes.

Moreover, with the size of Japan's economy, the 1 percent of GNP Tokyo allocates to defense approaches in absolute terms the military budgets of Germany, Britain, and France, even though their military establishments receive a higher proportion of their GNPs.

Iraq's invasion of Kuwait in August 1990 presented a classic example of the Japanese dilemma. Tokyo, which imports 70 percent of its oil from Persian Gulf countries, could not mobilize itself politically to make a meaningful contribution to protect its vital interests in Operation Desert Shield/Storm. Despite its $30-billion defense budget and its 250,000-man Self-Defense Forces, Japanese soldiers—who have not gone abroad even as part of a U.N. or multilateral peacekeeping force—never left their barracks. Instead, Tokyo contributed by reluctantly reaching into its wallet.

After sharp criticism of its first offer of a $1-billion contribution in September 1990, Japanese politicians desperately searched for a new policy consistent with international demands and domestic apprehensions. Some proposed a "Peace Cooperation Corps" consisting of troops who would broadly support U.N. goals and work on humanitarian programs but who would remain unarmed and would not participate specifically in the mission of collective self-defense. One legislator demanded that soldiers resign from the Self-Defense Forces before participating in such a corps. When this idea suffered an agonizing death in a prolonged and confused debate in the Japanese Diet, Tokyo offered to toss an additional $1-billion contribution into the pot in December 1990, which most observers derided as paltry. After sustained diplomatic arm-twisting from the United States, Japan finally committed $11 billion in financial support and managed to deploy a small unarmed medical unit and—after the fighting —four minesweepers.

Japan was paralyzed by its debate about what to do, when

to do it, and how much to give. Its factional political system failed to produce a timely decision on an issue that involved its vital interests and that required an immediate response. Tokyo lacked the national will to act when it mattered. When the Japanese did finally act, they did so hesitantly and equivocally, dodging greater responsibilities through legalistic pretexts based on tortured readings of its constitutional provisions. Most significant, the Persian Gulf War demonstrated that Japan simply cannot step up to the military responsibilities inherent in any wider regional role.

Instead of browbeating Japan to increase its military budget, the United States should work toward increasing Tokyo's geopolitical role in five ways:

Enhance cooperative development of defense-related technologies. The link between Japan's technological advancements and U.S. military development should be strengthened. Both countries would benefit from the integration of Japanese research in lasers, computers, sensors, and space technology into U.S. weapons research. At a minimum, we must prevent rising protectionist sentiments from stifling technological cooperation. At the same time, we should seek to develop major joint projects targeted at high-tech defense requirements, especially SDI-related programs.

Increase Japanese economic aid to strategic countries. To compensate for its low level of defense spending, Japan should allocate substantially more resources to helping those developing countries in which the West has a strategic stake. Already Tokyo's foreign aid budget of over $15 billion exceeds that of the United States. But Japanese aid policies have been deeply flawed. Since most of its money has been tied to the purchase of Japanese goods, these programs have sought to advance Japan's unilateral economic objectives more than our mutual security interests. As one Southeast Asian official observed to me in 1985, "When the Japanese provide foreign aid, they are like semiconductors. They take everything in and give nothing in return."

In addition, Japan's aid has not been channeled sufficiently to strategic countries, such as Egypt or the East European democracies. While Japanese military policies will be debated and possibly changed in the future, Japanese economic strength is a reality today and should be strategically targeted. We should not ask the Japanese to be philanthropists or to flip open their checkbook to fund every faddish idea from Washington. Instead, we should ask that they use their enormous economic power to serve our interests as well as theirs.

Provide funds to facilitate solutions of regional conflicts. Japan lacks the political muscle to help resolve the world's difficult regional conflicts, such as the Arab-Israeli dispute or the wars in Afghanistan, Cambodia, and Central America. It should stand ready, however, to provide the financial support needed for the internationally supervised elections, multilateral peacekeeping forces, economic compensation, or follow-up aid packages often mandated as part of wider settlements.

Subsidize U.S.-led efforts to develop security arrangements for the Persian Gulf. In view of Japan's dependence on Persian Gulf oil, it should provide economic assistance to help the United States and other Western powers preposition supplies and develop the infrastructure to guarantee the region's security from Iraq and other potential aggressors. Domestic constraints prevent Japan from taking a more ambitious role. But we are entitled to expect financial support for these collaborative Western security efforts.

Provide economic aid to the democratic republics of the former Soviet Union as part of a comprehensive geopolitical accommodation. In stark contrast to the U.S. return of Okinawa to Japan in 1971, previous Soviet governments have refused to return the four Japanese islands seized by Stalin in 1945. With noncommunist governments now in power in the Kremlin and in the Russian republic, Japan should be able to negotiate a return of the islands and lay the groundwork for economic aid to reformist former Soviet republics, provided that the new governments adopt viable free-market reforms.

The worst move the United States could make would be to withdraw from its forward bases along the Pacific rim. If we cast aside our security alliance with Japan—which has served as an anchor of stability in the region—Tokyo will confront one nuclear superpower, Moscow, and another aspiring nuclear superpower, Beijing, a few miles off its shores. Without credible U.S. security guarantees, Japan would have two grim options. First, it could develop its own nuclear forces. Second, it could strike a deal—trading economic support for military protection—with either of the other two corners of the Pacific triangle. While Japan would be reluctant to move in either of these directions, it will have little choice if abandoned by the United States.

The greatest threat to the U.S.-Japanese relationship, however, lies not in security disputes but in economic antagonisms. Many Americans decry the specter of the Japanese "buying up America." The Japanese, they suspect, are turning America into an economic colony. Yet despite their acquisition of highly visible assets—Universal Pictures, Rockefeller Center, and even Michael Jackson's $1-billion contract with Sony—Japanese-owned firms and assets account for only 17 percent of foreign investments in the United States, while those of Great Britain represent 30 percent. Ironically, many who strongly support U.S. investment abroad have xenophobically denounced businessmen who happen to be Japanese and who simply wish to invest in America.

The trade imbalance between our countries is the crux of the problem. The U.S. trade deficit with Japan was $46 billion in 1985, $55 billion in 1986, $60 billion in 1987, and $65 billion in 1990. The most important causes of the imbalance—exchange rates, budget deficits, economic cycles, varied growth rates, and domestic savings and investment levels —have been lost in the emotional melee of finger-pointing on both sides of the Pacific.

Japan's critics point out that Tokyo has exploited its low defense spending to enhance its competitiveness unfairly. In addition, they contend, the Japanese have made a fetish out of keeping foreign goods out of their markets. Japan outlaws some potential imports such as certain fruits and vegetables, inflicts astronomical duties on other goods such as telecommunications and medical equipment, turns a blind eye as domestic cartels vanquish international competitors, and sabotages some imports with red tape. When U.S. pressure builds up, the Japanese do not address our concerns but rather engage, as one critic put it, in an ingenious export shell game, shipping products to the U.S. market not from factories in Japan but from Japanese-owned facilities in such countries as Thailand. As sociologist Daniel Bell noted in a paraphrase of Clausewitz, "Economics is a continuation of war by other means."

America's critics blame the federal deficit and lagging competitiveness for the trade gap. Japan produces top-quality goods, they argue, while America turns out junk. Japan has a strong work ethic, while Americans are lazy. Japanese save, while Americans spend. Japan's economy grows by leaps and bounds, while America's grows by inches. Energy wasted demanding more open markets in Japan, they conclude, would be more productively used in undertaking needed structural adjustments in the United States, particularly decreasing the federal deficit, increasing the private savings rate, and ending the obsession in capital markets with short-term returns.

While those who coined the term *Japan, Inc.* exaggerate, some legitimate concerns exist about Japanese trade practices. Japan's government and business firms often work together so closely that they become virtually indistinguishable. Large industrial groups connected through interlocking directorates, shareholdings, and cartel membership and backed by guidance from government bureaucrats make the Japanese market a political as well as an economic battlefield. Many retail outlets, for example, are not independent but locked into subcontracts and controlled by dealer associations that give the most powerful manufacturers political control over the market. Monopolies, price-fixing, and other predatory economic tactics rule the intertwining business and political spheres. And both officials and manufacturers have a pernicious vested interest in maintaining this unfair system.

These individual power clusters operate internationally as well. The Ministry of Finance coordinates the important international moves of banks, security houses, and insurance firms. By contrast, rather than working as a partner of major U.S. multinational corporations or at least pursuing a policy of benign neglect, the U.S. government often acts as an antagonist.

Instead of complaining about an "economic evil empire," we must begin with the recognition that legitimate reasons exist for the trade deficit. Japan, for example, must generate a dollar trade surplus to pay for its huge oil-import bill. Moreover, Japan's tremendous economic success represents an easy scapegoat for American politicians seeking to deflect attention from our own economic problems. First, the combination of a high federal deficit and a low domestic savings rate requires capital imports, which, in turn, are reflected in a trade deficit in goods and services. Second, many U.S. companies lack the long-term horizons needed to cultivate the Japanese markets. Third, since 95 percent of Japan's young people but only 75 percent of America's graduate from high school, we have failed to invest sufficiently in our human capital. Some studies have pointed out that even if Japan eliminated all its import barriers, the U.S. trade deficit would drop by only $5–8 billion. They suggest that primarily the fault is ours, not theirs.

At the same time, we should not overlook Japan's economic weaknesses because of its great strengths. Japan's population is growing increasingly older. Today, 11 percent of the population is aged sixty-five or over. By 2025, that figure will rise to over 25 percent. More people will be going into retirement than entering the labor force. This employee vacuum must be filled if Japan is to sustain its economic growth. Because much of the generation under the age of twenty-five grew up relatively wealthy, however, they tend to leave jobs they do not like, to marry later in life, and to have fewer children. They reject the grueling work ethic of their elders, opting to spend ninety hours a week in recreation rather than in the workplace.

Women account for 40 percent of Japan's work force, but their talents are left largely untapped. Today, most Japanese women are channeled into traditionally "female" jobs, such as elevator hostesses and receptionists. Some Japanese firms require their female employees to wear uniforms, obey evening curfews, and live in company dormitories. Women are seldom appointed to high-level positions, with only 1 percent of women in the work force involved in management. Even when a woman holds a relatively prestigious position, she is expected to cater to her male counterparts by serving tea and cleaning the office.

Such subservience perpetuates the glass ceiling that blocks the professional and social advancement of Japanese women. While attitudes are slowly changing, women are strongly pressured to limit themselves to staying home and raising children, which the government encourages through $6,700 grants for women to have a third child. One edge we have over Japan is that we are far ahead in providing equal opportunities for women. Japan's economy would soar to even greater heights if women's capabilities and talents were unleashed by following our example.

The U.S.-Japanese relationship can only be saved if both sides make concessions. The United States can begin by reducing the federal deficit and improving its competitiveness. We should not fear but rather learn from competition. The Japanese can learn from us, and we can learn from them. We should reverse the trend toward retaliatory protectionism because trade barriers always backfire by triggering ever-escalating countermeasures. Broad-based trade retaliation leads to economic isolation. We should pursue carrot-and-stick policies vis-à-vis Japan in coordination with our European allies at the GATT talks and at the annual economic summits. Only as a last resort should we employ selective retaliation if the Japanese refuse to abandon clear and identifiable unfair trade practices.

Meanwhile, Japan must reduce its tariff and nontariff trade barriers. We should insist on structural reforms in the Japanese economic system that will eliminate monopolistic and anticompetitive practices of individual firms and cartels. If the Japanese want access to our markets, we must have access to theirs. Japan has already begun to open up its rice markets, which were traditionally closed to all imports. While such steps slowly build confidence between our two countries, they must be rapidly accelerated in order to prevent U.S.-Japanese economic competition from escalating into a trade war.

Despite forty-five years of close cooperation as allies, cultural barriers and suspicions compounded by economic antagonisms have fueled "Japan bashing" in the United States and "America bashing" in Japan. On both sides, this stems from the changing dynamics of our relationship: Japan no longer accepts America's tutelage, and America no longer accepts Japan's free ride. As these two great powers search for a new foundation for their alliance, special interests in both countries will seek to turn this friction into an explosion that would serve neither of our long-term interests. Because our natural economic competition spurs greater growth for both countries, we must not allow those who wish to inflame national passions to prevail.

These obstacles cannot be overcome easily, but can be reduced and eventually dismantled only if we curb needless rhetorical attacks and gradually cultivate mutual confidence. Because of the lack of a common heritage and social roots— best typified by America's exultation of and Japan's suppression of individualism—a lack of understanding often leads to mutual incomprehension, which, in turn, creates deep distrust. Despite the many Americans of Japanese descent and the many diverse ties between our two countries, we are still very different peoples. In fact, the greatest cultural link between the two countries is a common love of baseball.

Yet we share values and interests that naturally pull us together. We both believe in democratic government and free-market economics. We both have a major stake in the survival and expansion of global free trade. We both want to prevent international instability and to develop initiatives to manage environmental problems. We both are fiercely competitive and committed to excellence. Those Americans who feel most threatened by Japanese investments—and whose anxieties are mirrored and exaggerated by their representatives in Congress—work primarily in industries such as automaking, electronics, and textiles that have been most hurt by Japanese imports. Elsewhere, local and state officials compete eagerly for Japanese investment. Polls measuring U.S. attitudes toward other countries reveal that Americans associate the Japanese with qualities they apply to themselves: hardworking, creative, competitive, and peaceful.

While we should recognize our cultural and economic differences, we must find a way to work with them. Cultural barriers should be leveled, but not the cultures themselves. We should not try to be alike. We should respect and learn from our differences. Americans should continue to enjoy sushi, and the Japanese should continue to visit the Tokyo Disney World. Also, the political demands of U.S. and Japanese special interests should be kept in perspective. To allow differences over such issues to poison our relationship would be unworthy of the world's two strongest economic powers. Instead of wasting time chastising each other and instituting self-defeating policies, we must cooperate with each other constructively, maturely, and responsibly. America needs Japan, and Japan needs America. If we contribute from our strengths, our relationship will be even more complementary and mutually reinforcing. Working against each other will weaken us both. Working together we can ensure that the twenty-first century will be not only a century of peace for the Pacific but also a century of the greatest prosperity the world has ever known.

A greater global role for Japan is inevitable. Singapore's

former prime minister, Lee Kuan Yew, foresaw this development twenty-five years ago, long before the Japanese economic miracle was recognized worldwide. He told me, "The Japanese inevitably will again play a major role in the world. They are a great people. They cannot and should not be satisfied with a world role that limits them to making better transistor radios and sewing machines, and teaching other Asians how to grow rice." The open-ended Japanese debate during the Persian Gulf War was the first tenuous step for Japan toward playing that major role. The next steps will come more easily and quickly. The United States at this time has a major opportunity to work with Japan as it redefines its national purpose internationally. If we seize the moment, our renewed relationship could be a powerful force in solving the problems of today and tomorrow.

China—whose 1.1 billion people represent one-fifth of the world's population—has not only become a key political player but could also become a major global economic power in the coming decades. As one of the corners in the Pacific triangle, China is a voice in the world that cannot be ignored and a force in the world that cannot be isolated. Exactly twenty years ago, we opened the door to China. In the next twenty years, we must keep the door open as China secures its place in and integrates itself into world affairs.

China's emergence as a global heavyweight is inevitable. With a significant nuclear capability and the largest conventional army in the world, it could become a military superpower within decades. Its population has increased by more than 200 million since 1978, a figure only slightly smaller than the entire population of the United States. If its per capita income were to rise to half of Hong Kong's—a feasible objective over the next fifty years—its GNP would be $5.1 trillion higher than today, an increase about equal in size to the current U.S. economy. If its economic reforms continue, the creative enterprise of its people could make China not only the world's most populous but also the world's richest nation in the twenty-first century.

To understand where we should take the U.S.-Chinese relationship, we must understand where we have been. For a generation after the Communist revolution in 1949, the two countries squared off against each other in angry confrontation. While the United States recognized the Republic of China on Taiwan as the country's sole legitimate government, the Communist Chinese became the junior partner in a close alliance with the Soviet Union under Stalin and Khrushchev. While the United States provided aid and troops to prevent Communist victories in Korea and South Vietnam, the Communist Chinese sacrificed tens of thousands of soldiers—including Mao Zedong's only son—to support the aggression of North Korea and provided indispensable economic and military assistance to the aggressors in North Vietnam.

Despite these profound differences, I had decided before the 1968 presidential election that the time had come for a rapprochement with the People's Republic of China. I did so not because I had changed my views about the Communist regime but because its leaders were in the process of changing their foreign policies. From 1959 to 1963, the Sino-Soviet bloc disintegrated over ideological disputes about whose brand of communism was purest and over geopolitical conflicts about whether China would move from junior to full partner in the alliance. As a result of the split with Moscow, China found itself isolated and surrounded by hostile powers by the late 1960s:

—To the northeast, Japan possessed minimal military forces but posed an enormous potential challenge because of its economic might.

—To the south, India had the world's second-largest population, had an active program to develop nuclear weapons, had crossed swords with China in a series of border clashes, and had the capacity to become a dangerous threat with Soviet support.

—To the north, the Soviet Union had strategic forces capable of knocking out China's nuclear forces in a surgical first strike, had deployed more than forty fully modernized divisions on the border, and had engaged in armed clashes over disputed territories along the Sino-Soviet frontier.

—Across the Pacific, the United States represented the Communist regime's most deadly ideological enemy but was the only major Pacific power that had no designs, present or future, on China.

This geopolitical isolation forced Communist China's leaders not only to look to themselves rather than to rely on foreign aid to foster economic development at home but also to retrench from their adventurist policies abroad. After I took office in 1969, I probed their intentions, concluded that this represented a genuine sea change in foreign policy, and decided that it was time to end our mutual enmity. On February 27, 1972, I signed the Shanghai Communiqué in Beijing, which was the culmination of three years of behind-the-scenes negotiations and which set the stage for the eventual restoration of full diplomatic relations in 1979.

Foreign policy analysts have since speculated that the primary motivation behind our diplomatic overtures was a desire to enlist China's help in ending the Vietnam War or to recruit Beijing as a counterweight to Moscow in Asia. Both were important reasons for my initiative. The primary reason

I changed our policy toward China, however, was that China was changing its policies toward the world. Even if there had been no war in Vietnam or no Soviet threat, it was vital for the United States to end China's isolation. As I observed in an article in *Foreign Affairs* in 1967, "Taking the long view, we simply cannot afford to leave China forever outside the family of nations, there to nurture its fantasies, cherish its hates, and threaten its neighbors."

As a consequence partly of our initiative, China slowly awakened to the modern world, gradually moving away from the nightmares of the Cultural Revolution, and began to look to the West for solutions to its economic problems. Our rapprochement opened the door for China to the world community, and it opened the eyes of the Chinese to the world.

When Deng Xiaoping took power in 1977, he launched an ambitious economic reform program. He decollectivized agriculture, granting 750 million farmers twenty-year leases on their land and freeing them not only to decide what, when, and how to produce but also to receive the returns from their own labor. He allowed private firms to compete with state-owned enterprises in cities. His protégés, Hu Yaobang and Zhao Ziyang, took these reforms even further after 1984. They opened "special economic zones" with free-market institutions in China's coastal provinces, thereby unleashing the talents of the Chinese people and attracting massive foreign investment. Deng and his pro-reform lieutenants cast aside ideological rigidity in favor of economic progress. As he once remarked, "It does not matter what color the cat is as long as it catches mice."

The results were stunning. While Soviet per capita income has declined after seven years of Gorbachev's reforms, Deng's initiatives doubled China's rural incomes in six years and its per capita income in ten years. The growth rate in agricultural output quadrupled, from a 2 percent average annual increase during 1958–1978 to 8 percent during 1979–1984. China today produces enough to feed its 1.1 billion people with some left over for export. The Soviet Union, with over twice the territory of China, has to import food for a population one-fourth the size of China's. The share of industrial output produced by state-owned enterprises declined from 80 percent in the late 1970s to 50 percent in 1991, thus channeling resources into the highly productive private sector. If these reforms remain in place for a generation, China will become a major economic power and bring one-fifth of mankind out of poverty and into the global middle class—in spite of, not because of, its Communist government.

As China broadened its contacts with the world economy, these ties transformed Chinese society. After 1972, basic goods and conveniences of modern life—televisions, washing machines, refrigerators, sewing machines, and bicycles—became widely available. More important, people who had been locked into their towns and provinces began to broaden their horizons. They took advantage of their new job mobility and of the easing of residency restrictions. They were exposed to the world through greater freedom for travel and through television coverage of events abroad. They began to express themselves more freely as the state retreated from efforts to police the thoughts of its citizens. More than two hundred thousand students traveled abroad to study and brought back with them the Western ideas of human rights and democratic government.

While calm on the surface, pro-democracy political currents ran deep within Chinese society. Those ideas were openly advocated by Beijing students in pro-reform posters pasted on the so-called Democracy Wall in 1978 and later in large-scale demonstrations in 1986. Communist officials—including Hu and Zhao—began to speak of the need to match economic change with political reforms. The globalization of the Chinese economy, the communications revolution, and the increase in international exchange of ideas and people broke the hold of the Communist ideology on China's society.

The old regime and these new ideas clashed at Tiananmen Square in June 1989. For more than six weeks, over 1 million students and workers engaged in peaceful demonstrations—triggered by Hu's death—not to overthrow the state, but to engage officials in a dialogue on the need for political reform. Their calls were met not with reason and understanding but with tanks and bullets. An estimated 1,300 demonstrators were killed and 10,000 wounded in the one-sided battle. Another 10,000 were taken into custody, most of whom were sentenced to prison or to hard labor on state work farms and some of whom were executed. Nineteen eighty-nine was a year of triumph for the 90 million people of Eastern Europe, with rule by law replacing rule by terror. It was a year of tragedy for the 1.1 billion people of China, as high hopes for political reforms were dashed by the harsh realities of martial law.

The global political effect of Tiananmen Square was magnified by the fact that unlike the killing of peaceful demonstrators in Lithuania in 1990 by the Soviet Black Berets, the massacre in China took place under the microscope of live international television. Although not the most brutal event in Chinese history—more than 5 million Chinese were slaughtered during and after the 1949 revolution and more than 1 million were killed and 100 million brutally persecuted during the Cultural Revolution—the cold-blooded killings in Tiananmen Square were undoubtedly the most widely witnessed. The images of brave pro-democracy demonstrators standing up to army tanks were beamed into millions of homes and seared into the memories of America and the world. The excessive use of lethal force, the show trials and cruel sentences meted out to demonstrators, the Orwellian lies and disinformation disseminated by Communist officials, and the callous refusal of the regime to express any regret for its actions squandered the goodwill China had built up since the U.S.-Chinese rapprochement in 1972.

The Beijing regime's brutal actions deserved the universal condemnation they received. President Bush's actions—an arms sales cutoff, a suspension of most senior-level discussions, an extension of visas for Chinese citizens studying in the United States, and an offer of humanitarian assistance for victims of the violence—represented a proper, measured response. But the additional sanctions advocated by administration critics, including even a total economic boycott, would have been not only useless but also counterproductive.

Our objective must be to keep the process of reforms alive until the current hard-line leadership passes from the scene. This might not be the most emotionally satisfying course of action, but it is the most sound strategically. And it also holds the greatest promise of success. No sanctions, however draconian, will induce Beijing's leaders to bow to the demands of foreign powers with respect to China's domestic affairs. It would be futile to try to extract a formal recantation through external coercion. Instead, the challenge for those who support political liberalization in China is to develop the U.S.-Chinese relationship in ways that foster conditions conducive to peaceful internal change.

Too much is at stake in our relationship to substitute emotionalism for foreign policy. China is one of the world's five major geopolitical power centers. It is a nuclear power. It continues to be a key player in the crucial regional conflicts in Afghanistan, Cambodia, and the Middle East and the Persian Gulf. It exercises a veto over any North Korean actions against South Korea. Taiwan's interests and Hong Kong's political and economic future are best served by close ties between their friends in the West and Beijing. For example, the fact that the PRC must choose between using force to conquer Taiwan and forfeiting its relationship with the United States is the best guarantee of Taipei's security. The United States and China also share common interests on a wide range of bilateral issues, such as intelligence cooperation, trade, and cultural exchange. It will be impossible to deal with environmental problems on a global level without the cooperation of those who rule one-fifth of all the people in the world. Those who call for total economic sanctions as a response to Chinese human rights violations are like surgeons who would perform a delicate operation with a butcher knife instead of a scalpel.

Moreover, as a permanent member of the U.N. Security Council, China has veto power over resolutions authorizing actions to block or reverse aggression. While Gorbachev was widely praised for his support of the U.N. resolutions against Iraq, too little credit has been given to China for abstaining from using the veto. If the Bush administration had alienated and isolated China, we would have had no influence with China on those resolutions or any other critical matters before the U.N. Security Council.

To determine the proper course, Americans must take the long view. Today, China has arrived at a critical moment in its evolution. Its leaders must ask themselves three questions. Will they replace the bold economic reforms Deng initiated fifteen years ago with the old-style Communist policies that almost suffocated China previously? Will they forfeit China's potential greatness and consign their nation to the backwater of oppression and stagnation? Will they make common cause with the unrepentant Communist leaders of Cuba, Vietnam, and North Korea or join countries from Mongolia to Albania in the search for ways to introduce needed political reforms?

Economically, China has moved halfway to a free-market system. It now has two economies—one private and one state-owned—locked in mortal competition. The state sector, inefficient and unimaginative, depends on the graces of government leaders to survive. The private sector, productive and creative, is sustained by the process of economic reforms, the initiative and talents of individual Chinese, and the links between China and the world economy. Since Deng launched his reforms, these two sectors—and the millions of bureaucrats and entrepreneurs whose interests are inextricably intertwined with them—have been circling each other warily. While each side has experienced progress and setbacks over time, this battle is far from settled.

Economic reforms, thrown into reverse gear after Tiananmen Square, are getting back on track. At first, Communist hard-liners, by imposing strict austerity on the private sector, tried to restore the dominance of state-owned enterprises. Available capital went to the state sector. Price controls were imposed. Controls over foreign trade were recentralized. As a result, economic growth plummeted from an annual average of 11 percent during 1983–1989 to 3.6 percent in 1991. Soon, however, the hard-liners were forced into making concessions to China's private sector. The spirit of free enterprise refused to die. Local, provincial, and even some national officials—all of whom had increased their power as a result of Deng's decentralization of economic power—rejected the new restrictions. In addition, hard-liners had to face the fact that workers had adopted the ethos of the free market and that the nation had become a consumer society. Because of the free-market reforms, the economic train left the station. To maintain stability, the hard-liners had to temper their assault on the reforms.

Politically, China's human rights situation continues to be abysmal. In contrast to the dramatic democratic reforms in the Soviet Union, China has come under the rule of neo-Stalinists. Imprisoned demonstrators—many held without charges and without hope of release—have received no amnesties. Many prisoners work in forced labor camps for substandard wages or none at all. Propaganda campaigns against "spiritual pollution" from the West and in favor of communism dominate Chinese news media. Censors monitor all publications. Intellectual exchange has been stifled. While the noose of martial law has been loosened, it still rings the neck of Chinese society.

This does not mean that the hard-liners have totally consolidated their grip on power. The drama in Tiananmen Square—where the demonstrations lasted more than six weeks before the crackdown—had been protracted because even the Communist leadership, particularly in the Central Committee, had split down the middle over how to respond. Those who had opposed the use of lethal force have not been totally vanquished. For every Li Peng—the most hated man in China—who wants to maintain totalitarian control over Chinese society there is still another Zhao Ziyang who wants to begin the process of political liberalization.

The current leadership in China is split into three generational levels. On top are the hard-liners, led by Deng Xiaoping. Mostly octogenarians, they led the original revolution and still serve as the ideological anchors of Chinese communism. The second level is China's current leadership. These men—mainly in their sixties and including Li Peng and Jiang Zemin—take a hard line on ideological issues and control the instruments of power. The third level holds the future of China. This group of younger, local and provincial leaders is more pragmatic. By setting aside ideology, they want to bring China into the world and prosperity to China. Though the hard-liners hold the upper hand today, the moment of truth will come when these two forces struggle for power after Deng passes from the scene.

Internationally, China must choose between playing a responsible role in the international community and pursuing a narrow agenda that will alienate its friends and end in self-defeating isolation. Its leaders have sold arms to the repressive regime in Myanmar. They have continued to provide arms and supplies to the Khmer Rouge, who slaughtered 2 million Cambodians during their three-year rule in the 1970s. They have not only refused to join international conventions to control the spread of ballistic missiles but have also sold M-9 missiles to Syria—thereby enabling Damascus to target every major city in Israel—and M-11 missiles to Pakistan, as well as the CSS-2 medium-range ballistic missile to Saudi Arabia. In addition, they have assisted Pakistan's nuclear program and built a reactor in Algeria that could be used to develop nuclear weapons. As the self-appointed leaders of the underdeveloped world, Chinese officials claim such actions are within their prerogatives, but they will be ousted from the inner circle of major powers if they continue to engage in them.

In order to influence China's evolution toward political and economic progress, the United States should work along four fronts:

Increase U.S. economic engagement in China. We should not stand idly by as the future of China's dual economy hangs in the balance. Examples of state-imposed economic irrationality still abound in China. Today, state-owned or state-regulated enterprises produce more than two thousand brands of cigarettes, while private firms are permitted only thirteen. Battles between the center and provinces and localities over fiscal policy result in arbitrary taxation. Local governments strike deals with the provinces about how much they will hand over, and in turn the provinces make deals with the center, which results in wildly inconsistent payments, particularly between centrally planned and more market-oriented regions. In an isolated China, stop-and-go cycles of reform and retrenchment will enable the state sector to consolidate its position. If we remain engaged in China, we can play a critical role in helping the private economy gradually eclipse the state sector.

In this respect, the most counterproductive thing we could do would be to revoke China's most-favored-nation trade status. Despite its elitist tone, MFN status is a routine international allowance conferred by the United States on all but a few hostile international outlaws such as North Korea, Vietnam, and Libya. Since the 1980 ratification of the Sino-American trade agreement, the President must certify annually that China—as a nonmarket economy—fulfills legal requirements on immigration practices and human rights. Under MFN status, Chinese goods can compete in the U.S. market under the same terms as those of any other country. Without it, China would face punitive tariffs that would undercut its exports and halt some altogether.

Many human rights advocates argue that this should be the price we exact for Tiananmen Square. But the United States cannot effect positive change by ruining China's economy. The withdrawal of MFN status would most hurt not those in power but rather those who depend on the free-market sector. China's transition toward a market economy has made steady progress, though with some digressions. Foreign trade and investment have been the driving forces behind the growth of the private sector. If the United States revoked MFN status, tariffs would skyrocket on the goods such as textiles, shoes, and toys that are primarily produced by private enterprises. Coastal provinces, such as Guangdong near Hong Kong and Fukien near Taiwan, that have served as the beachhead for free-market economics would suffer the worst blow. Higher tariffs would send Guangdong's 65 million people—who represent only 6 percent of China's population but who produce one-third of the country's exports—into an economic nosedive.

A revocation of MFN status would devastate Hong Kong, a conduit for over 70 percent of China's exports. Skyrocketing tariff rates would cause up to a 50 percent drop in these exports, costing Hong Kong thousands of jobs and 2.5 percent of its GNP. To accelerate China's evolution toward a market economy, we must do nothing that would jeopardize Hong Kong's role as a model for the mainland, particularly in light of the scheduled termination of British control in 1997. Once withdrawn, MFN status cannot easily be reissued. Since political pressures would mount to keep the sanctions in place until all human rights issues were resolved, they would become an open-ended policy. In the meantime, the sanctions would inflict irreparable damage to the economy of Hong Kong.

Repeal of MFN status for China would actually help the Chinese hard-liners turn the clock back on the economic revolution started by Deng. Many whose power depends on the state sector would like to see the free-market experiment collapse, particularly if the West unwittingly conspired in destroying private and semiprivate firms. In addition to hurting American investors and trade companies, denying MFN status would undercut the political positions of the pro-reform elements in the Chinese government and the Communist party, whose rise to power represents the sine qua non of political reform. In trying to punish China's hard-line leaders, we would punish the Chinese people more. Instead of helping the cause of human rights, we would hurt it. We must face up to the fact that there would have been no demonstrations in Tiananmen Square in 1989 had we not opened the door to China in 1972. It would be a tragic mistake to close that door now.

This does not mean that we should ignore unfair Chinese trade practices or reject any use of our economic power in our relationship with China. Beijing's estimated $15 billion trade surplus with the United States in 1991—which was second in the world only to Japan's—stemmed in large part from prohibitive trade barriers. Eighty consumer products cannot be imported at all. Others, such as automobiles, motorcycles, and appliances, face astronomical tariffs and bureaucratic red tape. Auto importers, for example, must provide two free samples, pay about $40,000 for "testing," and subsidize a trip by Chinese officials to inspect the factories where the cars are built. In addition, U.S. companies lose about $400 million each year in copyright and patent royalties for such products as software because China fails to protect intellectual property rights.

Our response, however, should not be across-the-board tariff increases but rather more discriminating tactics such as blocking China's entry into GATT or cutting back China's export quota under the International Multifibre Agreement of 1974, which regulates all textile imports into the United States. If we want to have an impact on the changes occurring in China, we should not pull the plug on trade. Increasing economic progress will bring progress on human rights and civil liberties.

Foster peaceful political change. Some human rights advocates argue that the United States should adopt a tougher policy toward China to punish its leaders for the massacre in Tiananmen Square. While we should strongly condemn China's human rights abuses in all appropriate forums, we must recognize that our only viable strategy to promote political reform—continued economic and political contact— will work only in the longer term. If we adopt either policy extreme—handling Chinese leaders with kid gloves or striking them with an iron fist—we will fail. Though we might be frustrated with the slow pace of change, economic reform without political reform is ultimately unsustainable, as the cases of South Korea and Taiwan demonstrated.

Our moral outrage over Tiananmen Square is not a policy. The question we face is whether any of our interests—not only national security but also human rights—would be advanced by isolating China and backing its leaders into a xenophobic corner. They would not. A quarantined China may make us feel better temporarily, but it would do nothing for the people suffering in China, whom we are ostensibly trying to help. If we isolate China, the psychological damage to those pushing for greater reform within China would be irreparable.

Moreover, sustained pressure works. Progress will not come instantly or easily. But China has already taken several significant though inadequate steps. Some political dissidents, including Fang Lizhi, have been released, and many have received far lighter sentences than they would have without American leaders lodging public and private complaints and private human rights organizations watching over China's track record. While we lack the power to make

Beijing capitulate on every case, we have the leverage to extract incremental concessions. If we use our ultimate weapon—total economic sanctions—we will squander our greatest asset for only marginal returns. Sanctions held in reserve are more powerful than sanctions put in place.

Chinese hard-liners have accused the United States of conspiring to subvert their rule and promote democracy through "peaceful evolution." In response, they seek to close the door to the outside world. They might even welcome political, if not economic, isolation. They thrive on isolation because it means guaranteed and unquestioned power for them. They know that before our opening in 1972, there was no reform whatsoever, economic or political. They recognize that contact with the West stimulates pressures for political reforms that threaten their power. Rather than playing into their hands, we should promote peaceful change, just as we do in other countries around the world.

First, we should resume the high-level dialogue between China and the United States. The fact that we are meeting is not as important as what we say during the sessions. Legislative-branch leaders and executive-branch officials should go to China. Tough language on human rights and political reform should always be included in their talking points. In particular, we must strongly condemn the abuse of political prisoners in forced labor programs. The Chinese will not welcome their remarks, but the hard-liners must understand that the way they treat their own people is a legitimate international concern. We should not facilely judge China by the American standard of democracy, but its current human rights violations are beyond the pale. At the same time, we should not suspend our relationship because of the human rights issue. If we had always refused to deal with leaders who violated human rights, there would have been no opening to China in 1972.

Second, we should increase, not decrease, cultural and educational exchange programs with China. Contact with the West has been a major impetus for peaceful change. Without these programs, the ideas of inalienable rights and popular self-government that fueled the democracy movement would have remained largely unknown in China. Although the Tiananmen Square demonstrations overlapped with Gorbachev's visit to Beijing, his reforms were not their inspiration. It was not accidental that the symbol the Chinese students and workers chose for their cause strikingly resembled our Statue of Liberty.

Third, we should open up two new international broadcasting stations—Radio Free China and Radio Free Tibet—to provide these nations with independent information and commentary. The repression at Tiananmen Square dealt a serious but not fatal blow to the pro-democracy movement. It has been forced to lie dormant until a future moment of opportunity. As the revolutions in Eastern Europe proved, however, that moment will eventually come. In the meantime, we can assist the forces of freedom best through broadcasts of news and information, not just about the world at large, but particularly about the internal situation in China. It is significant, incidentally, that during the coup attempt in the Soviet Union broadcasts by Radio Liberty provided important information about developments to the people who played a role in mobilizing resistance to it. Because the Voice of America is part of the U.S. government and because its charter limits its programs to warmed-over international news and trivial rock-and-roll shows, the new station for China must be an independent organization patterned on Radio Free Europe and Radio Liberty.

The people of Tibet represent a separate case. Conquered by the Chinese in 1950, occupied brutally by troops who killed thousands, desecrated local cultural and religious sites, and denied reasonable demands for autonomy, Tibetans have elicited much sympathy but little support from the outside world. The outrage over the brutal killings of peaceful demonstrators in Lhasa in March 1989 quickly faded after the massacres in Beijing in June. While there is a limit to what we can do, we should do more than we have done. In addition to raising the issue of Tibet in bilateral talks, we should establish Radio Free Tibet so that its people, though isolated, will no longer feel abandoned.

Make China pay a price for geopolitical irresponsibility. The United States must apply discriminating pressure on China to alter those foreign policies that threaten our interests. Until its recent decision to sign the Nuclear Nonproliferation Treaty, China acted as the developing world's nuclear door-to-door salesman. China's announcement is an encouraging first step, but we must watch its actions as well as its words. If Beijing fails to curtail its sales of not only nuclear technologies but also ballistic missiles, we should take actions against them through multilateral organizations and inflict costs for such irresponsibility by placing embargoes on the high-tech items China wants to import.

At the same time, we should not overreact and should provide rewards for changes in Chinese policy. If we isolate China economically, politically, or diplomatically, Beijing will have no incentive to curtail its destabilizing foreign policies in Cambodia and elsewhere. On the contrary, that might even create greater incentives for China to seek export earnings through irresponsible weapons sales. If China uses its leverage to rein in North Korea's nuclear aspirations—which represent a menace in East Asia comparable to those of Saddam Hussein in the Middle East—we should reward Beijing by loosening access to the high-tech exports China needs.

Enhance Taiwan's international political standing. Since 1979, the United States has maintained only informal relations with the government in Taipei through the U.S. Institute in Taiwan, an organization officially separate from but fully funded and staffed by the State Department. In the Shanghai Communiqué of 1972, we recognized the fact that both Beijing and Taipei viewed Taiwan as part of China but unequivocally expressed our support for a peaceful settlement of the unification issue. While we should not alter the fundamental pillars of our policy, we should consider certain steps that will raise Taiwan's international standing. For example, Taiwan's application for membership in GATT should be approved based on its formidable economic achievements, not on the status of Beijing's application. Since Hong Kong already belongs to GATT, the free-market and democratizing Chinese regime on Taiwan should no longer be denied membership.

To assume its rightful place in the world, China must modernize. It cannot succeed without contact with the countries of the West, but its success depends ultimately on the Chinese people themselves. We should provide moral and material support to those who favor economic and political reform, but we must not try to force through changes before China itself is ready to make them work. Our two countries have very different political systems, economies, cultures, and even national interests. China will reform, but change must come from the Chinese, in their own way, according to their own traditions, and at their own pace. This change will be brought about by the two-thirds of China's population who were born after the 1949 revolution. They have no memories of warlords, foreign exploitation, wartime occupation, or civil war. Instead, they will be influenced by the success not only of the West but also of their neighbors in Taiwan and

Hong Kong. At this defining moment, America should not walk away.

After forty years of competing for top billing among the major powers in the world Communist movement, China finds itself starring in a one-man show. The fall of Communist systems around the world has raised the hopes of the Chinese people and the fears of the Chinese leadership. In the August 1991 revolution, the Chinese people witnessed the overthrow of the world's first Communist government. The Chinese leaders interpreted the same event as the consequence of Moscow's fatally flawed policy. Gorbachev allowed political liberalization but stumbled in economic reform. Deng promoted economic reform but stifled political change. With the demise of Soviet communism, the Chinese hard-liners may escalate their repression and retreat further into isolation. It therefore becomes doubly important that the United States and the West maintain economic contacts with Chinese society in order to nurture the growth of peaceful change.

It is imperative that we work with China as an equal partner rather than work against China as a bitter enemy. To restore the momentum to our crucial bilateral relationship requires skillful statesmanship by leaders on both sides. Despite Tiananmen Square, the United States should reestablish a working relationship in order to move forward in all areas of common interest. Until China redresses the worst of its human rights violations, however, our two governments can be partners but they cannot be friends. While we cannot yet be friends, we cannot afford to be enemies. We must avoid the animosity and isolation of the first twenty years of our relationship, which produced two Asian wars that cost both our nations dearly. But the burden for resurrecting the close cooperation we had before June 1989 lies in Beijing, not Washington.

The Great Wall of China is one of the Seven Wonders of the World. While it is difficult enough to be heard when you are inside the wall, it is impossible to be heard when you are on the outside. Cooperation might work only slowly in bringing about change, but isolation would not work at all. In the long run, China will become part of the great changes that have swept Communist regimes from power in Eastern Europe, the Soviet Union, and the underdeveloped world. It will not be able to cling to the failed revolution of communism if it continues to have contacts with the new revolution of freedom. Because of the communications revolution, instead of going through or burrowing under the Great Wall, ideas will travel into China over the Great Wall—and no ideological SDI exists to shoot them down.

The Chinese are a great people with an incredibly rich cultural heritage. When Europe was mired in the Dark Ages, China was the most advanced nation in the world. In the eighteenth century, Voltaire called it "the finest, the most ancient, the most extensive, the most populous and well-regulated kingdom on earth." We need only see the economic miracles that Chinese people have achieved in Hong Kong, Taiwan, Singapore, and in their overseas communities all over the world to appreciate the enormous potential of the over 1 billion people in China itself once their energies are unleashed from the dead hand of Communist economic and political repression.

Almost two centuries ago, Napoleon observed, "China? There lies a sleeping giant. Let him sleep! For when he wakes, he will move the world." The giant is awake. Which way he moves the world will primarily depend on the Chinese people but will also depend on us. To isolate China now would be a historical tragedy of inestimable magnitude.

. . .

With the world's attention riveted on Soviet actions in Europe, Moscow's policies along the Pacific rim have traditionally been overlooked. A longtime expansionist power in the region—the Russian flag flew over settlements in Alaska in 1784 and California in 1811—the Kremlin never slackened its eastern push into the Pacific. As a Eurasian power, it has treated Europe as its most visible front, but Asia has always been an equally vital one.

Even with the rise of a noncommunist government in Moscow, the prospects for a rapid improvement in Soviet relations with other members of the Pacific triangle are limited. Before August 1991, the Soviet Union and China were divided by ideological differences. Today, they still stand on opposite sides of an ideological chasm. Japan, wary of the uncertain political situation in Moscow and adamant about the return of the Northern Territories, wants to keep Moscow at arm's length at this time. Both China and Japan have known the Kremlin as the seat of power of not only the Soviet Union but also the Russian Empire. They respect—and fear—the potential influence Russian nationalism can have on Moscow's foreign policy. And they know that in the postcommunist Soviet Union, this traditional nationalism could eventually come to the fore.

Zhou Enlai remarked to me in 1972 that Moscow seeks "to fish in troubled waters." With its political turbulence, the Pacific has always been a rich fishing ground. After expanding its territorial control across Eurasia to the Pacific three centuries ago, Russia clashed with the other two principal regional powers. It participated in the European division of China into spheres of influence. It engaged in a fierce rivalry with Japan, which culminated in the Russo-Japanese War of 1904, a conflict settled through the mediation of the United States under President Theodore Roosevelt. In the postwar period, not only did Moscow fail to sign a peace treaty with Japan to end World War II, but the Sino-Soviet bloc collapsed amid mutual recrimination, with Brezhnev at one point even toying with the idea of a first-strike attack on Beijing's nuclear forces.

When Gorbachev came to power, he cast his line into the politics of the Pacific. The partnership between Japan and the United States, united by a security treaty but divided by economic bickering, had an uncertain future. China and the United States, brought together by the Soviet threat and the Chinese need for modernization but driven apart by China's human rights record, had clouded the prospects for their long-term relationship. In addition, Indochina and the Korean peninsula continued to be hotbeds of great-power rivalries, while the large-scale presence of U.S. and Soviet naval forces added an explosive element to the region.

Until the revolutionary events that brought noncommunist governments to power in the Soviet Union on August 24, 1991, Gorbachev's approach to the Pacific involved a mix of "old thinking" and "new thinking." His principal goal—to increase Moscow's presence in the short term in order to set the stage for regional preeminence in the long term—dovetailed with traditional Soviet policy. But he developed a three-tiered strategy far more subtle and effective than the heavy-handed saber rattling of his predecessors. A military buildup that earned the Kremlin a voice in Pacific affairs, a political "peace offensive" that opened doors long closed to its diplomats, and an economic opening that sought to capitalize on the region's dynamism dealt Gorbachev a hand in a geopolitical game in which he had little to offer but much to gain.

While he did not want increased tensions in the region, he did seek a decreased U.S. presence. He wanted to break out of the Soviet Union's traditional political isolation and embark on an active engagement in the Pacific. He wanted to establish beachheads diplomatically and economically that would not only help Moscow solve its domestic crisis but would also enable him to expand the Soviet sphere of influence along the Pacific rim.

Military power was Gorbachev's most concrete lever of influence in the Pacific. Without it, the other members of the Pacific triangle would not have taken the Soviet Union seriously. Because of this power, however, they could not have afforded to ignore Moscow's concerns. This leverage was earned by a comprehensive military buildup larger in many ways than Soviet efforts in Europe:

—It has doubled its deployments in the Far East since 1970 to a total of fifty-five divisions—which account for 43 percent of its ground troops east of the Ural Mountains.

—It has quadrupled its combat aircraft in the region, with its deployments accounting for 54 percent of its tactical aircraft east of the Urals and including its most advanced Backfire long-range bombers and MiG-31 fighter-bombers.

—It has developed a vast military infrastructure—bases, airfields, supply depots, roads, and railroads—in some of the world's most inhospitable terrain to support the 500,000 troops in active units in the area.

—It has modernized its Far Eastern ground forces with equipment withdrawn from Eastern Europe and areas west of the Urals.

—It has redeployed 120,000 troops removed from Eastern Europe to the Sino-Soviet border, negating the effects of its earlier withdrawals in the late 1980s.

—It has built up the Soviet Pacific Fleet—particularly its 110-strong nuclear attack and ballistic-missile submarine force—in an effort to counter the maritime power of the United States.

—It has brought its total ICBM force in the Far Eastern military districts to 493, adding 85 missiles in 1990 and 1991 and thereby enabling its planners to cover all Pacific targets assigned to SS-20 missiles before they were destroyed under the INF treaty.

—It trimmed its permanent naval deployments at Cam Ranh Bay and aircraft at Da Nang in Vietnam in the late 1980s, but Moscow's military presence in Indochina vastly exceeded its deployments in the area even during the Vietnam War.

At a time when lessening East-West tensions prompted the United States to reduce its forces in the Pacific, the Soviet Union's peaked in terms of numbers and capabilities. This did not mean that Moscow intended to launch a Pacific blitzkrieg. But it did mean that its efforts to advance its political and economic presence in the region were built upon the rock-hard foundation of military power.

Gorbachev's political "peace offensive" was the main axis of his strategy in the Pacific. Unlike his predecessors from Stalin through Chernenko, he knew that overt threats and bullying would win little ground among the region's major powers. Instead, he borrowed successful lessons from his diplomacy in Europe. Soviet officials called for the development of "an Asian common home" and "a single Eurasian area of stability and security." Both concepts would have excluded the United States. By making political inroads now, Gorbachev wanted to tap the Pacific rim's dynamic economy to save his Communist system. His subtle tactics—which sought to address China's and Japan's demands in form but to hold back in substance—were designed to parlay diplomatic initiatives into political gains.

The centerpiece of his diplomatic offensive was the rapprochement with China in 1989. For forty years, the relationship with China served as the driving force behind

Soviet policy in East Asia. Ideological and geopolitical competition between the two major Communist powers spawned diplomatic maneuvering and even military clashes between them. When Gorbachev realized the depth of the Soviet internal crisis, he concluded that he could no longer afford the Sino-Soviet enmity. Both powers buried the ideological hatchet, accepting each other's brand of socialism as legitimate interpretations of the Marxist-Leninist canons, and began diplomatic exchanges to bridge the key issues dividing them.

Most important, Gorbachev yielded on Deng's "three conditions" for normalization of relations—a reduction in Soviet forces on the Sino-Soviet border, a Soviet withdrawal from Afghanistan, and a Vietnamese withdrawal from Cambodia. But he did so in measured and qualified steps. Soviet force levels still remained much higher along the Chinese border after the withdrawals than before the Soviet regional buildup began in the 1970s. Gorbachev kept a significant number of "advisers" in Afghanistan and continued to keep the Kabul regime in power through massive military and economic aid. Despite Hanoi's pullout from Cambodia and the 1989 Sino-Soviet agreement on a process to end the Indochina conflict, the Vietnamese-backed Hun Sen government continued to impede a final peace settlement. While Gorbachev got his half of the bargain up front, the Chinese have had to work to collect on theirs.

Gorbachev sought to employ the same formula—concessions in form but not in substance—to the third corner of the Pacific triangle, Japan. He knew that Moscow could not be a credible Pacific power without a cooperative relationship with Japan. In order to win normal relations with and massive economic aid from Tokyo, he tantalized the Japanese with rumors of Soviet flexibility on the crucial issue of the four islands seized by the Soviet Union in the last days of World War II. He floated trial balloons calling for a swap of territory for billions in aid, hoping to crown his visit to Japan with a major political breakthrough. But the Soviet concessions actually put on the table, such as easing visa requirements for Japanese visiting some of the islands, left Tokyo cold. Gorbachev best encapsulated his bottom line when he remarked in September 1990 that the Soviet Union had "no land to spare" for Japan.

His economic opening to the Pacific was the element of his policy that Gorbachev most needed but for which he had the least to offer. Although Sino-Soviet trade has doubled over three years and totaled $4.5 billion in 1991, it lags far behind the $18 billion in U.S.-Chinese trade. Even though Moscow and Beijing have reached several long-term trade agreements, their trade will not exceed modest levels in the near future, particularly because much of it must occur through barter agreements. For Gorbachev, however, Japan represented the real catch. On his state visit in March 1991, Tokyo refused to rise to his bait. Genuine opportunities for investment would have hooked the Japanese, but Gorbachev had been fishing for aid, not trade.

Gorbachev played a skillful diplomatic game in Asia. While enhancing Soviet relations with South Korea—moving from no ties to full diplomatic relations in only three years—he continued to back North Korea, though slapping its leader on the wrist for its nuclear program. While Soviet trade with South Korea will rise from $85 million in 1985 to an estimated $1 billion in 1995, Moscow continued to provide $1 billion in aid to North Korea and to equip the 1.1 million troops in its armed forces with Soviet weapons.

Gorbachev's strategy was to use his military, political, and economic policies to supplant the United States as the principal power along the Pacific rim. We should seek to make the new noncommunist leadership in the Kremlin and the Russian republic a partner in resolving the issues on which Gorbachev would accept only a partial accommodation. Unburdened by the totalitarian baggage of the past, the new noncommunist leaders should be more willing to demilitarize the Sino-Soviet border, to phase down Soviet naval deployments in the Pacific, to accept a political settlement in Afghanistan based on elections, to cut off the Communist regimes in Vietnam and North Korea from military and economic aid, and to return the Northern Territories to Japan.

With modernist, democratic leaders instead of insular, Communist despots, the Soviet Union can begin to make a constructive contribution to Pacific security. But the United States cannot assume that this process will occur in a fortnight. The nations of the Pacific triangle harbor deep national suspicions of each other. Unlike Americans, the Soviets have traditionally had great difficulties relating to China and Japan, not only because of their political differences, but also because of their clashing cultures and centuries of geopolitical antagonism. A closed and parochial society for much of this century, the Soviet Union has a strong streak of xenophobia that will influence its Pacific policies even in the postcommunist period. Because the new leaders in Moscow have ceased being Communists does not mean that they have ceased being Russians.

China, Japan, and the smaller countries in the region want a continuing, strong U.S. military presence in the Pacific. Current U.S. ten-year defense plans—which foresee a 12 percent cut in Pacific troop deployments in the first phase alone —must not reduce our forces to the point at which we would lack the forward-based infrastructure needed for a major intervention into the region. The 16 percent of U.S. forces stationed in the Pacific are stretched thin already. Cuts proportional to those made in our European forces would seriously weaken our ability to deter countries that might harbor ambitions of dominating the region through military coercion or intimidation.

Compared to Europe, our deployments in the Pacific are not great. But they make an enormous contribution to regional stability. Japan, South Korea, Taiwan, China, Australia, New Zealand, and the countries of the Association of Southeast Asian Nations spend a total of over $50 billion a year on defense, a figure that will rise to $120 billion by the year 2000. To cap this growth, the United States should maintain a high profile in the region, keeping both its naval forces in the South Pacific and its ground forces in South Korea and Japan. In addition, it should work with friendly countries, such as Singapore, that will allow an increased U.S. presence through short-term rotation of aircraft at their air bases and ship maintenance at their naval yards. While these measures might pack little military punch, their symbolic value is vital to keeping potential escalations of arms spending in check.

Our military presence must be sufficient to prevent a security vacuum from developing in the Pacific. Over the last forty-five years, U.S. security guarantees have enabled the countries of East Asia to develop politically and economically, and our own standard of living has benefited significantly as a result. Other countries might be able to match our economic, political, or military power. But unlike the three members of the Pacific triangle, the United States has no history of hegemonic aspirations. We may think of China's, Japan's, and even Russia's imperialism as ancient history, but in the region they are as fresh as the morning's news.

. . .

Although we must avoid pretensions of acting as the prime mover in the geopolitics of the Pacific rim, we have a unique role to play. Only the United States has the credibility to maintain the balance of power in the region, an essential precondition for Pacific prosperity.

The conflicts between the powers of the Pacific triangle did not begin with the cold war and will not end with the end of the cold war. As a nation, Americans have difficulty grasping the depth of historical antagonisms between other nations. But these intractable conflicts have dominated the politics of the Pacific triangle for decades. The record of the rivalry between Japan and Russia reaches back far beyond the postwar period. The centuries-old, visceral antipathy between Russia and China and between Japan and China cannot be overcome by a cleverly worded communiqué. Though a more democratic and less aggressive Soviet Union should be able to tamp down the most acute conflicts, it would be foolhardy to assume that all the great rivalries between Pacific nations that predated the Communist era will remain dormant.

Japan, a democratic ally and a technological power capable of building nuclear weapons, must remain our intimate geopolitical partner, regardless of our commercial disputes. The new governments in the Kremlin and the Russian republic have created the possibility of closer economic and political relations with Tokyo, once the Northern Territories are returned to Japan, but these would be short-lived in the absence of an active U.S engagement in the Pacific. Without a security link to the United States, Tokyo might temporarily strike a security deal with Moscow but would inevitably develop its own nuclear weapons, thereby rekindling its historical antagonisms with Russia and China.

Just as Japan is a political ally but an economic competitor, China is a potential strategic partner despite its totally unacceptable violations of human rights. A stable and modernizing China is vital to Pacific security. We cannot ignore China's internal repression, but it should not be ostracized or endlessly harangued. Besides the United States, no great power—neither Japan, the Soviet Union, nor any country in Europe—can foster peaceful change in China. While we may have to work with repugnant hard-line leaders in the short term, a continuing engagement with China will serve our interests and those of the Chinese people in the long term.

Most important, as a result of the dramatic changes in the Soviet Union, a window of opportunity has opened to explore the possibility of what Gorbachev might have called a "common transpacific home." We should recognize that the Soviet Union, like the United States, has a proper role to play and legitimate interests to protect in Pacific affairs. But before we can welcome even the new Kremlin leaders as constructive geopolitical partners, they must first check their guns at the door.

A continued U.S. presence in Europe is important, but a continued U.S. role in the Pacific is indispensable. Without the United States, the Pacific triangle will be like a three-legged stool: unstable and potentially dangerous. The competition among Japan, China, and the Soviet Union would be unbridled, with each driven to seek preeminence in the region. The United States must serve as a stabilizer—the fourth leg of the stool—in order to advance the interests of all East Asian nations. Whether or not East-West relations continue to improve, America's role as regional balancer, honest broker, and security guarantor in the Pacific will only increase in importance.

5

THE
MUSLIM
WORLD

MANY AMERICANS TEND TO STEREOTYPE Muslims as uncivilized, unwashed, barbaric, and irrational people who command our attention only because some of their leaders have the good fortune to rule territory containing over two-

---

thirds of the world's proven oil reserves. They remember the three wars waged by the Arab states to try to exterminate Israel, the seizure of American hostages by the fanatical Ayatollah Khomeini, the terrorist attack at the Munich Olympics by the Palestinian commandos from the Black September organization, the endless and senseless slaughter by rival Muslim militias in Lebanon, the bombing of civilian airliners by Syria and Libya, and the attempted annexation of Kuwait by a Hitler-like Saddam Hussein. No nations, not even Communist China, have a more negative image in the American consciousness than those of the Muslim world.

Some observers warn that Islam will become a monolithic and fanatical geopolitical force, that its growing population and significant financial power will pose a major challenge, and that the West will be forced to form a new alliance with Moscow to confront a hostile and aggressive Muslim world. This view holds that Islam and the West are antithetical and that Muslims view the world as two irreconcilable camps of Dar al-Islam and Dar al-Harb—the house of Islam and the house of war where the forces of Islam have yet to prevail. It foresees the forces of resurgent Muslim fundamentalism orchestrating a region-wide revolution from Iran and other states and prompting the need for a comprehensive Western and Soviet policy of containment.

This nightmare scenario will never materialize. The Muslim world is too large and too diverse to march to the beat of a single drummer. Many mistakenly assume that the Muslim world is equivalent to the Middle East. But more than 850 million people—one-sixth of humanity—live in the thirty-seven countries of the Muslim world. These nations have 190 ethnic groups who speak hundreds of distinct languages and dialects and who belong to three main religious sects—the Sunnis, the Shias, and the Sufis—and dozens of minor ones. They cover a 10,000-mile-long swath of territory extending from Morocco to Yugoslavia, from Turkey to Pakistan, from the Central Asian republics of the Soviet Union to the tropics of Indonesia. More Muslims live in China than on the Arabian peninsula, and more live in Indonesia than in the entire Middle East. The former Soviet Union, with over 50 million Muslims, has more than any Middle Eastern country except Turkey. At current birth rates, there will be more Muslims than Russians in the former Soviet Union in the next century.

Only two common elements exist in the Muslim world: the faith of Islam and the problems of political turbulence. Islam is not only a religion but also the foundation of a major civilization. We speak of the "Muslim world" as a single entity not because of any Islamic politburo guiding its policies but because individual nations share common political and cultural currents with the entire Muslim civilization. The same political rhythms are played throughout the Muslim world, regardless of the differences between the individual countries. Just as all Western countries have parties that advocate the free market, the welfare state, and socialism, the Islamic countries have groups that subscribe to the main political currents of the Muslim world—fundamentalism, radicalism, and modernism. This commonalty of faith and politics breeds a loose but real solidarity: when a major event occurs in one part of the Muslim world, it inevitably reverberates in the others.

The rivalries in the Muslim world have made it a caldron of conflict. The short list of these conflicts includes Morocco versus Algeria; Libya versus Algeria; Libya versus Chad; the Arab world against Israel; Jordan versus Saudi Arabia; Syria versus Jordan; Syria versus Lebanon; Saudi Arabia versus the small Gulf states; Saudi Arabia versus Yemen; Iraq versus

Syria; Iraq versus Kuwait and Saudi Arabia; Iraq versus Iran; the Arab Gulf states versus Iran; Pakistan versus Afghanistan; India versus Pakistan and Bangladesh; and Indonesia versus Malaysia and New Guinea. Since many countries are artificial composites of several nations or ethnic groups, potential internal strife pervades the region. Many states in the Muslim world are future Lebanons waiting to happen.

Demographic, economic, and political trends make conflict increasingly inevitable. The global population explosion centers in the Muslim world. The population of the Middle East alone will double by the year 2010. At the same time, the economies of the region will not grow sufficiently to prevent a drop in living standards, thereby undercutting the meager ability of governments to buy off threats to stability and peace. In many areas, basic resources—such as water—will become ever more scarce, prompting disputes or even wars over their control. National borders, many of which are artificial creations of the European colonial powers, have increasingly been challenged, both between countries and from minorities within countries. Brittle political regimes, mostly authoritarian dictatorships or traditional monarchies, depend on their monopoly of force rather than support of their people to stay in power. Political liberalization has led more often to fragmentation than to democracy.

All of these conflicts and problems have unfolded in the most militarized region of the underdeveloped world. In 1990, the countries of the Muslim world spent a total of over 8 percent of their GNP on the military, while the Western figure was less than 5 percent. Iraq allocated over 8 percent of its GNP to the military; Syria, 11 percent; Saudi Arabia, 17 percent; Egypt, 8 percent; and Pakistan, 7 percent. More ominously, the area has become the focal point of the proliferation of weapons of mass destruction and ballistic missiles.

Some of its most aggressive states—Iraq, Syria, and Libya—already have the capacity to build chemical weapons. Of the fifteen developing countries armed with ballistic missiles, nine are part of the Muslim world. Iraq and Pakistan have made great strides toward developing their own nuclear weapons, and Algeria has embarked on a similar program. The two most perilous nuclear flash points—Israel versus its Arab neighbors and Pakistan versus India—involve countries of the Muslim world.

I have visited thirteen of the thirty-seven Muslim countries over the past thirty-eight years—Indonesia, Malaysia, Pakistan, Sudan, Iran, Saudi Arabia, Libya, Egypt, Afghanistan, Morocco, Tunisia, Jordan, and Syria. I have also traveled to the Muslim Soviet republics of Kazakhstan and Uzbekistan. Their leaders and people are proud of their heritage. Most of them have staunchly opposed communism. Whittaker Chambers once observed, "Communism is never stronger than the failure of other faiths." Islam has stood up to that test in many ways better than Christianity has. Except for the former South Yemen, Soviet influence in the Muslim world has been based not on the appeal of Communist ideas but on the persuasive power of Soviet arms sales to such countries as Iraq, Syria, Libya, and Somalia, and to Egypt before 1973. More often, religious opposition to the ideology of communism has been an insurmountable obstacle to Soviet expansionism in the Muslim world.

Few Americans are aware of the rich heritage of the Islamic world. They remember only that the sword of Muhammad and his followers advanced the Muslim faith into Asia, Africa, and even Europe and look condescendingly on the religious wars of the region. They overlook the fact that Islam has no doctrine of terrorism and that only three centuries have passed since Christians engaged in religious wars in Europe.

While Europe languished in the Middle Ages, the Islamic civilization enjoyed its golden age. The Muslim world made enormous contributions to science, medicine, and philosophy. In his book *The Age of Faith*, Will Durant observed that key advances in virtually all fields were achieved by Muslims in this period. Avicenna was the greatest writer on medicine, al-Razi the greatest physician, al-Biruni the greatest geographer, al-Haitham the greatest optician, Jabir the greatest chemist, and Averroës one of the greatest philosophers. Arab scholars were instrumental in developing the scientific method. As Durant commented, "When Roger Bacon proclaimed that method to Europe, five hundred years after Jabir, he owed his illumination to the Moors of Spain, whose light had come from the Moslem East." When the great figures of the European Renaissance pushed forward the frontier of knowledge, they saw further because they stood on the shoulders of the giants of the Muslim world.

Those achievements represent what the Muslim world has been in the past. They also point to what it could become in the future, if the deadly cycles of war and political instability can be arrested. We should adopt policies to channel the long-term historical evolution of the Muslim world in constructive directions. At the same time, we should tackle the immediate problems—such as Persian Gulf security and the Arab-Israeli conflict—that threaten to trigger further bloodshed. Unless we succeed in meeting these challenges, the cradle of civilization could become its grave.

The Muslim world is a vital civilization searching for its historical identity. In the 1950s and 1960s, it escaped the bonds of colonialism. It subsequently drove down the ideological blind alleys of nonalignment, pan-Arabism, and reactionary fundamentalism. In the 1990s and beyond, these countries will renew the search for their place in the world. The United States needs an active policy to affect that evolution in constructive ways.

The greatest stumbling block to developing such policies has been the tendency to lump all these countries into one category. Many Americans, weary of the endless array of fanatics chanting anti-Western slogans in the streets, tend to view all Muslim nations as adversaries. The Muslim faith represents a thread of unity that binds the politics of these countries together, but it does not weave them into a cohesive bloc. The policies of each country in the Muslim world have less to do with Islam than with how Islam has interacted with its national culture and traditions.

Some political solidarity does exist among Muslim nations. When the Soviet Union invaded Afghanistan, Moscow's relations with Muslim countries from Morocco to Indonesia chilled, and those with states such as Saudi Arabia went into the deep freeze. The perception that the United States backs Israel uncritically—providing billions of dollars in aid but not demanding action on the Palestinian issue—has been a major impediment to closer U.S. ties with all Muslim countries. Generally, however, while Islam provides these nations with a common worldview, it does not come with a ready-made political platform.

Islam is not monolithic politically. Every great faith is susceptible to multiple interpretations that support multiple political approaches or orientations. In the West, Christianity once blessed monarchies through the belief in the divine right of kings and now provides a key pillar of democratic thought through the belief in the fundamental dignity of the individual. The reinterpretation of the Christian political tradition accompanied the transformation of the dominant form of Western government. Islam is also susceptible to varied interpretations and evolutionary change, as made evident by the fact that such disparate figures as Khomeini, Saddam Hussein, Anwar Sadat, and Zia ul-Haq have all claimed its mandate for their rule.

To operate in the Muslim world, U.S. policymakers must maneuver within a snake pit of venomous ideological conflicts and national rivalries. Even among fundamentalists, doctrinal clashes are sharp and sometimes violent. In tiny Lebanon, fundamentalist terrorists were unified only in the loosest sense, with virtually every cell differing with the others over doctrine. We should recognize that the Muslim world's diverse political movements fall within three basic currents of thought:

Fundamentalism. Painfully familiar televised images— blind-folded U.S. hostages paraded before our embassy in Teheran, 241 Marines killed in the truck bombing of their barracks in Beirut, and the ghostly figures of Americans kidnapped and held prisoner in southern Lebanon—sum up the political thrust of extreme Islamic fundamentalists on the world scene. They are motivated by a consuming hatred of the West and a determination to restore the superiority of Islamic civilization by resuscitating the past. They seek to impose the shari'a, the code of law based on the Koran that recognizes no separation of church and state. Though they look to the past as a guide for the future, they are not conservatives but revolutionaries. Before they build the new, they intend to destroy the old.

Radicalism. Dictators and one-party states—legitimized by radical nationalistic ideologies—control several of the countries in the Muslim world. Some, such as Libya's Qaddafi, resemble Mussolini's dictatorship. Others, such as Syria's Hafiz Assad and Iraq's Saddam Hussein, command brutal totalitarian regimes that would have made Stalin proud. Just as hostile to the West as the fundamentalists, the radicals trade on their opposition to "imperialism" to mobilize support among the people and have often made common cause with the Soviet Union to undermine the United States and its allies. Their power rests not on the charisma of their leaders, but on the ruthless efficiency of their police and security apparatus. In the town of Hama in 1982, for example, Assad brutally slaughtered twenty thousand men, women, and children who dared to oppose his rule.

Modernism. Most prominent but least visible, the modernist political current seeks to integrate the countries of the Muslim world into the modern world, both economically and politically. Tolerance marks the key thrust of modernist Islam, with the nations of the West not condemned as "unbelievers" but embraced as other peoples "of the book." Some modernist states, such as Turkey and Pakistan, are democracies. Others, such as Egypt and Indonesia, are relatively open societies but fall short of Western democratic standards. The ballot box, however, is the recognized source of political legitimacy. The central message of modernist political leaders is that their countries must combine the best of the West with their own nations' cultures and social mores.

We should never equate the actions of Islamic extremists with the faith of Islam. The extreme fundamentalists are highly visible, but their electoral appeal is weak. Though their numbers have grown in Jordan, Morocco, Tunisia, Malaysia, Pakistan, and Algeria in recent years, they have taken power only in Iran, where they have been discredited by a decade of thuggery and pointless carnage in the Iran-Iraq war. Fundamentalists can fill the streets in the Muslim world with vocal demonstrators, but they cannot yet take power through the polls.

The people of the Muslim world are candidates for revolution. They are young: over 60 percent are under twenty-five years of age. They are poor: their average per capita income, including the oil-rich Gulf states, is only $1,600 a year compared with $21,000 in the United States. Most have no voice in their government: only 27 percent of the people in the Muslim world live in democratic countries. Muslim fundamentalists appeal to the people less for what they stand for than for what they stand against—the status quo, which provides no relief from the present and no hope for the future, and the empty materialist ideologies of Soviet communism and Western consumerism.

We should support the modernists in the Muslim world, in their interest and in ours. They need to give their people a positive alternative to the ideologies of extreme fundamentalism and radical secularism. The refusal of the Kuwaiti royal family to adopt meaningful democratic reforms after the liberation of their country from Saddam Hussein is a shocking example of the insensitivity of too many nonelected authoritarian rulers in the Muslim world. In supporting a friendly but nondemocratic ruler, we should make it clear that we do not support government systems that give no voice to the people over whom they rule.

In charting our course, we must know who are our friends and who are our enemies. Though this might sound like a truism, U.S. policymakers have repeatedly honored this basic principle in the breach. Trading arms for hostages with the extreme fundamentalist regime in Iran and selling billions of dollars of arms to the radical leaders of Iraq are just two recent examples of the United States viewing its sworn enemies through rose-colored glasses. Those who would praise Syria and Iran for winning the release of some Western hostages in Lebanon would repeat the error. You do not praise a kidnapper for releasing his captives. Damascus and Teheran should not derive any benefits for doing today what they should have done seven years ago. It is unlikely that the Assads, Rafsanjanis, and Qaddafis of the Islamic world will choose to become Muslim Havels.

The key to a U.S. policy of discriminating engagement is to undertake *strategic* cooperation only with modernist regimes and to limit our ties with extreme fundamentalist and radical regimes to *tactical* cooperation. Because we share common goals with the modernists, our cooperation should cover the full range of economic and security issues. Because our values and interests clash with those of the extreme fundamentalists and radicals, our links with them should not move beyond the requirements of the moment. We should work with them when their power earns them a place at the table, but we should not enter a wide-ranging partnership with them. We should not completely isolate the radicals and fundamentalists through trade embargoes and similar policies, but we should not naively try to search out "moderates" in regimes such as Iran's or to court leaders such as Iraq's by taking no position on their border disputes with their neighbors. While we should not cut them off, we should certainly not build them up. We should adopt a hardheaded policy of quid pro quo cooperation on a case-by-case basis.

Many observers in retrospect condemn U.S. policy during the Iran-Iraq war. They express shock that we alternately helped one side and then the other depending on the tide of battle. They are only partly right. Our interests demanded that neither side emerge as a clear-cut victor, and the Reagan administration acted correctly in playing both sides. In allowing arms sales to Iraq, the mistake was to exceed the amounts needed to check Iran's offensive capabilities, thereby enabling Saddam Hussein to become a military menace after the war. We should maintain a deliberate distance when engaging in unavoidable tactical cooperation with such regimes. The hard lesson of our experience with Iraq is that today's tacit friend can become tomorrow's mortal enemy. In the case of Saddam Hussein, it cost $100 billion and 148 American lives to reverse the error.

Today, many analysts contend that a "window of opportunity" exists to developing cooperative relations with President Assad of Syria. Prudence argues otherwise. We should have no illusions in dealing with Assad. He did not join the U.S.-led coalition against Iraq because of a change of heart. Instead, he saw the chance to knock his rival, Saddam Hussein, out of contention for the title of champion of the radical Arab world. Syria also won a free hand in Lebanon and cashed in with a $3-billion aid package from Saudi Arabia, Kuwait, and the United Arab Emirates. We must remember that Assad still seeks to advance his geopolitical goals through military might and remains one of the principal supporters of international terrorism.

To affect the historical evolution of the Muslim world, we should not fashion a grand "Muslimpolitik" that applies one policy to all these countries. Instead, we should identify key pivot points for our presence. We should cultivate partnerships with select modernist countries that share common interests or parallel agendas and that carry real weight in the region. By working with them on political and security issues and by providing advice and assistance to further their economic development, their gradual emergence as success stories within the Muslim world will enhance the prospects for modernist forces throughout the region. Over one or two decades, they could become economic and political magnets, poles of attraction moving the entire region in a positive direction through peaceful change.

Four countries stand out as the most logical partners with which to pursue this approach:

—Turkey—the geographic and cultural bridge connecting

the Muslim and Western worlds—has had a working democratic government for nine years and provides more troops for NATO than any other member of the alliance. We should prod our European allies to admit Turkey into the European Community and the Western European Union. At the same time, we should encourage Turkey to take advantage of its historical and cultural ties to become more involved economically and politically in the Middle East. If the Arab-Israeli peace process moves forward, the issue of regional water supplies will move to the top of the agenda. In cooperation with the United States, Turkey, a water-rich country, could ease the problems of Israel, Syria, and other water-poor countries in the area through new aqueducts.

—Pakistan—the only major U.S. strategic partner situated between Turkey and Japan—has cooperated with the United States in recent decades to support the Afghan resistance, as well as to facilitate the rapprochement with China in 1972. Though Islamabad's policies sometimes clash with ours—especially regarding nuclear proliferation—no other country has shown comparable courage in serving as a frontline state against Soviet aggression. In order to avoid a potential nuclear conflict between Pakistan and India over Kashmir, we should urge New Delhi to end the massive violations of human rights by its security forces in the province and to negotiate an autonomy agreement with Kashmiri leaders. After winning democratic elections in 1990, Prime Minister Nawaz Sharif moved Pakistan decisively toward free-market reforms, including lower tax rates, denationalization, and deregulation. As Islamabad implements these reforms, we should encourage U.S. businesses to invest in Pakistan, thereby reinforcing the process of reform.

—Egypt—whose population represents 35 percent of the Arab world—remains the only Arab state to have signed a peace treaty with Israel. Ten years after the Camp David accords resulted in its expulsion from the Arab League, Cairo has reemerged as its natural leader. In advancing the Arab-Israeli peace process, we should form a united front with the Egyptians, who have earned a great deal of political capital through their actions in the Persian Gulf crisis. Also, as a result of the debt cancellations and aid packages Egypt received during the Gulf War, Cairo has a critical but momentary opportunity to set its economy on a free-market course without the danger of large-scale domestic unrest. We should help the Egyptian leaders adopt the right reforms so that future aid will feed Egypt's people, not its voracious bureaucracy.

—Indonesia—a 2,000-mile-long archipelago with the fifth-largest population in the world—has begun to make important strides economically, though it continues to be ruled by an authoritarian regime. Since President Suharto took power in 1967, Indonesia's per capita income has risen from $50 to $500 today. He adopted successful programs to slow his country's explosive population growth. A pioneer in free-market reforms in the Muslim world, Indonesia has opened its markets, lowered tariffs, and cut bureaucratic red tape. One of the world's largest oil exporters, Indonesia's earnings from nonoil exports exceeded those from oil exports by a two-to-one ratio by 1991. In addition, it has not defaulted on or rescheduled any loans from the United States or international lenders since 1967. This fiscal responsibility and commitment to free-market principles should be rewarded with a close U.S. partnership.

This does not mean that we should place on the back burner our relations with other modernist and pro-Western regimes. King Hassan, one of the Muslim world's most enlightened rulers, has instituted progressive policies in Morocco and has worked closely with the United States on strategic issues. The Saudi monarchy has also forged important ties with the West, despite its authoritarian domestic system. But neither of these states represent viable pivot points. They lack the political weight to tip the evolution of the Muslim world in one direction or another.

Our policy of selective partnerships will not yield immediate success, but over a generation the United States could have a profound—though unintrusive—effect on the historical evolution of the Muslim world. Some extreme fundamentalist and radical regimes, particularly Iran and Syria, have recently entered severe economic downturns. Though their leaders could hold on to power through repression, they might have to strike a new bargain with their people because they lack the resources to buy social peace. If internal pressures erupt, these countries might look elsewhere for direction. If modernist states have succeeded, other nations will be more likely to see them as models.

At the same time, we must not embrace the modernist states so tightly that our relationship becomes a target for their domestic critics. Because the memories of colonialism in much of the Muslim world make Western influence a sensitive issue, our special relationship must not be patronizing. We should address modernist leaders not as errand boys, but as full and equal partners. The quickest way to nail their coffins shut would be to create the impression that they are merely convenient mouthpieces for the West.

Americans respond with outrage and confusion when a friendly foreign government is forced by domestic politics to oppose our policies. When Mexico votes against us in the United Nations, for example, most Americans decry its actions as irresponsible. But despite these votes—which are typically dictated by domestic opinion—the Mexicans remain valued and important U.S. partners. Another recurring example can be found in our sometimes difficult relationship with the Philippines. On my visit to the Philippines in 1953, I expressed concerns to my host about reports of a speech by a prominent Filipino senator attacking U.S. foreign policy. My host reassured me that the senator was very pro-American. When I responded that he had a strange way of showing it, my host answered, "You don't understand Filipino politics. The recipe for success in the Philippines is to give the Americans hell and pray that they don't go away." Regardless of the rhetoric in its domestic debates, the Philippines has been a crucial U.S. friend ever since its independence in 1946.

We must also accept the fact that at times it does not serve our interests for our friends in the Muslim world to support our positions on issues that are highly sensitive politically in their countries. When the United States bombed Libya in April 1986 in retaliation for terrorist attacks against American servicemen, many leaders in the region denounced us in public but cheered us in private. We should learn to look the other way when circumstances force our friends to give lip service to our foes.

The vital importance of developing special relationships in the Muslim world was evident during the Persian Gulf War. Troops from six Muslim nations—including Pakistan, Egypt, Morocco, and even the moderate elements of the Afghan resistance—joined the U.S.-led coalition. Though their contribution may have been minimal militarily, it was critical politically.

The Muslim world poses one of the greatest challenges to U.S. foreign policy in the twenty-first century. As the cold war has waned, traditional rivalries frozen for forty-five years have begun to thaw. In a region where virtually every neighbor is at best a rival and at worst an enemy, potential instability poses a major threat to our interests. In two key zones of conflict—the Persian Gulf and the Arab-Israeli dispute—the need for U.S. action has become particularly pressing.

The victory in the Persian Gulf War has spawned dozens of easy recipes for enhancing the security of the region. If the United States is to forge an effective policy to strengthen Gulf security, it must recognize that the inherent complexity of the politics of the Muslim world will likely frustrate comprehensive solutions. Our policy must first avoid three fatal illusions:

The illusion of a comprehensive security framework. Many academics argue that the Middle East needs a security pact. Some want to involve the United Nations, while others want to create an organization patterned on NATO or CSCE. But the deserts of the Middle East are littered with the skeletons of failed regional security arrangements:

—In 1950, Britain, France, and the United States issued the Tripartite Declaration, which provided unilateral guarantees of Middle East borders in return for pledges of nonaggression. The system collapsed when Britain and France used force to seize the Suez Canal in 1956.

—In 1951, Britain and the United States formed the Middle East Command to coordinate the efforts of all powers inside and outside the region who wished to strengthen its defenses. It failed after proving too unwieldy to work.

—In 1951, the West European powers and the United States launched the Middle East Defense Organization to develop defense plans for the region and to enforce limits on outside arms sales. It soon fell into disuse.

—In 1955, Britain, Turkey, Iran, Iraq, Pakistan, and later the United States formed the Baghdad Pact to provide regional security. Four years later, all of these nations, with the exception of Iraq, revamped the organization, changing its name to the Central Treaty Organization. Both pacts fell victim to anti-Western coups in some member countries and languished in neglect.

—In 1957, the Eisenhower Doctrine announced that the United States would use armed force if necessary to protect the countries of the Persian Gulf from "armed aggression from any nation controlled by international communism." Though useful, the doctrine could not cope with the rise of threats of aggression by local powers.

—In 1980, the Carter Doctrine declared the Persian Gulf to be a "vital" U.S. interest and that any attempt by an outside power to seize it would be repelled by any means necessary, including military force. Since the United States lacked the forces required to back up its words, the doctrine represented a hollow warning at the time.

—In 1981, the Reagan administration sought to organize a "strategic consensus" in the Middle East in order to blunt the threat of Soviet expansionism. It failed because countries considered the threat from outside the region insignificant compared to threats from within the region.

The absence of stable regimes in key countries, the dearth of shared values, and the lack of a perceived common threat render the current fascination with comprehensive security systems for the Persian Gulf futile. Any such organization— which would inevitably grant veto authority over collective actions to every member—would short-circuit when local conflicts or even internal threats overloaded its capacity to respond. In the Muslim world, security structures sometimes serve as useful forums for discussion, but the rubber meets the road only through concrete arrangements made at the bilateral level.

The illusion of regional arms control. America's obsession with arms control flowered fully in the wake of the Persian Gulf War. Some analysts advocated a moratorium on arms sales to the Middle East. Others promoted the idea of an arms sellers' cartel to manage the flow of weapons into the region. Still others proposed strict restrictions on exports of technology related to chemical, biological, or nuclear weapons or to ballistic missiles. A few even wanted to craft arms control treaties that would make the Middle East a zone free from weapons of mass destruction.

There are four reasons why conventional arms control proposals are inadvisable and unfeasible. First, a moratorium on arms sales would impede the ability of all states in the region—both friendly and hostile—to equip themselves to meet their legitimate defense requirements. Second, since most Middle East countries face multiple potential threats and varied terrain, no simple cookbook solution can create the equivalent of the CFE treaty or enable a cartel to determine the appropriate arms levels for each state. Third, the economic incentives for arms exporters—not only the Soviet Union but also secondary powers such as China, Brazil, and North Korea—would soon lead to evasions or violations of agreed-upon limits. Fourth, conventional arms control, especially if imposed on the region by outside powers, would likely have the perverse effect of prompting countries to develop weapons of mass destruction as force equalizers.

Instead of comprehensive approaches, the United States should pursue a policy of discriminatory arms control that seeks to restrict arms flows only to states, such as Syria and Iraq, that pose threats to their neighbors. Arms sales to defensive powers, such as Israel and Saudi Arabia, enhance rather than diminish regional security. Top priority should go to restricting the availability of nuclear and ballistic-missile technologies. The Convention for the Limitation of the Spread of Missile Technology represents a good first step. We should not, however, delude ourselves about how much it can achieve. It can slow down but not stop the diffusion of weapons technologies. Maintaining the balance of military power remains the best formula for Middle East security, and selling arms represents an indispensable instrument in preserving that balance.

The illusion of redistributing regional wealth. As soon as the guns fell silent in the Persian Gulf War, Western policymakers began calling for share-the-wealth schemes that would transfer billions of dollars from the oil-rich Arab states to the poorer Arab countries. The Gulf Cooperation Council quickly fell into line, endorsing a proposed $10-billion regional development fund. Unfortunately, the past history of such efforts provides few reasons for high hopes. Their focus has traditionally been political patronage rather than economic development. Funds, dispersed through government-to-government aid programs, have usually been spent without sound economic rationales, subsidizing state-run enterprises or wasteful infrastructure projects.

The problem of rich versus poor in the Arab world has less to do with the distribution of oil revenues than with the overall poverty of the region. Saudi Arabia and the Gulf states appear rich only because of their tiny combined population of 20 million. The perception that these states have endless cash reserves is based on the image of jet-setting Arab princes, not the reality of their significant but not limitless wealth. The entire Saudi GNP—$82 billion—represents less than what the U.S. government spends on Medicare in a single year. Moreover, even if all oil revenues were redistributed equally among all Arabs, the region's per capita income would reach only $2,300, compared with $20,000 in Western Europe. The answer to the problem of Middle East poverty lies in free-market economic development rather than Robin Hood—like money grabs or handouts that would permanently consign the poorer nations to an international welfare role.

There is no single magical solution to the security dilemmas of the Persian Gulf. Unless Saddam Hussein's lieutenants overthrow him, the military threat to Saudi Arabia and the Gulf states will remain acute. Because the Persian Gulf possesses 65 percent of the world's proven oil reserves—and because it is projected to be the only source of significant exportable oil in the world for the next twenty-five years—we have no choice but to remain engaged in the area.

Since World War II, the Soviet Union has sought to stake a geopolitical claim to the Persian Gulf. It tried to carve off parts of Iran in 1946 and established close relations with Iraq after Arab radicals took power in 1958. It sought to hijack the fundamentalist revolution in Iran in 1979 by infiltrating Communists into its government, a plot that might have worked if the chief of the KGB residence in Teheran had not defected to the West. In the Persian Gulf War, the Soviets faced a dilemma. Gorbachev had to decide if supporting the principal pillar of Soviet regional influence, Iraq, was worth forfeiting any chance for large-scale economic assistance from the West. Moscow's internal crisis gave Gorbachev no viable alternative to reluctantly acquiescing to the U.S. position at least in the short run. One of our top priorities in working with the new noncommunist leaders in the former Soviet Union should be to convince them that their long-term interests will be served by supporting us unequivocally in our search for peace in the Middle East.

In the Gulf War, the U.S.-led coalition scored a knock-down but not a knockout. We won round one, but Saddam Hussein's strategy is to go the distance. Because he knows that he cannot fight us toe-to-toe, Saddam will try to win on points by staying in power, recovering gradually, retaining his weapons of mass destruction, and waiting for the United States to lose patience and throw in the towel. While we should allow Iraq to purchase some humanitarian supplies, we must keep the sanctions in place as long as he remains in power. We should insist that Iraq fully comply with the U.N. resolutions calling for the destruction of its chemical, biological, and nuclear weapons facilities. If Saddam Hussein persists in playing cat and mouse with U.N. officials, we should bomb sites suspected of containing equipment and material related to producing weapons of mass destruction.

We should view with skepticism Iran's expressed interest in closer ties to the West. While a moderate Iran would help stabilize the region, the extreme fundamentalists clearly want Teheran to reclaim the throne as the dominant regional power. Those who blame the United States for the poor relations with Iran miss the mark. Iran has continued to finance international terrorist networks that target the United States, including those that bombed the U.S. embassy and the Marine barracks in Lebanon in October 1983 and that downed Pan Am flight 103 over Scotland in December 1988. Its extreme fundamentalist regime, which has used its embassies to coordinate anti-Western terrorist groups, has been linked to more than four hundred terrorist incidents worldwide. Moreover, Iran played a spoiler role in the Persian Gulf War, pitting each side against the other until Iraq's fate had been clearly sealed.

As President, I authored what was called the Nixon Doctrine. It stipulated that we would help train and supply the forces of friendly developing countries combating internal threats instigated by foreign foes but that we would intervene with our own forces only when our friends were threatened by an external enemy that overwhelmed their capacity to respond. While some interpreted this doctrine as an indication that the United States was getting out of the underdeveloped world, it actually outlined the only sound basis for a sustained U.S. engagement in the third world as a whole and in the Persian Gulf in particular.

Until the fall of the shah in 1979, the United States could protect its interests through Iran and Saudi Arabia, the two pillars of our Gulf policy for more than a decade. With a hostile regime in Teheran after 1979, we lacked a major regional player who could act as a surrogate and therefore had to take steps to ensure our ability to protect vital Western interests. President Carter concluded initial agreements to allow prepositioning of U.S. equipment and supplies in regional states and created the Rapid Deployment Force, which later became the U.S. Central Command. President Reagan followed up with extensive, low-profile cooperation in the Gulf to establish the infrastructure needed to support a major U.S. intervention to defend Saudi Arabia and the southern Gulf. Without these facilities, Operation Desert Shield/Storm would have become a modern-day Gallipoli.

The key to Gulf security is sturdy U.S. bilateral military ties in support of cooperative defense efforts among the moderate Arab states. While many have called for institutionalizing U.S. security relations and even for the establishment of a new Central Command headquarters in a Persian Gulf country, the same results can be achieved without a high-profile U.S. presence. We should use our influence behind the scenes to ensure that Egypt and other Muslim countries work out multilateral arrangements to bolster the defense of the weaker Gulf states. We should also negotiate informal agreements for the prepositioning of equipment and supplies for any potential future U.S. intervention. Maintaining too high a profile would undercut our objectives. We would fatally undermine our friends and our interests if we appear to treat the Persian Gulf as our own protectorate. Our presence, rather than the threat posed by our adversaries, would become the central issue for our friends.

Our two immediate interests in the Middle East—oil and Israel—are not always fully compatible. On the one hand, our commitment to Israel has sometimes carried a high price in terms of our access to Persian Gulf oil at free-market prices, as the 1973 Arab oil embargo demonstrated. On the other hand, our commitment to the security of Saudi Arabia and the Gulf states has at times complicated relations with Israel. While the decision to sell Awacs early-warning aircraft to the Saudis in 1982 prompted a bitter fight with supporters of Israel in Congress, those arms sales—and other informal security cooperation—proved indispensable during Operation Desert Shield/Storm.

Our interests require a difficult geopolitical calculus: we must both ensure the survival of Israel and work with moderate Arab states to enhance the security of the Persian Gulf. The Arab-Israeli conflict represents a central obstacle. For forty-five years, both sides have poured endless resources into arms to destroy each other rather than investing in their economies to improve the welfare of their citizens. They have waged five wars—in 1948, 1956, 1967, 1973, and 1982— and engaged in countless military skirmishes. This conflict, exacerbated but not created by the cold war, has repeatedly pitted our key interests against each other. The only way we can square the circle is to press forward actively with the Arab-Israeli peace process.

Time has never been on the side of peace in the Middle East. An Arab-Israeli war has broken out in every decade of the postwar period because a political stalemate was permitted to develop during peacetime. The peace process is not a panacea. But it is critical to the U.S. position in the Muslim world. Although many exaggerated the degree to which the U.S.-led victory in the Persian Gulf would enhance our diplomatic influence in the region, President Bush's skillful leadership has opened an opportunity for progress. While still not hopeful, the situation at least is no longer hopeless.

Our commitment to the survival and security of Israel runs deep. We are not formal allies, but we are bound together by something much stronger than a piece of paper: a moral commitment. Contrary to the conventional wisdom, Israel is not a strategic interest of the United States. Our cooperation in intelligence sharing and military prepositioning and exercises is helpful but not vital. While Israel's armed forces have brilliantly proven themselves on the battlefield, the Persian Gulf War—where they contributed not by participating in but by staying out of the conflict—proved their limited utility in the most important regional contingencies. Our commitment to Israel stems from the legacy of World War II and from our moral and ideological interest in ensuring the survival of embattled democracies. No American President or Congress will ever allow the destruction of the state of Israel.

Many supporters of Israel argue that the United States should back to the hilt the hard-line positions of the current Likud government. They insist that Israel cannot return to the Arabs any of the occupied territories—the West Bank, the Gaza Strip, and the Golan Heights—without endangering its security. Others even endorse the Likud leaders' biblically based claim that the West Bank—which they call Judea and Samaria—belongs historically to Israel. All advocate support for Israel's adamant refusal to talk with Palestinians linked with the PLO, to enter negotiations about the final status of the occupied lands, and even to contemplate any settlement that would reverse the Israeli annexation of East Jerusalem and the Golan Heights.

While we are right to support Israel's survival and security, we would be wrong to back the current Israeli government's extreme demands. Without engaging in "moral equivalency" between offensive and defensive states, we should understand how the occupied territories came into Israel's possession through the 1967 war. Aggressive military moves by Arab states created the crisis—perhaps even made the war inevitable—but Israel launched the first attacks. Former prime minister Menachem Begin said in August 1982, "In June 1967, we again had a choice. The Egyptian army concentrations in the Sinai do not prove that Nasser was really about to attack us. We must be honest with ourselves. We decided to attack him." Because the war resulted from actions by both sides, the subsequent U.N. Security Council resolutions—242 and 338—demanded not unilateral concessions, but bilateral trade-offs of land for peace.

There are three reasons why we must press forward with the peace process based on the land-for-peace formula. First, the Arab-Israeli conflict totally distorts our foreign aid budget. In 1991, the 60 million people of Israel and Egypt received more than 40 percent of the almost $15 billion the United States allocated to foreign aid, while the over 4 billion people in the rest of the underdeveloped world competed for the leftovers. Since the mid-1970s, the United States has given Israel $49 billion in direct and indirect foreign aid. In addition, Israel received $16.4 billion in loans between 1974 and 1989 that were subsequently converted into grants. To balance the Middle East equation, the United States has provided Egypt with $28 billion in foreign aid between 1980 and 1991. Besides having underwritten large portions of the Israeli and Egyptian defense budgets, we also canceled $6.8 billion of debt that Cairo could never hope to repay. By channeling such a disproportionate amount of assistance into coping with the Arab-Israeli conflict, we lack sufficient money to help the emerging democracies of Eastern Europe, the struggling economies in Latin America, and the destitute peoples of Africa and South Asia.

Second, the Arab-Israeli conflict poisons our relations with the Muslim world and undercuts our ability to cooperate with countries with modernist, pro-Western leaders. Israel's occupation of Arab lands—and particularly its increasingly harsh treatment of the Palestinians—polarizes and radicalizes the Muslim world. It undermines the moderates, such as President Mubarak of Egypt. All Muslim leaders support the legitimate aspirations of the Palestinian people and view the harassment of Israeli occupation forces in the so-called *intifada* as legitimate armed resistance, not terrorism. While many may criticize the leadership of the PLO, especially after its shameless support for Saddam Hussein's invasion of Kuwait, they have not backed away from the Palestinian cause and will never drop it from the agenda. President Sadat could not have signed the Camp David accords without Israel's commitment to establish "transitional arrangements for the West Bank and Gaza for a period not to exceed five years." Under the agreement, Palestinians were to receive local autonomy as soon as arrangements could be worked out, with negotiations over the final status of the territories to start within three years. With that timetable, the entire process should have been concluded in 1984. Nothing has happened.

To put it bluntly, Israel stonewalled the United States and Egypt.

Third, more than any other flash point, the Arab-Israeli conflict poses the danger of dragging the United States into a war involving the use of nuclear weapons. While any future conflict between India and Pakistan could cross the nuclear threshold, the likelihood of direct U.S. involvement remains low. But we would almost certainly become engaged in a future Middle East conflict. I vividly recall a meeting with legislative leaders during the 1973 Middle East war. In the opening rounds of the conflict, the tide of battle had run against Israel. Meanwhile, the Soviets had initiated a massive airlift to Egypt and Syria. When a congressman asked whether the United States would take measures to counter Moscow's actions, I flatly answered, "No American President will ever let Israel go down the tube." I subsequently ordered a massive airlift to prevent Israel's defeat and later put U.S. nuclear forces on alert to forestall a threatened unilateral Soviet intervention in the region. If war comes, the U.S. commitment to Israel will inevitably mean our direct or indirect involvement. Particularly since Israel has built nuclear weapons and its Arab adversaries possess chemical and biological arms, the United States cannot afford to let the peace process languish.

Both American and Israeli interests would be best served by a settlement based on land for peace. If Israel retains the occupied territories, it will corrupt its moral cause. One of Israel's founders and a leader whom John Foster Dulles once described as an "Old Testament prophet," David Ben-Gurion, rightly observed that the "extremists" who advocated the absorption of Arab lands would deprive Israel of its mission: "If they succeed, Israel will be neither Jewish nor democratic. The Arabs will outnumber us, and undemocratic, repressive measures will be needed to keep them under control." While the more than 4 million Israelis and the more than 1 million estimated Jewish émigrés from the Soviet Union will exceed the 2 million Arabs in Israel and the occupied territories, it is destabilizing and dangerous to keep the Arabs captive. If Israel annexes these lands, its security problem will become a national problem, as intractable as those in multinational states such as Iraq and the Soviet Union. Israel would inevitably become a binational garrison state, thereby not only corrupting the spirit of the Jewish nation but also undermining the moral purpose that undergirds the U.S. commitment to its survival.

Ironically, Israel's current leaders appear reluctant to pursue peace at a time when the circumstances for striking the best deal are the best they have been in the forty-four years of Israel's existence as a nation.

—Iraq, crushed in war, isolated in the Arab world, and burdened by debt and reparations, can no longer pose a conventional offensive military threat to Israel.

—The PLO, discredited by its alliance with Saddam Hussein and cut off from former creditors such as Saudi Arabia, has lost its appeal for many Palestinians, as well as its supporters abroad.

—Syria, economically feeble and financially broke, can entertain no illusions after the Persian Gulf War that its Soviet-made weaponry could prevail against Israel.

—Jordan, squeezed between the twin threats of political radicalism and economic collapse, cannot pose a real threat to Israel and wants a deal that would restore its ties with the West after its support for Iraq in the Gulf War.

—Egypt, the only Arab state to sign a peace treaty with Israel and the principal moderate Arab power, has regained its position as the leader of the Arab world.

—Given the massive influx of Soviet émigrés into Israel—
now arriving at a rate of 30,000 per month—Arab leaders
know that this will be their last chance to prevent Israel's
annexation of the territories through new settlements.

—Moscow, too preoccupied at home to play its traditional
role as spoiler of the peace process, will have no choice but
to follow whatever course the United States chooses.

Israel's strong hand will inevitably weaken over time. Exploiting Israeli obstinance, the PLO may rehabilitate its
image. Syria will tap new sources of support among the Gulf
states. The new leaders in the former Soviet Union could
resuscitate the Kremlin's historical policy of seeking a foot-
hold in the Middle East. As the death toll in the suppression
of the Palestinian uprising surges past eight hundred, the
erosion of Israel's political standing abroad will accelerate.
The Israeli people—40 percent of whom now support talks
with the PLO and would accept a Palestinian ministate in the
occupied territories—appear to recognize that the status quo
has become intolerable. Israel should negotiate now when it
is stronger than any of its potential enemies rather than waiting until the increased strength of its enemies forces it to do
so. The essence of successful statecraft is to strike a deal at
the most favorable moment. For Israel, that time is now.

U.S. mediation is the sine qua non of success in the peace
process. The idea that the issue should be turned over to the
United Nations is a nonstarter. Israel will not—and should
not—submit its fate to a stacked jury. Though U.N. forces
have played a useful buffer role in other hot spots, their track
record in the Arab-Israeli conflict has been abysmal. Four
times U.N. troops have come to bat in the Middle East. In all
four trips to the plate, they have struck out.

Many Israeli moderates, as well as the hard-liners, hesitate
about accepting a land-for-peace deal. They suspect that the

return of land will be permanent but the peace will be temporary. They view skeptically the idea of international guarantees, especially since those offered after the 1948 and 1956 wars evaporated when the chips were down. They strongly believe that a prospective settlement must not depend on trust between the two sides. They are only partly right. No such trust exists or can be generated through a treaty. But a peace between adversaries is possible. This peace must be grounded in concrete security arrangements reinforced with a balance of power. A peace based on power is a sturdy one. If peace depends on trust, the peace disappears when the trust evaporates. If peace depends on power, the peace endures even in the absence of trust.

Any U.S.-mediated peace settlement must have four objectives: (1) full diplomatic recognition of Israel by its neighbors, (2) secure borders for Israel, (3) return to Arab states of territories captured in 1967, and (4) self-government for the Palestinians.

In the past, interim agreements—some of which have lasted more than fifteen years—have avoided the issue of Arab acceptance of Israel's existence. That is no longer acceptable. If Arab leaders will not accept the reality of Israel after forty-four years, they are interested not in a peace settlement, but in a temporary armistice.

Israel faces two potential threats that security arrangements must address—full-scale invasion by conventional forces and small-scale strikes by guerrilla and terrorist units. To cope with the conventional threat, the United States should work at two levels. First, if Israel agrees to return the occupied territories, we should enter a mutual security treaty with Israel stipulating that a conventional attack on Israel will be treated like an attack on the United States. After the Persian Gulf War, there can be no lingering doubts about our willingness to fulfill such a pledge. We had no alliance with, no commitment to, and no deep sympathy for Kuwait. Yet we moved manpower equivalent to the population of two cities the size of Madison, Wisconsin, halfway around the world to free the country. Although President Bush had to lobby for votes on the Persian Gulf War resolutions in Congress, senators and congressmen would line up to support Israel.

Second, the United States needs to craft additional measures to ensure that the loss of land would not mean a loss of security for Israel. In all the returned territories, for example, conventional forces with offensive capabilities should be prohibited. The Golan Heights and the West Bank would in effect become buffer zones. While Syria might administer the Golan Heights and Jordan the West Bank, neither state could station military forces on these territories, thereby neutralizing their utility as a launching pad for invasion or harassing artillery strikes. We should also insist on a thinning out of Arab forces stationed along current cease-fire lines and on international or joint U.S.–Israeli–Arab League reconnaissance and early-warning stations in the territories to frustrate any plans to seize the buffer zone through a surprise attack. An international force—equipped not to observe, but to enforce the agreement by arms if necessary—could be deployed as well. With the right security measures, a land-for-peace deal can enhance rather than diminish Israel's physical security.

Confronting the guerrilla and terrorist threat will be more difficult. Israeli hard-liners argue that the return of the West Bank would allow irregular Palestinian forces to fire mortars —some of which are small enough to fit in a knapsack—on Israeli cities from positions a couple of miles across the border. That concern is genuine, but could be addressed with security measures. Today, Israeli checkpoints along the cease-fire line with Jordan prevent the smuggling of small arms and munitions into the West Bank. There is no reason that a similar control regime—staffed partly by Israelis— could not remain in place on the ground, as well as at airports. Moreover, a peace settlement should explicitly recognize an Israeli right of retaliation in the event of unconventional attacks coming from the current occupied territories, thereby creating an incentive for Jordanian and Palestinian leaders to keep their own people in check.

To achieve Palestinian self-government, the United States should seek to resuscitate the Camp David formula—local Palestinian autonomy in association with Jordan phased in over a multiyear transition period. Although this means convincing King Hussein to retract his 1988 renunciation of the Jordanian claim to the West Bank, such flexibility is not unknown in Middle East diplomacy. In the meantime, elections should be held in the occupied territories to select Palestinian representatives for the peace talks. Israeli leaders have insisted on advance approval of those who might serve in that role and on blackballing anyone with any association —no matter how distant—with the PLO. That is unreasonable. We did not like negotiating with Stalin or his successors, but since they held power, we had to deal with them. Unless Israel comes to terms with its enemies, no peace agreement will enhance its security.

Both the Israeli and Palestinian hard-liners must abandon their ultimate aspirations. Although some adjustments in the pre-1967 control lines should be negotiated to provide secure borders for Israel, the Israelis must give up their settlements on the West Bank and Gaza Strip. In turn, Palestinians must accept the fact that refugees from the 1948 war—who together with their descendants now number 3 million—will not return to their homes in Israel proper. To an extent, the

PLO has already accepted that reality in public statements. At the same time, the Israeli settlers withdrawn from occupied territory and the Palestinians who lost their homes in Israel proper should be compensated for their property. We should persuade the Saudis and the Gulf states, as well as Japan, to provide the financial salve that will ease the sting of these concessions. The control of East Jerusalem—a neuralgic issue for both sides—cannot easily be settled. At a minimum, the Israelis should Vaticanize the Muslim and Christian holy places, but dividing the city along pre-1967 lines has become nonnegotiable.

A settlement with those general provisions would serve the core interests of both sides. Nothing is sacrosanct, however, about those particular security arrangements. They are only one possible approach. But we must recognize that it is possible for measures to be negotiated that will cope with the difficult security problems inherent in an Arab-Israeli land-for-peace deal.

Our tactics are another matter. We should not start the process by trotting out a comprehensive U.S. peace plan. Both sides will instantly shoot it down. Instead, we should engage in broad discussions with each side to explore their ideas for an adequate security framework. We should then determine what kind of settlement would be fair and feasible. Only after we identify the general outlines of such an agreement should we embark on the contentious task of crafting provisions and language for a formal treaty. At that point, we should lean on both sides for the needed concessions. Our leverage, though limited, is significant. Israel needs billions of dollars to facilitate the settlement of Soviet émigrés. The moderate Arab states—Egypt, Saudi Arabia, the Gulf states, and Jordan—need U.S. arms sales and security cooperation. Saudi Arabia and Moscow can put pressure on Syria.

We should not impose a settlement but rather convince the

parties of the merits of its terms. In the power politics of Middle East diplomacy, that requires more than eloquent talking points. It also means pointedly reminding obstinate leaders of what the United States can do for and do to their countries. Progress in the peace process has come only when the parties believed the status quo was more painful than a potential compromise. While heavy-handed bullying would be counterproductive, we should remember that we have the leverage to *make* the status quo more painful than a proposed settlement.

As they approach the prospective Arab-Israeli peace talks, U.S. policymakers should observe five basic rules:

Emphasize substance, not process. With the difficulty in convincing Arabs and Israelis to sit down at the conference table, the talks threaten to become bogged down in the minutiae of the process rather than grappling with the critical substantive issues. All leaders in the Middle East are masters at avoiding concessions by erecting procedural obstacles. The idea that a peace settlement can be reached if only both sides negotiate face-to-face is well intended, but totally unrealistic. The problem is not a lack of understanding between Israel and its neighbors. On the contrary, both understand each other too well. They want totally different things. The Arabs want land without peace. The Israelis want peace without giving up land. Israel and Syria do not have to meet face-to-face to understand that both want the Golan Heights.

Pursue a phased, not a comprehensive, agreement. Progress in the peace process comes not in great strides, but in small steps. Each side will attempt to forge links between issues. Syria, for example, will not grant full recognition to Israel until movement takes place on the Palestinian issue. No single agreement will overcome every issue that has arisen during the years of tension that have divided the two sides. It is therefore better to narrow the agenda early in the process to the key items that represent achievable and significant objectives.

Maintain strict secrecy in negotiations. The American people instinctively agree with President Wilson's famous call for "open covenants, openly arrived at." But secrecy is indispensable to success in the peace process. Unless covenants are arrived at secretly, there will be none to agree to openly. Without secrecy, none of the parties will feel free to float potential compromise formulas. If negotiating positions leak to the news media—thereby exposing leaders to attacks by domestic critics—both sides will instantly set their maximum demands in concrete.

Conduct talks only at the highest levels. Success in mediation will come only as a result of the direct, active, and sustained personal engagement of the President. Although the secretary of state can serve as an effective surrogate, the President must clearly indicate that the U.S. position has his personal imprimatur. I took this approach during the negotiations that led to the Syrian-Israeli disengagement accords after the 1973 war. President Carter did so in negotiating the landmark Camp David Agreements in 1978. If the peace process is delegated to an assistant secretary of state or to another one of a long succession of personal envoys, no Middle East leader will take it seriously. History is strewn with failed missions of special presidential representatives who broke their picks on the hard rock of Arab-Israeli hostility. Only negotiations at the highest level have any chance of succeeding.

Prepare for the long haul. The 1974 disengagement agreements took four months of virtually nonstop shuttle diplomacy by Henry Kissinger to achieve. Egypt, Israel, and the United States signed the Camp David accords only after eleven months of often-contentious talks, including two summit-level meetings. Because of the geography of the Sinai, those agreements were relatively uncomplicated compared to what will be required for the remaining occupied territories. Any settlement will require not a quick sprint of negotiations but rather will come at the end of a diplomatic marathon. The optimal time to put negotiations on the front burner is during a nonelection year in the United States. In election years, political pressures will stymie any significant progress.

In coping with the Arab-Israeli conflict, we must recognize a key fact of international life: a treaty can change the behavior of states, but not the attitudes of people. Peace in the Middle East is not a matter of Arabs and Israelis learning to like each other. They have hated each other for centuries and will continue to do so. At most, it means learning to live peacefully with their differences. A lasting settlement requires that they be separated and kept apart by concrete security arrangements that, if violated, will cost the aggressor more than he could ever hope to gain.

As we develop our policies to engage the Muslim world, we must begin with respect and understanding for peoples who feel that they have been misunderstood, discriminated against, and exploited by Western powers. We should not try to impose our values on them. Though the Muslim world lags behind the West in political development—only two Muslim nations have democratic governments—our civilization is not inherently superior to theirs. The people of the Muslim world were more resilient against the appeal of communism than those of the West, and their widespread rejection of the materialism and moral permissiveness of Western culture redounds to their credit.

For five centuries—from 700 to 1200—the Muslim world led the Christian world in terms of geopolitical power, standard of living, religious toleration, sophistication of laws, and level of learning in philosophy, science, and culture. Decades of warfare turned the tables. As Durant wrote, "The West lost the Crusades, but won the war of creeds. Every Christian warrior was expelled from the Holy Land of Judaism and Christianity; but Islam, bled by its tardy victory, and ravaged by Mongols, fell in turn into a Dark Age of obscurantism and poverty; while the beaten West, matured by its effort and forgetting its defeat, learned avidly from its enemy, lifted cathedrals into the sky, wandered out on the high seas of reason, transformed its crude new languages into Dante, Chaucer, and Villon, and moved with high spirit into the Renaissance."

Just as knowledge from the East helped trigger the Renaissance in the West, the time has come for the West to contribute to a renaissance of the Muslim world. If we engage the modernist states of the Muslim world as full and equal partners, and if we seek to resolve the difficult security issues plaguing the Middle East, we can lay the foundation for such a rebirth. If we work together and combine the best of our civilizations, the next period of our history will be one of constructive cooperation, not destructive conflict.

6

THE
SOUTHERN
HEMISPHERE

W HEN I TRAVELED THROUGH noncommunist Asia as vice
president in 1953, I always made a point of not just meeting
with leaders in their regal offices, but also making stops to
examine conditions in the poorer neighborhoods. With the

---

grinding poverty I saw—children with distended stomachs, jobless men milling in coffee shops, and open sewers befouling the air—I could understand why these slums were a fertile breeding ground for communism. Many of the leaders whom I met at that time viewed communism as an attractive shortcut to economic prosperity. When I visited those same countries in 1985, no one entertained such illusions. With the collapse of the Soviet economy, the allure of socialist central planning had vanished. As a model for political and economic development, Soviet communism had been swept into the dustbin of history.

The defeat of communism in the underdeveloped world does not mean the victory of freedom. I visited more than a dozen nations and colonies on that 1953 trip, including Indonesia, Malaysia, Cambodia, Laos, Vietnam, Singapore, Burma, the Philippines, South Korea, Taiwan, Hong Kong, Ceylon, India, Pakistan, Iran, and Afghanistan. Some, such as Vietnam and Afghanistan, took the fatal detour of communism. Others, such as India and Burma, turned down the dead end of socialism. Only a few, such as South Korea, Taiwan, Singapore, and Hong Kong, drove down the road to prosperity by adopting free-market economics.

Among the developing nations of Africa, Latin America, East Asia, and South Asia—regions that can figuratively be described as the southern hemisphere—the path to economic development remains strewn with obstacles. Corrupt government officials, mismanaged economic policies, and misguided development strategies hold back the potential of talented and hard-working peoples on every continent. These problems—most self-inflicted—have locked these countries into a vicious cycle of poverty from which they seem powerless to escape. Only if we work with them to overcome these obstacles can we ensure that the success of freedom in the southern hemisphere follows the failure of communism around the world.

If we wash our hands of these concerns, the future will become a tale of two worlds—one rich and the other poor, one surging ahead with high technology and the other lagging behind with obsolete industrial plants and subsistence agriculture, one smug in its ease and comfort and the other increasingly resentful and hostile. The average annual per capita income of the more than 4 billion people of the underdeveloped world has stagnated at less than $800, compared with $21,000 in the United States. If we ignore those less fortunate than ourselves, we will not only disregard our moral responsibility, but also imperil our vital economic and strategic interests.

One quarter of the people in the underdeveloped world live below the threshold of poverty. Thirty thousand people die every day from dirty water and unsanitary conditions. Average life expectancy is twenty years shorter than in the United States. Because population growth is three times greater than in the West, the average per capita income will fall by the end of the century. We cannot stand back and watch from afar as the underdeveloped world sinks in an economic morass. We should not allow it, and the billions of people who live there will not tolerate it.

Contrary to the Marxist cant in many American universities, the West did not cause the poverty, famine, malnutrition, and disease that afflict poorer nations. The West, however, must not ignore their problems. As the world's only superpower, the United States has a particular responsibility to act. Until the collapse of communism in the Soviet Union, the rationale for most of our aid to developing nations was to counter the threat of direct and indirect Soviet aggression. Now we must recognize that even in the absence of a Soviet threat, it is imperative to continue to provide aid to the developing nations. Without our help, they cannot succeed. This does not mean that we should write a blank check to ineffective or corrupt governments. It does mean that we need a new aid program that will encourage developing nations to help themselves.

In addition to our moral obligation, we have major economic and strategic interests at stake. First, we will benefit if we can unlock the vast untapped economic potential of these countries. Seventy-five percent of the world's oil, as well as other critical raw materials, is in the underdeveloped world. By the year 2000, four out of five people will be living there. In 1900, the ten largest cities in the world were in Europe. By the end of the decade, eight out of ten will be in the southern hemisphere. If the per capita incomes of these countries were to rise to Western European standards over the next century, annual U.S. exports would increase by $3 trillion, infusing new vitality into our economy. Since every $1 billion in new exports produces 25,000 jobs, the United States could over the coming decades generate 75 million new jobs for future generations of Americans. Greater economic prosperity in the underdeveloped world means money in the pockets of American workers.

Second, if we ignore the southern hemisphere, we risk being dragged into potentially deadly regional conflicts. Poverty will no longer produce communism, but it can still produce brutal, radical regimes. Since the end of World War II, millions of people have died in over 120 wars in the underdeveloped world, forty of which are still being fought today. As the Persian Gulf War demonstrated, instability half a world away can have a profound effect here at home. Such conflicts could disrupt the flow of oil or other resources that are crucial to our national security. Our economic destiny could be held hostage by capricious and hostile rulers such as Saddam Hussein. The danger to the United States has been heightened because many of these countries are acquiring the technologies to manufacture nuclear weapons and ballistic missiles. While our allies in the underdeveloped world face the most immediate threat, we will not be immune from future threats.

Third, unless we foster economic opportunity in the underdeveloped world, our borders will be overwhelmed by a flood of economic refugees. The developing countries have a total population of over 4 billion people today and will have an estimated 7.2 billion in the year 2025. The ranks of unemployed and underemployed workers could swell from the hundreds of millions to the billions in the next century. The developed world cannot draw artificial lines in the sand to keep these people from fleeing their hopeless poverty. Even now, more than two thousand Mexican workers emigrate illegally to the United States every day. If we turn our back on their problems today, we will find them on our doorstep tomorrow.

Many on both the American right and left advocate a policy of disengagement from the underdeveloped world. Some argue that these countries are no-man's-lands of corruption —"kleptocracies" in which a few rulers rake in millions of dollars through theft while millions of workers eke out a few dollars through backbreaking labor. Others contend that we should focus our energies and resources on the poor and homeless in New York and Los Angeles rather than on those in Ouagadougou and Calcutta. But most responsible observers recognize our moral and strategic interests in assisting the people of the underdeveloped world. The question then becomes not *whether* we should help but *how* we can help most effectively.

More than other developed countries, the United States ought to know the paths to success. Only a hundred years ago—a passing moment in terms of human history—America was part of the underdeveloped world, with a per capita income of only $210. Also, the success of the four Asian tigers—Taiwan, South Korea, Hong Kong, and Singapore—should serve as a positive example that less developed countries can make the transition from poverty to prosperity. Many of our previous aid programs have amounted to nothing more than conscience money thrown at the problem of world poverty or spent to prevent Communist expansion. Today, we must reorient our approach to the southern hemisphere, applying the lessons of the successful development of East Asia's newly industrialized countries.

During my 1953 trip, two of my most discouraging stops were in Taipei and Seoul. Both appeared to be economic basket cases, capitals of countries artificially divided by the pull and tug of the cold war, saddled with massive expenditures for national defense, and preoccupied with short-term survival rather than long-term prosperity. Hong Kong and Singapore, still British colonies, seemed to face equally dim futures. By avoiding the economic dead end of communism and embracing the market, however, these countries turned the corner. Within thirty-five years, they moved from the periphery of the underdeveloped world to the threshold of entering the developed world.

After the Communist victory in China's civil war in 1949, Taiwan stood on the brink of collapse. Its industrial and agricultural output was less than half of that of 1937. In 1949, its per capita income was $50, roughly the same as the Communist mainland. Taiwan today has become one of the world's most dynamic economies, with annual real growth averaging over 9 percent over the past three decades. It possesses $73 billion in foreign exchange reserves, the world's fourth largest after the United States, Germany, and Japan. The 21 million Chinese in Taiwan export $14 billion more a year than do the 1.1 billion Chinese on the mainland. Taiwan's per capita income is $6,335, more than nineteen times higher than that of the People's Republic of China across the Straits of Formosa.

With its territory overrun three times by Communist armies in the Korean War, South Korea emerged as an economic wasteland, with a per capita income of $50 in 1953. Despite allocating over 5 percent of its GNP to national defense over the past forty years, it has grown from an economic pygmy of the 1960s to a potential economic giant of the 1990s. In 1989, South Korea's per capita income reached $4,600, nearly four times that of its Communist counterpart to the north. This success—which has been fueled by a 20 percent annual growth rate in exports over the past quarter of a century—not only raised the ire of protectionists in the United States, but also piqued the interest of leaders in Moscow and Beijing, who distanced themselves from their longtime North Korean Communist allies to gain economic benefit from their former South Korean capitalist enemies.

Even though it lives in the shadow of the People's Republic of China, Hong Kong has maintained a consistent policy of free-market economics over the past four decades. Despite its tenuous existence as a British protectorate six thousand miles from London, Hong Kong's main problem has not been an exodus of emigrants but a tide of immigrants. Its economy had an annual growth rate of 6.3 percent in 1989, yielding a per capita income of $10,350. We must insist that Beijing build upon this success when Britain returns this territory in

1997. Hong Kong could then serve as a catalyst for the prosperity of one-fifth of the world's people.

Under the leadership of Prime Minister Lee Kuan Yew, Singapore has catapulted itself into the ranks of the world's fastest-growing economies. While exploiting its geographic position to serve as a major transshipment point for East Asian trade, it has also made its own economic mark. With a territory of 225 square miles—one-fifth the size of the smallest U.S. state, Rhode Island—and a GNP of $24 billion, Singapore is mile for mile the most economically dynamic country in the world. Over the past quarter of a century, its economy has grown at an annual rate of 7 percent, pushing its per capita income to $10,450 in 1989. With little territory and even fewer natural resources, growth could have come only through developing its human resources. As Lee once said, "This place will survive only if it has got the will to make the grade. It's got nothing else but will and work."

The four Asian tigers succeeded because their governments adopted policies that unleashed the creative potential of their people. Though this appears mundane at first glance, anyone who has studied the underdeveloped world knows that most of its governments have spent enormous time and resources sapping the energies of their peoples. The leaders of the Asian tigers understood that the most basic human motivation— the desire to better the condition of one's self and family—is the mainspring of economic growth. People, regardless of their education and background, have responded to such basic economic incentives from the dawn of time in every corner of the world.

The first correct move of the successful developing countries was to ignore the advice of Western academics who, like snake oil salesmen, pushed development strategies based on import substitution and statism. Advocates of import substitution believed that economic contact with the industrialized world hindered development. They therefore urged high tariffs, prohibitive barriers to multinational investment, major subsidies to favored industries, and rigid self-reliance through the elimination of imports wherever possible. Domestically, their premise was that economic development was unnatural and that governments had to adopt comprehensive programs to compel their people to produce. They insisted that the state not only had to provide the needed infrastructure, but also had to fashion industrial strategies and to mobilize—through coercion if necessary—an apathetic people. As one prominent Western development theorist wrote, "The special advisers to underdeveloped countries who have taken the time and trouble to acquaint themselves with the problem, no matter who they are . . . all recommend central planning as the first condition of progress."

Ne Win, Burma's longtime dictator, epitomized this approach. When I met with him in 1985, I asked why he did not follow China's example of providing economic incentives for his people to produce, particularly since Burma was the poorest nation in Asia. He replied candidly, "The Chinese people are different. They respond to positive incentives. The Burmese people are lazy. They will only respond to negative incentives." Not surprisingly, Burma's economy atrophied during his rule.

The Asian tigers rejected this theory. They understood that there were five keys to successful development:

Base development on the foundation of competitive markets. Free-market institutions—private property and floating prices—create the incentives for people to produce. Only through the right to own private property can an iron link be forged between work and reward. And only market-based prices can provide the indispensable signals to consumers and producers that drive an economy toward greater efficiency. Yet in much of the underdeveloped world, governments have continually undermined confidence in the sanctity of property by nationalizing entire industries and have systematically meddled with free prices through controls and subsidies.

A hint of condescending racism exists in the views of development academics who depict the people of the underdeveloped world as torpid, unenterprising, and shortsighted. Though some of these countries have low literacy rates, their peoples have always responded when presented with incentives to produce. It has been the peculiar genius of many of their leaders to contrive elaborate ways to give them incentives not to produce. No psychological difference exists between the Chinese on the mainland and those in Taiwan, Hong Kong, and Singapore. The poverty of the former and the prosperity of the latter results from a difference not in talent but in incentives. Deng Xiaoping understood this. While he is still a committed Marxist, his economic reforms gave millions of Chinese incentives to work their way out of poverty rather than insisting on doctrinaire socialism, which guarantees everyone an equal share of poverty.

Facing stiff economic competition is the key to becoming a stiff economic competitor. Those who argue that developing countries should protect their "infant" industries with tariffs until they mature as world-class producers fail to realize that unless they face international competition, these firms will never learn to walk on their own. While many underdeveloped countries hunkered down behind protectionist walls and erected domestic cartels and monopolies, the Asian tigers threw themselves in the fray of the world market and also maintained a competitive environment domestically.

Some say that Japan's international success supports the need for protectionist development strategies. That argument captures only half the picture. While Japan has maintained high tariff barriers, its producers faced a highly competitive domestic market. Few American cars were permitted to slip into Japan in the 1950s and 1960s. But the competition between domestic producers—Nissan, Honda, Toyota, Mitsubishi, and others—was intense, thereby priming Japanese automobile companies for their expansion abroad.

Invest in human capital. The leaders of the Asian tigers understood that the critical component of development was human capital. Although its abundance in land and natural resources significantly helped the development of the United States, the key was the enterprising nature of its people and the value they placed on education. The same has been true among the four successful developing countries. Each has invested a high proportion of its GNP in education—as high as 4.4 percent in Singapore—and has encouraged its people to study abroad. All four have literacy rates far above the underdeveloped world's average, with Taiwan and South Korea even matching Western standards.

Keep the economic burden of government low. Though many today scoff at the theories of supply-side economics, they have refocused attention on an important truth: the more you tax something, the less you will get of it. If government imposes high taxes on the fruits of work—incomes and profits—there will be less economic activity just as surely as night follows day. While many countries in the underdeveloped world raised taxes to try to capture more revenue, the successful developing nations in East Asia understood that low taxes produce high growth, which eventually generates more government revenue even at lower tax rates. Governments in unsuccessful developing countries have sought to carve out for themselves a bigger piece of the pie, while the successful ones have focused on increasing the size of the pie.

Taxes are not the only problem. In much of the under-developed world, there is an almost cultish worship of state intervention in the economy. The state reserves monopoly industries for itself, controls all imports and exports, maintains an iron grip on new businesses through the licensing of commercial and industrial activities, restricts the mobility of labor and capital, enforces wage and price controls, and subsidizes enterprises and sectors in accordance with an overall plan or at the behest of certain interest groups. In none of the Asian tigers did such idiocy infect the thinking of economic policymakers.

This has been particularly true in the area of investment. It is almost a cliché to criticize developing countries for their senseless investments in economic white elephants. Steel plants, government airlines, six-lane superhighways leading nowhere, and newly built capital cities—all status symbols of development—have been the focus of billions of dollars of state-directed spending. While such "industrial strategies" continue to seduce Western academics and liberal pundits, virtually all of those resources were wasted. Anyone who has spent time discussing economics with government bureaucrats in the underdeveloped world knows that they are the last people on earth who should control national investment. The contrast with the policies of the Asian tigers—where investment remained under the control of the private sector —could not be more stark. When their governments did intervene in the economy, the purpose has been to strengthen —not to weaken or displace—the private economy.

Create conditions to attract foreign investment. While much of the underdeveloped world handed the West's multinational corporations their walking papers, the successful developing countries were rolling out the red carpet for them. They understood that foreign investment meant new jobs and that by attracting such investment they were not losing control of their economic destiny but were creating the prospects for a better economic future. They never cavalierly nationalized foreign firms, as many underdeveloped countries did in the 1960s and 1970s, but rather let these companies profit according to the dictates of the market. While the Asian tigers ascended the economic ladder, the others dropped into economic sinkholes. In Africa, only the Ivory Coast under President Félix Houphouët-Boigny followed this lesson and welcomed foreign investment.

Make exports the engine of economic growth. Since few countries in the underdeveloped world have sufficient size to fully exploit economies of scale with modern production techniques, they can succeed only through exports to the world market. Since the early 1960s, all of the successful developing countries of East Asia adopted some kind of export-oriented strategy. In 1990, their total export revenues accounted for 60 percent of their aggregate GNP. Exports made up 34 percent of GNP in South Korea and 55 percent in Taiwan. With their role as transshipment points for regional trade, those figures were even higher for Hong Kong and Singapore, reaching 135 percent and 191 percent, respectively.

These lessons—the keys to the success of the Asian tigers—should not be startling. In a contest that pits a strategy based on state control and intervention in every aspect of economic life against one based on free markets, private initiative, and competition, the latter will always prevail. The collapse of the Soviet economy proved this point dramatically. Many observers explain the success of the four Asian tigers as a product of East Asia's Confucian heritage, with its emphasis on a strong work ethic. While culture does affect economic performance, the decisions of their leaders to unleash market forces represent the real secret to their success. Not only do their policies have little to do with the philosophies of East Asia, they are also not unique to Asia. If other countries free the mainsprings of the market, they will enjoy the same success as the Asian tigers.

For most of the underdeveloped world, learning the lessons of the successful developing countries represents only half of the battle. Before these maxims can begin to generate economic growth, many less developed countries must overcome the hurdles of political instability and economic mismanagement that have blocked them since they won their independence from the European powers. Without sound and stable government, neither foreign firms nor domestic entrepreneurs will risk their capital through investments. Without responsible fiscal and monetary policies, incentives to produce will evaporate. While we should seek to help those in poorer nations, we should not deceive ourselves into believing that any aid will make a difference until a solid foundation of political stability and economic common sense has been laid.

There are many different reasons for the poverty and turmoil in the underdeveloped world. In Latin America, fledgling democracies wage an uphill battle against massive governmental corruption, narrow-minded economic thinking, powerful drug cartels, and brutal Communist insurgencies. In Pakistan and India, human and economic resources are not applied to development projects but are instead squandered on the military. In Africa, incompetent and corrupt leadership has severely handicapped a continent that has yet to struggle to its feet, much less enter the global economic race. Most African nations have rejected communism, but too many have adopted socialism. In the Middle East, the Arab-Israeli dispute has been matched by the growing intensity of inter-Arab strife.

Internal political instability remains the most debilitating feature of the underdeveloped world. Since my 1957 trip to Ghana, the first sub-Saharan nation to be granted independence from a colonial power, forty-seven other nations in Africa have become independent. There have been more than sixty coups and thirty-five assassinations of high government leaders. More than 10 million people have been killed in civil wars, and more than 15 million have died of starvation. No end to this pattern is in sight. Only three of the continent's fifty countries have had stable governments over the last twenty years. In Liberia, a brutal dictatorship was replaced in a bloody civil war in which three tribally based guerrilla bands sacked the country and killed more than ten thousand people. In Ethiopia, two ethnically based "liberation fronts" toppled the barbaric Communist regime of President Mengistu Haile Mariam. In South Africa, progress toward ending apartheid has not produced progress toward peaceful change, with black-on-black violence killing thousands of people.

In Latin America, there are still fifteen different groups of Communist insurgents and three major drug cartels holed up in jungle hideouts. In Colombia, successive governments have fended off repeated assaults by drug barons and Communist guerrillas, with violence directly related to drugs and terrorist groups claiming the lives of tens of thousands of Colombians over the past decade. More than 300 judges and court personnel were murdered between 1985 and 1991, and a total of 18,000 assassinations occurred in 1989 alone. In

Chile, Communist terrorists have unleashed a campaign to overthrow the government of President Patricio Aylwin, striking 279 times in 1990. In Peru, the Shining Path—numbering an estimated 5,000 hard-core Communist guerrillas—has murdered more than 11,000 people since its founding in the late 1970s. Political violence in Peru, predominantly committed by the Shining Path, has caused $10 billion in damage over the past decade.

In Asia, democratic governments have landed on hard times in recent years. In India, where political parties have long been the source of corruption in domestic politics, they are now becoming the instigators of ethnic and religious strife. In the state of Uttar Pradesh, Hindu extremists have battled Muslims for control of the Babri Mosque, leading directly and indirectly to more than two thousand deaths. At the same time, open armed conflict has raged in three areas. In the last eight years, India has had five different prime ministers, two of whom have been assassinated by radical factions. In Myanmar, formerly Burma, a military government seized power in a bloody coup in 1989, with the junta now permitting drug traffickers to ply their trade and launder their money from bases on its territory. In the Philippines, Communist rebels continue to undermine President Corazon Aquino's fragile base of power, while the competence of her own leadership has been called into doubt. There have been six coup attempts since she came to power in 1986, and many of her original ministers have resigned out of frustration with her directionless policies.

Many believe that democracy is the answer to the underdeveloped world's problems. According to this logic, because democratic government has proved to be the best form of government in the developed world, the West should export it to the rest of the world. In this view, the United States should use its influence and leverage to force the dictators in the developing world to hold elections so that these countries can enjoy the fruits of political stability and escape poverty.

But democracy is not an Alice in Wonderland solution to these problems. Much of the underdeveloped world lacks the political traditions necessary to make democracy function properly. In some countries, ethnic hatreds, class divisions, and even tribal rivalries would frustrate the most well-intentioned advocates of democracy. A spirit of compromise and a willingness to accept defeat in elections are not universal human traits. Many political figures still adhere to Mao's dictum that political power comes from the barrel of a gun. For democracy to work, these nations must first transform their political cultures.

Democracy is not a potted plant that can be transplanted into any soil. Instead, it must take root naturally, growing stronger with work and time. As the countries of Eastern Europe are realizing, the seeds of democracy have difficulty growing in the barren soil left behind by communism. It took the Western world hundreds of years to develop working democratic systems. We should not deceive ourselves into believing that the nations of the underdeveloped world can do so in one year. Democracy is government by people. Since people are not perfect, we must not expect democracy to be perfect. While democracy is the best form of government, it does not guarantee good government.

Some democratic leaders have instituted economic policies as bad—if not worse—than those of the worst dictators of nondemocratic nations, while some authoritarian regimes have pursued enlightened economic strategies. We welcome the fact that twelve nations in Latin America moved from dictatorship to democracy in the 1980s, but political progress has not been matched by economic progress. To the contrary, the per capita income of the more than 400 million people in Latin America declined in that same period. More often than not, a majority of people in a developing country will not support the temporary cuts in wages and welfare that might be necessary to build a sound foundation for economic progress.

Many democratically elected leaders in the underdeveloped world have irresponsibly played politics with the national economy, flooding their countries with cheap money to buy votes before an election and reaping the whirlwind of hyperinflation after they have been safely returned to office. While this strategy wins votes, the ensuing inflation erases any short-term economic benefit that the people may have gained. Brazil, Peru, Argentina, Bolivia, and Colombia—where leaders repeatedly exploited this tactic—all experienced four-digit inflation in the 1980s.

Chile is a classic example of a country in which the seeds of economic reform grew in authoritarian soil. In the 1980s, Chile under President Augusto Pinochet scaled the economic ladder, while the rest of Latin America fell down the ladder. From 1986 to 1989, the average annual growth rate of the Chilean economy was 7 percent. Foreign investment grew 11 percent in 1990, totaling $1.1 billion in a $26-billion economy. While we rightly condemned Pinochet's political repression, the fact that an authoritarian government triggered this growth did not lessen the economic benefits to the average worker.

Nor are democratic governments immune from political corruption. In the Philippines, democracy has gone astray. Since her election in 1986, President Aquino's government has been ravaged by corruption and intracabinet strife. Instead of working to improve conditions for the Filipino people, many ministers have worked to improve the balances in their own checkbooks. Unfortunately, the Aquino regime has fallen victim to the "Philippine disease," the mixture of nepotism and corruption that has infected Filipino politics for much of the past century.

This does not mean that we should not support the aspirations for democracy of the peoples of the underdeveloped world. We should encourage the rise of democratic governments when the conditions exist for their success, while not falling prey to the idea that it represents a universal quick fix. In recent years, democracy has made some meaningful inroads. In Latin America, Cuba remains the last bastion of totalitarian government, and some of the new democracies in the rest of the region, such as in Brazil, Argentina, and Mexico, have begun to improve their economic performance. In East Asia, South Korea held free elections in 1988, while Taiwan, Hong Kong, and Singapore have significantly opened up their political systems. Africa's track record has also improved. In Mali, President Moussa Traore's military government was driven from power in March 1991 by a group of army officers who committed themselves to democratic elections. In Zambia, President Kenneth Kaunda agreed last year to end two decades of one-party rule with elections in October 1991. In Benin, dictator Mathieu Kerekou was ousted in March 1991 in the country's first free elections in history. In the Cape Verde Islands, the electoral victory of Movement for Democracy ushered out sixteen years of one-party rule. In Ethiopia, seventeen years of Communist repression ended with the victory of the Eritrean Liberation Front and the Tigre People's Liberation Front, both of which have pledged to implement free-market reforms and institute democratic pluralism.

While we cannot, and should not, transplant our system into the underdeveloped world or micromanage every developing country, we can make meaningful contributions. We should invest resources in helping these nations develop the social and political institutions needed for democracy to work. In 1982, President Reagan established the National Endowment for Democracy (NED) to encourage the growth of democratic government around the world, not only by sending teams to observe the fairness of elections, but also by funding a wide range of organizations, including pro-democratic think tanks, newspapers, civic groups, and labor unions. It has also done important work, particularly in Eastern Europe, in training democratic political parties in the basics of grass-roots organization. It represents a practical and realistic approach to promoting Western ideals in what is still a largely undemocratic world. Despite its successes, however, it must fight tooth and nail in Congress for its pitifully inadequate $25-million budget. If we are truly committed to seeing freedom and democracy flourish in the underdeveloped world, we should start by substantially increasing the funds for the NED.

The theology of state economic interventionism—epitomized by nationalized industry, state subsidies, and price controls —still attracts a large following in the underdeveloped world, producing scores of economic horror stories.

In the 1980s, Latin America—despite its abundant natural resources and talented peoples—went into reverse gear economically. While the world enjoyed a major boom, Latin America's economy went bust. In nineteen out of its twenty-one countries, living standards have declined. Per capita income fell by more than 10 percent for the entire region. In Peru, Argentina, and Nicaragua, it fell by 25 percent. The average annual rate of inflation among Latin American countries exceeded 1,000 percent in 1990, over ten times higher than in 1982. The region's total foreign debt rose from $116 billion in 1980 to $421 billion in 1990. Mexico—whose stability is a vital interest of the United States—saw the peso's dollar exchange rate escalate from 23 to 1 to 2,813 to 1 in less than ten years.

In sub-Saharan Africa, living standards went from bad to worse. Sixteen of the world's twenty poorest nations are located on the continent. In 1990, nineteen of sub-Saharan Africa's fifty countries had a per capita income of $300 or less. Six—including Ethiopia, Chad, Somalia, and Tanzania—had per capita incomes of less than $200. Torn by civil war and sapped by socialist policies, Mozambique, whose real GNP declined by 1.4 percent annually for a decade, managed to generate a per capita income of only $80. Between 1981 and 1987, per capita GNP for sub-Saharan Africa's six most populous countries fell at an annual rate of 4 percent. Over the past decade, the area has experienced a negative growth rate of 2.2 percent. Over the past two decades, African exports as a proportion of total world exports fell by 50 percent, while foreign investment in Africa dropped from $2.3 billion in 1982 to $500 million in 1986. Today, one-fourth of Africa's population faces a chronic shortage of food.

While it is generally assumed that Israel's economic problems are caused by its high defense budget, Israel is actually a textbook case of an economy hobbled by a tradition of socialist economic policies. The Israeli government owns and operates 190 companies, which account for one-fifth of Israel's industrial output and are worth more than $15 billion. In addition, the government owns 93 percent of all land. One-quarter of all Israeli goods and services are under price controls. Taxes consume 50 percent of Israel's GNP. Worse,

Israel's protectionist policies—in the form of customs and nontariff barriers—force Israelis to pay twice the world price for many consumer goods.

Some of the world's most highly capable and talented people live in Israel. Its population not only has the highest literacy rates and the best math skills in the world, but also has more scientists per capita than any other country. Israel publishes more technical and scientific papers per capita than any other nation—ten times more than the runner-up, the United States. If Israel abandons its destructive economic policies and embraces the free market, it could enjoy enormous prosperity.

Not even generous U.S. economic assistance has been able to counteract the effects of these socialist policies. Over the past ten years, Israel has received $15 billion in U.S. economic assistance, an amount per capita fifteen times greater than that given to the next largest aid recipient, Egypt. Yet Israel's real growth in 1989 was only 1.1 percent, while inflation ran at 21 percent and unemployment hit 9 percent. Israel's foreign debt totaled $16.4 billion, one of the highest per capita totals in the world. Instead of serving as a helping hand, U.S. aid to Israel has become an economic crutch.

India's economic and political policies represent another case of flawed priorities. Its leaders deserve great credit for integrating an extraordinarily diverse population into a relatively stable democracy. It has 702 million Hindus, 97 million Muslims, 20 million Christians, 17 million Sikhs, 4 million Buddhists, 3 million Jains, and 7 million members of other religions. Its people speak 23 main languages and more than 200 dialects and are divided into more than 2,400 castes. India's leaders committed a colossal error, however, when they bought into Western academic development theories emphasizing government intervention and import substitution. With the natural industriousness of the Indian people—the average Indian immigrant to the United States enjoys a higher income than the average American—India's economy should have experienced booming growth in the 1970s and 1980s. Instead, real per capita growth bumped along at a 1.8 percent annual rate over the past twenty-five years, with its economic progress barely keeping pace with its massive population growth.

These mistakes were compounded by the misguided geopolitical ambitions of India's leaders. Instead of focusing on the dire needs of its people, whose per capita income reached only $340 in 1990, India's political leadership squandered vast resources trying to elevate their country to the status of a regional superpower. From 1970 to 1990, the Indian government spent ten times more on the military than on education and eleven times more than on health care. Even the rivalry with Pakistan—over which India easily prevailed in battle in 1948, 1965, and 1971—does not represent an external threat sufficient to justify astronomic military spending levels. With a population of 850 million and a GNP of $333 billion, India dwarfs Pakistan's 107 million people and $43 billion economy. Moreover, New Delhi's military—the fourth largest in the world—fields twice as many combat aircraft and tanks and seven times more artillery than Islamabad's.

It is obscene that together India and Pakistan—two of the world's poorest countries—spend over $11 billion annually on defense and even worse, have active nuclear weapons programs. While the United States has been rightly concerned with nuclear proliferation in South Asia, the exclusive focus on Pakistan's program has been unbalanced. India, after detonating a nuclear device in 1974, has reportedly developed a small but significant nuclear stockpile. Since India's leadership has yet to fully accept the legitimacy of Pakistan's existence—and since New Delhi dismembered East and West Pakistan in the 1971 war—Islamabad concluded that it had no choice but to try to acquire its nuclear deterrent. Though we should seek to curb proliferation, particularly in volatile regions such as South Asia, we will not succeed if we ignore the security concerns that originally prompted countries to seek to develop nuclear weapons. We must therefore seek a region-wide solution, based on Pakistan's proposals for a South Asian nuclear-free zone, that will not only advance our nonproliferation objectives but also enhance security and stability.

India and Pakistan are symptomatic of a wider problem. Military spending in the underdeveloped world is spiraling upward by 7.5 percent a year, with the growth of its spending on military hardware outpacing that of the West by a three-to-one margin. A freeze on military budgets would free up $15 billion for economic development and for the dire humanitarian needs of the 180 million malnourished children in the underdeveloped world, 3 million of whom perish each year from preventable diseases because of inadequate medical care.

Many Western analysts argue that because of their problems, the countries of the underdeveloped world deserve massive foreign aid. Their view of the world comes from a Charles Dickens novel. A cause-and-effect relationship, they contend, links the wealth of the industrialized world and the poverty of developing countries. Exploitation by multinational corporations and unbalanced terms of trade keep making the rich countries richer, while the poor nations grow poorer. Only vast transfers of resources from north to south through credits, low-interest loans, and development grants can balance the moral equation. They call in effect for an international entitlement program that would make the West the world's welfare agency.

Generous humanitarian assistance should be provided for those in desperate straits in the poorer countries of Africa. The infant mortality rate of Africa stands at 11 percent, reaching 18 percent in the Western Sahara. Half of the continent's 480 million people are infected with malaria. But filling Africa's tin cup with Western money is a stopgap measure. It will not solve Africa's chronic economic and social problems.

But if Africa's leaders want to know who is responsible for its economic disasters, they should just look at themselves. To blame the West—or the legacy of European colonialism —ignores the socialist policies that have transformed once-prosperous agricultural areas from breadbaskets into basket cases. All the aid in the world will achieve nothing unless combined with sound market-oriented policies. Over the past decade, the United States and other Western industrialized countries have injected over $100 billion in aid and credits into sub-Saharan Africa. Most was wasted because inefficient and corrupt governments refused to put into place policies to provide average farmers and workers with incentives to produce. If we attempt to carry these countries on our back, the moment they are on their own they will fall flat on their faces.

The argument that developing countries need the international dole to progress at a reasonable rate, if at all, is wrong. Those who contend, as one Western academic has, that "foreign aid is the central component of world development" are naive. Neither the Western world nor the Asian tigers needed infusions of external aid to industrialize their economies. We should reject the patronizing notion that underdeveloped nations need handouts to achieve what so many others did on their own. While that should not lessen our desire to help the less fortunate, we must remember that foreign aid goes not to people but to governments. Only if those governments, in turn, institute the right economic policies will we help the peoples of the underdeveloped world, not just its government bureaucrats.

Western policies toward the world's pariah states—South Africa and the Communist regimes in Cuba and Vietnam—must address circumstances complicated by human rights and geopolitical considerations. In these cases, establishing normal relations—particularly in the economic sphere—must also serve our interests and values.

The United States, as well as the rest of the world, has rightly condemned South Africa's apartheid system since its inception in 1948. Worse than the notion of "separate but equal," apartheid was based on the principle that races should be separate because they *were* unequal. It violated the fundamental precept of Western morality that every individual deserves to be treated with basic human dignity and granted equal rights. Although blacks in South Africa had a higher per capita income than in any other sub-Saharan African nation, and although far more brutal regimes existed elsewhere on the continent, apartheid's formal legal inequalities made it different in kind, not just degree. South Africa's system was not only morally repugnant but also economically stupid. No country can afford to squander the talents and productivity of 86 percent of its people, as Pretoria did by discriminating against all nonwhites. By denying them equal economic opportunities, the South African regime undercut its own potential prosperity.

The economic sanctions imposed by most countries of the

West, however, were the wrong response. Though satisfying the self-righteousness of antiapartheid activists, the policy hurt the people we most wanted to help. The economic boycott against South Africa was color-blind, affecting both the white and black communities. But unlike the blacks, the whites were in a better position economically to withstand its effects. The 215 American corporations that divested from South Africa were no longer able to enforce their fair employment practices and spend millions of dollars on social programs that improved the working and living conditions of their black employees. Many American companies, such as Ford Motor Company, had financed black housing, schooling, recreation, and health facilities. If sanctions had remained in place until the year 2000, they would have cost South Africa's blacks an estimated 2 million jobs. Some key black leaders, who backed sanctions at the time they were imposed, have recently conceded the damage they did to South Africa's blacks.

Despite the criticism from Western foes of the South African government, President Bush acted correctly in repealing the sanctions in July 1991. President Frederik W. de Klerk had not only met all the conditions stipulated in the sanctions legislation—such as the repeal of the Population Registration and Group Areas Act and the release of all political prisoners —but had also signaled a clear intention to move toward a multiracial society. In addition to the negotiation of a new constitution, further progress toward a just and stable South Africa requires work on two fronts. First, the leaders of black organizations such as the African National Congress and the Inkatha Movement must curb black-on-black violence. A democracy cannot be built while blood flows in the streets. Second, the white government must prepare to redress the economic consequences of apartheid and block efforts by white extremists who do not want South African blacks to play an equal role in society. This means not only equality of opportunity in education and employment but also reparations to blacks whose land and property were seized under apartheid. Only after these steps are taken can South Africa be fully welcomed into the community of nations.

The junkyard relics of Moscow's former empire in the underdeveloped world pose different problems. Some pundits argue that now is the time to normalize relations with Cuba and Vietnam, that the reasons for our mutual enmity have faded with the cold war, and that the West should extend trade and foreign aid as a peace offering. This view is wrong. The United States must insist that each meet specific political and human rights conditions before establishing diplomatic or trade relations.

We must not allow the brilliant performance of Cuban athletes in the Pan American games to blind us to the fact that Cuba is an economic disaster area. Castro's government, not the Cuban people, is to blame. Cuban Americans in southern Florida enjoy extraordinary prosperity, while Cubans ninety miles away who stayed behind suffer in abject poverty. After relying for decades on Soviet aid and subsidized trade, Cuba has been squeezed by the twin problems of incompetent government planning and cutbacks in Moscow's largess. Castro has tried pathetically to rally the Cuban people by calling for a "special time of peace"—a euphemism for wartime austerity. More than 240 items, including fish, fruit, milk, rice, and other basic foodstuffs, are now rationed. Fuel shortages forced state farms to draft over 600,000 bulls and oxen to replace their tractors. Instead of moving Cuba forward, communism has pushed it backward.

Vietnam faces similar problems. While the Soviets have

pumped in $33 billion in economic and military aid since 1979, the Vietnamese have sunk into a self-inflicted economic malaise. Poor harvests in the late 1980s pushed 7 million people to the verge of starvation. Today, Vietnam has a 20 percent unemployment rate and cannot absorb the 1 million new workers who enter the labor force every year. Trade with the Soviet Union and Eastern Europe, which accounts for 60 percent of its total trade, has plummeted. Hanoi is scrambling to service its $18-billion debt to Moscow. Vietnam now sells old U.S. military equipment, such as tanks and armored personnel carriers, as scrap metal to earn hard currency on the international market. With a per capita income of $130, it is one of the five poorest nations in the world.

Because Cuba and Vietnam continue to challenge our interests, the United States must link diplomatic and trade ties to changes in their foreign policies. Castro continues to funnel millions of dollars of arms and ammunition to the Communist guerrillas in El Salvador and to encourage their obstructionism in the ongoing peace talks. During the past twelve years, the Salvadoran civil war has caused over $2 billion in economic losses and seventy thousand deaths. The United States must not expand political or economic contacts that would increase Cuba's ability to undermine democratic governments in Central America.

Vietnam's leadership has continued its quest for regional domination. It is sadly ironic that those who fought to expel French colonial rule from Indochina now view that region as their natural imperial domain. Despite the withdrawal of Vietnamese forces from Cambodia in 1989, Hanoi provides the essential economic and military support needed to keep its client, Hun Sen, in power in Phnom Penh. In addition, the Vietnamese dominate Laos, where they have brutally used chemical weapons against the Hmong people in the southern part of the country.

Even if Vietnam were to facilitate a peace settlement in Cambodia and allow genuine self-determination for Laos, we should insist on two other conditions for normalization of relations. First, Hanoi's rulers must provide a full accounting of the 2,273 Americans still missing in action from the Vietnam War. Second, they must liberalize their totalitarian political system, particularly in the south. Since the borders of the unified Vietnam were established by conquest, not concord, we owe it to the Vietnamese people—millions of whom fought with us as allies—to demand improvements in the regime's human rights record before we restore economic and political ties.

Angola is a classic example of a country where Soviet-style communism has lost the battle, but freedom has not yet won the war. In June 1991, the Moscow-backed government in Luanda and the freedom fighters of the pro-Western Unita movement signed a political settlement that ended sixteen years of war and provided for multiparty elections. With the final pullout of Cuban troops from Angola in the summer of 1991, the conditions exist for ending the strife and poverty imposed on the Angolan people by communism. While we must exercise vigilance to ensure the fairness of the elections, the United States should also stand ready to assist Angola—rich in natural resources and human talent—to rebuild its economy once a freely elected government comes to power. We should help a free Angola, not only for its own sake, but also to create an example of what could await other former Soviet-client states if they choose to join the free world.

· · ·

For decades the underdeveloped world has been bleeding from self-inflicted wounds. While the world moved toward free trade, many underdeveloped countries isolated themselves in economic autarchy. Yet today there are many encouraging signs that these developing countries might finally integrate themselves into the world economy.

In his much-heralded work, *The Other Path*, Peruvian economist Hernando De Soto analyzes the lessons of Peru's massive underground economy and advocates a complete break from economic authoritarianism, with its stifling bureaucracy, government intervention, and state subsidies. While De Soto reminds his readers that economic and political freedom are the twin pillars of stability in the underdeveloped world, his main message is that developing countries must solve their own problems, not look for help from abroad. His book won plaudits throughout Latin America, indicating that many developing countries may be ready to take critically important steps on the road toward market-based prosperity.

This new sense of hope is evident throughout the underdeveloped world. In the early 1950s, many governments adopted the socialist model as a shortcut to industrialization. Today, many of these same countries have cast aside socialism and embraced capitalism. The success of the four Asian tigers has spread to Thailand, Indonesia, and Malaysia. In Latin America, the Chilean example of economic growth has attracted widespread interest. In South Asia, India and Pakistan are turning toward the market. In Africa, several heads of state have adopted the rhetoric of radical economic change, even though their actions still fall far short in practice.

Our policies must build on this hope. Our strategy should therefore advance along four fronts:

Assist population control programs. We must help break the link between spiraling population growth and poverty. At current rates, the underdeveloped world's population will increase 23 percent by the year 2000 and 77 percent by the year 2025. Countries such as Mozambique, Ethiopia, Tanzania, and Somalia will need to maintain real economic growth rates greater than 3 percent just to keep their per capita incomes from dropping. Unchecked population growth will put them on an ever-accelerating treadmill that will outpace any potential economic performance.

Where they have been tried, family planning programs have largely worked. Thailand reduced its population growth rate from 3.1 percent in the 1960s to 1.9 percent in the 1980s, which in turn helped sustain an average annual growth rate over 7 percent during the decade. But today only half the women in the underdeveloped world have access to standard birth control methods. More than 125 million additional couples would use birth control methods if they were available. Unless family planning programs are expanded, the economies of the underdeveloped world will forever languish behind the curve of population growth.

Many pro-life advocates argue that the United States should stand by the so-called Mexico City policy, which denies funding to any family planning organization that employs abortion in any of its activities. They contend that to condone abortion even implicitly is morally unconscionable. Their view is morally shortsighted. If we ban all funds to such organizations, we might prevent hundreds or thousands of abortions. But if we provide funds for birth control methods other than abortion—even if the same organizations we aid engage in abortion with money acquired from other sources—we will prevent the conception of millions of babies who would be doomed to the devastation of poverty in the underdeveloped world.

Abortion is a deeply divisive issue in the United States. We can honestly disagree on that issue insofar as it affects policy in this country. We should not, however, try to export our views on abortion to overpopulated countries in the underdeveloped world, whose values and circumstances differ so profoundly from our own. Unless the population growth rates are slowed, many developing countries will forfeit their only chance to provide a better standard of living for their peoples.

Reduce trade barriers to exports from the underdeveloped world. To promote economic growth, foreign trade, not foreign aid, should be our principal instrument. Over the past forty years, the United States has poured more than $400 billion in foreign aid into the underdeveloped world. The results have been meager. Foreign aid alone often only serves to prop up inefficient industries, increase industrial subsidies, and raise trade barriers. The developing countries cannot immerse themselves in the healing waters of free trade unless the industrialized world keeps its markets open to their goods.

By removing trade barriers, these countries have the chance to specialize in industries in which they enjoy a competitive advantage over the rest of the world. In the Uruguay Round of the GATT talks, we should push for the elimination of costly agricultural subsidies in the United States and the European Community that prevent the less developed countries from gaining access to our markets.

If we are to preach the gospel of free trade, we must practice it by eliminating our own self-serving agricultural subsidies. Sugar quotas, for example, deprive impoverished sugar-producing countries, such as Guatemala, Jamaica, the

Dominican Republic, Colombia, and the Philippines, of vitally important export earnings. These import restrictions also force Americans to pay twice the world price for sugar, which costs them $3 billion a year. In addition, the U.S. government coddles the nation's thirty thousand peanut farmers. It restricts foreign peanut imports to 1.7 million pounds per year, which is only two-tenths of one percent of total domestic consumption. This absurd quota leaves poor peanut-exporting countries out in the cold, while forcing U.S. consumers in effect to subsidize each American peanut grower an average of $16,000 annually.

By promoting the mutual economic interests of the United States and Mexico through the negotiation of a free-trade agreement, President Bush has taken a vitally important step in the right direction. The best way to promote the development of Mexico's economy is to grant free access to the U.S. market. This agreement would not be a one-way street. Free trade will increase our exports to Mexico, as well as reduce the flow of illegal workers into the United States.

Many liberals—who claim to be advocates of the underdeveloped world—raise the banner of protectionism in their campaign against the free-trade agreement. Though their hidden agenda seeks to shelter special interests, they have launched a two-pronged attack against the free-trade accord. They argue that U.S. firms will flock to Mexico because of its low wages and that Mexico's weaker environmental and worker safety laws will give Mexican firms an unfair competitive advantage. Both of these objections are unfounded. If U.S. corporations located their facilities simply on the basis of lower wages, they would all have moved to Mexico already. In addition to wage levels, other variables such as output per worker, transportation capabilities, and the quality of human resources are all part of the economic equation.

Moreover, Mexico has committed itself to enhancing protection of the environment and its workers. Free trade will help to provide Mexico with the resources needed to strengthen enforcement of its laws in these two areas.

The strongest argument in favor of the free-trade agreement, however, is not economic but political. Those who contend that we should keep Mexico at arm's length economically because its government is not fully democratic would compromise a vital U.S. interest. A free-trade agreement could be the key catalyst in moving Mexico toward greater political democracy. If we fail to work with President Salinas to develop Mexico's economy, we would not only throw U.S.-Mexican relations into a tailspin. We would also send Salinas to an early political grave and give his leftist rivals the hammer to nail his coffin shut.

A new generation of enlightened leaders in Mexico—led by Salinas—has emerged to defend the principles of free-market economics. Their commitment to those principles has been met with tough resistance from Mexico's entrenched bureaucracy, including rural chieftains, anti-U.S. populists, and corrupt politicians. By signing a free-trade accord with Mexico, the United States will help slay the bureaucratic dragon that has wreaked havoc on Mexico's economic and political system for the past century. A failure to complete a free-trade agreement with Mexico would not only deal a serious blow to free-market reformers, but it would also send a message throughout all of Latin America that the United States is not serious about helping developing countries achieve economic prosperity.

A U.S.-Mexican free-trade agreement could be the first step toward a western hemisphere free-trade zone. We would derive huge economic benefits from such a trading agreement. In 1989, 13 percent of our exports went to Latin

America and the Caribbean, more than our total exports to Japan. If we doubled our exports to this region, we would create 1.2 million jobs for American workers. The purpose of a hemispheric free-trade agreement would not be to form a potential trading bloc against Japan and the European Community, but to increase trade throughout the hemisphere. Free-trade agreements, both regional and multilateral, always serve our interests because they open up possibilities for greater economic growth.

Improve the effectiveness of economic assistance. We must face up to the fact that in the past our foreign aid has done as much harm as it has done good. Too often it has perpetuated bad habits rather than encouraged necessary change. Since foreign aid budgets will almost certainly shrink in the future, we need to overhaul these programs if we expect them to help the people of the underdeveloped world.

First, we need to give our aid on the basis of strict conditionality. We should not extend aid without attaching strings with clearly defined and measurable goals. While we cannot micromanage every dollar of aid distributed, we should monitor our funds to ensure they are not spent irresponsibly on wasteful infrastructure projects or siphoned off into government graft.

Second, we should extend more of our aid on a bilateral, not multilateral, basis. Multilateral organizations such as the World Bank have their own agenda, which does not always coincide with ours. Even though we provide 20 percent of the capital for these organizations, they have in the past made loans that sharply conflicted with our interests. They have, for example, provided discounted loans to Soviet-backed, anti-Western governments, such as Ethiopia, Somalia, and Vietnam. In addition, most multilateral organizations have omnivorous bureaucracies whose regal offices and padded payrolls rival those of the corrupt regimes to which they lend. Before we pour any more resources into these organizations, a major review of their overhead expenses and lending practices must be undertaken. It is wrong to spend millions of dollars on first-class travel accommodations for World Bank staff when the citizens of the underdeveloped world live a third-class existence.

Third, we should establish "enterprise funds" for those countries in the underdeveloped world that have adopted market-oriented reforms. These funds, which should be patterned on those in Eastern Europe, would fund viable business ventures, not frivolous government-to-government aid projects. They would lend money to individual entrepreneurs to start their own businesses, stimulating grass-roots economic activity rather than greasing the wheels of government bureaucracy.

Because of our budget constraints, we spent almost $15 billion on foreign aid in 1991, less than three-tenths of one percent of our GNP. While the needs of the underdeveloped world continue to grow, our aid budget cannot. We must therefore ensure that our aid is spent on projects that stimulate growth from the bottom up, not the top down. If we encourage aid recipients to undertake free-market reforms, open up entrepreneurial opportunities, and generate investment possibilities, our aid will be well spent. If not, we are throwing away not only our money but also any chance to better the lives of the people in the underdeveloped world.

After World War II, the United States extended a helping hand not only to its war-ravaged allies but also to its former enemies in Germany and Japan. Over the past forty-five years, Berlin and Tokyo have surged ahead, while most of the underdeveloped world has fallen behind. Until recently, the United States has shouldered most of the burden of foreign aid. Germany and Japan must now adopt a sense of global responsibility on a par with their burgeoning economic power. While Japan has taken encouraging steps by increasing its foreign aid budget to over $15 billion in 1991, both countries must do far more to give the underdeveloped world the same chance to grow and prosper that we gave them nearly half a century ago.

Facilitate debt relief. The ultimate answer to the debt crisis lies with the underdeveloped world. These countries must restore both domestic and foreign confidence in their economies before any long-term solution is possible. At the same time, Western governments must insist that the banks that recklessly lent billions to uncreditworthy states bear their share of the burden. Western leaders should do their part by not imposing draconian payback schemes that would crush the underdeveloped world's ability to finance its debt. Too much international pressure could create political instability, which would drive out responsible democratic leaders and drive in radicals who would rather cancel than carry their debt.

The underdeveloped world's $1.3 trillion debt not only restricts the potential growth of these countries but also serves as a deadly drag on the world economy. Some analysts have proposed elaborate debt-for-equity swaps, in which debtor states would trade ownership of enterprises and resources for cancellation of debt. While these proposals recognize the fact that the debt crisis must be solved by both the creditors and the debtors, they will not by themselves solve the critical economic problems that have forced many developing states to contract excessive debt in the first place.

. . .

The demise of communism does not mean the end of poverty any more than it means the victory of freedom. During the cold war, we addressed only half the problem. Many of these nations suffered from the twin depredations of Communist insurgency and grim poverty. While the Communists talked about the people's problems, we too often talked only about the Communists. That must now change.

In most of the underdeveloped world, the road toward economic and political reform has been the road less traveled. While some countries have made valiant efforts to escape poverty, they face overwhelming obstacles to success. If these nations have the courage to implement market-oriented reform, we must support them every step of the way. We should not try to run their economic affairs from Washington. Each country in the southern hemisphere has its own distinct traditions. Each country must find its own path to development. Our task is not to point our finger at these countries' failings. Instead, we should point out the lessons of the underdeveloped world's success stories. We must help these struggling nations foster their creative energies so that they can unlock their own potential to achieve freedom and prosperity.

To achieve these goals, we must have patience. Many developing countries see America through the eyes of the mass media and our pop culture. They think America is a problem-free society. The television programs we export—"Dallas," "Knots Landing," "Dynasty," and others—paint an unrealistically glamorous picture of America. The people of the southern hemisphere need to understand that maintaining freedom and prosperity requires constant effort and that our country has deep problems that our prosperity has not solved.

The southern hemisphere holds unlimited potential for

success, but it also faces daunting odds. We are therefore presented with an immense challenge. If we turn our backs on the countries of the southern hemisphere, we will never narrow the widening gap between the developed and under-developed worlds. And if the future becomes a "tale of two worlds," the foundation of future peace and stability will have been erected on soft ground.

7

THE
RENEWAL
OF AMERICA

I N A DRAMATIC ADDRESS before a joint session of Congress forty-six years ago, President Truman asked for military and economic aid for Greece and Turkey to meet the Communist threat to those countries. Two freshman con-

---

gressmen, John F. Kennedy and I, voted in favor of his proposal. It was a difficult vote for him because the liberal Democrats in his Massachusetts district opposed all *military* aid. It was a difficult vote for me because the conservative Republicans in my district opposed *all* foreign aid. We voted as we did because we were motivated by a great cause that transcended partisan politics: the defeat of communism. We thereby helped to launch the great bipartisan initiative that deterred Soviet aggression in Western Europe for over four decades.

Today, we are witnessing one of the great watersheds in history. The cold war world order—based on two clashing ideologies, two opposing geopolitical blocs, and two competing superpowers—has been irrevocably shattered. We now have a cause even greater than the defeat of communism— the victory of freedom. If we meet the challenges of peace, our legacy will be not just that we saved the world from communism but that we helped make the world safe for freedom.

Yet those who have hailed the beginning of a new order in which peace and freedom are secure speak prematurely. The peaceful revolution in Eastern Europe did not prevent the violent conquest of Kuwait by Iraq. Those who two years ago touted the conventional wisdom that economic power had replaced military power as the major instrument of foreign policy were exposed as false prophets when Japan and Germany proved impotent in responding to Saddam Hussein's aggression. Despite the great victories for freedom in 1989 and 1991, both the Persian Gulf crisis in 1990 and the coup attempt by Soviet hard-liners in 1991 demonstrated that the world remains a dangerous and unpredictable place.

America has an indispensable role to play in the world. No other nation can take our place. Some might eventually be able to replace us militarily. Others might be able to take our place economically. But only the United States has the military, economic, and political power to lead the way in defending and extending freedom and in deterring and resisting aggression. More important, our influence stems not only from our military and economic power but also from the enormous appeal of our ideals and our example. We are the only great power in history to have made its entrance onto the world stage not by the force of its arms but by the force of its ideas.

As we chart our course, we must ask ourselves four fundamental questions. Do we have the will to lead? Do we have the means to lead? How should we lead? How can we renew America at home so that we can lead abroad not only through our actions but also through our example?

André Malraux once observed that the United States is the only nation in the world to have become a world power without intending or trying to do so. We have traditionally been reluctant to play a world role commensurate with our enormous potential power. But when events have compelled America to become involved, we have led with skill and will equal to those of any European great power.

Idealism has been at once our greatest strength and our greatest weakness. American idealism—sometimes naive, sometimes misguided, sometimes overzealous—has always been at the center of our foreign policy. On the one hand, it has at times fostered a profound impulse toward isolationism. More comfortable with black-and-white moral choices than with the inevitable gray areas of world politics, we have often opted to withdraw into isolation in order to avoid tainting our idealism with the realities of power politics. On the other hand, this idealism has served as an indispensable foundation to sustain our commitment to the great moral causes of the twentieth century. It has enabled us to lead not on the basis of narrow and selfish interests but through the appeal of high ideals and common values.

When untempered by realism, our idealism has caused our foreign policy to swing between ideological crusades and shortsighted isolationism. When combined with hardheaded realism, America's idealism has left a record of world leadership that no nation, past or present, can match.

After playing a major role in the Allied victory in World War I, we refused to join the League of Nations and slashed our defense budgets so drastically that when Hitler came to power in 1933, our army was the sixteenth largest in the world, smaller than even Romania's. After World War II, we avoided that mistake, not by choice but by necessity. The British and the French were too weakened by war to play a leading role. The Germans and the Japanese were defeated enemies. The Soviet Union had become an adversary rather than an ally.

Never has a world power been more generous and responsible in exerting global leadership than the United States after World War II. We built the great transatlantic and transpacific alliances that deterred Soviet aggression. We helped to rebuild the economies of both our allies and our former enemies. We gave independence to the Philippines in 1946 and returned Okinawa to Japan in 1971. While we benefited by preserving the free world and by participating in a great cause, we asked for none of the geopolitical tributes traditionally claimed by victorious powers.

We parried dozens of Soviet political and military probes in every corner of the world. When Communist North Korea attacked South Korea in 1950, we provided 90 percent of the troops and suffered 95 percent of the fatalities in the U.N. expeditionary force that turned back the Communist aggression. When South Vietnam was attacked by Soviet- and Chinese-backed North Vietnam, we provided economic aid, training, and eventually armed forces to assist the South Vietnamese in their efforts to repel the aggressors.

In 1972, we opened the door to a new relationship with China and initiated an era of negotiations with the Soviet Union. We not only advanced our short-term interests but also began a process of fostering long-term peaceful change in the Communist world. Contact with the West helped seeds of free thought sprout into political movements that would later blossom into peaceful change.

But in the mid-1970s the United States began to lose its sense of purpose. One result was that after we withdrew our forces from Vietnam under the Paris Peace Agreements of 1973, the Congress irresponsibly slashed U.S. aid to South Vietnam by over 80 percent even as the Soviet Union and China were increasing their aid to Hanoi to record levels. Thus deprived of the military supplies needed to survive, South Vietnam fell to North Vietnam in 1975, two years after all American combat troops had returned home. While not a military defeat for the United States, it was a devastating defeat for the American spirit.

In the late 1970s, a malaise enveloped the nation's dominant elites. America's confidence was broken. We lost our geopolitical bearings. Our idealism steered us toward isolationism. Instead of shaping history, the nation let itself be buffeted by events. Emboldened by our lack of will, the Soviet Union rapidly established beachheads in Latin America, Africa, and Southeast Asia. We comforted ourselves with the notion that our previous world role had been overzealous because of our "inordinate fear of communism." By 1979, when the Red Army invaded Afghanistan, our reaction was primarily symbolic—refusing to participate in the Olympic games, curtailing grain sales to Moscow, and providing some antiquated arms to the Afghan resistance.

While not recognized as such at the time, that Soviet invasion marked the low-water mark of U.S. world leadership. It was shortly afterward, in 1981, that we began down the long road back to playing our indispensable role as leader of the free world. President Reagan has been credited with restoring American economic and military strength. His greatest contribution, however, was to restore America's spiritual strength. He renewed America's faith in its ideals and recommitted America to a responsible world role.

Ironically, the defeat of communism in Eastern Europe in 1989 and in the Soviet Union in 1991—the high-water mark for America's ideals—renewed the debate over whether we should remain a major player. Our sense of idealism fueled the arguments of both the isolationists and the internationalists. Isolationists, on both the right and the left, demanded that the United States "bring the boys home" and concentrate its resources on solving our domestic problems. Those on the right contended that we had accomplished our mission and had no further reason to pursue a global role. Those on the left argued either that America was a declining power that no longer had the resources to play such a role or that because of its problems at home, America was not worthy to lead abroad. Internationalists appealed to our idealism in their advocacy of a continued world role. Some urged that we rely on the U.N. to resist aggression. Others called for America to take on global crusades at the expense of America itself.

These views are narrowly myopic. We do not face a choice between dealing with domestic problems and playing an international role. Our challenge is to do both by setting realistic goals and by managing our limited resources. On both fronts—abroad and at home—America must be a dynamic innovator and leader. America cannot be at peace in a world of wars, and we cannot have a healthy American economy in a sick world economy. To lead abroad serves our interests at home, and to solve our problems at home enhances our leadership abroad. Americans will not support a strong foreign policy to deal with problems abroad unless we have an equally strong domestic policy to deal with our problems at home.

We can readily summon the will and resources to make practical idealism the hallmark of our role in the world. We should not set out to try to remake the world in our image, but neither should we retreat from our global responsibilities. We should set goals within the limits of our resources while working to the limits of our power. We should remain dedicated to the ideals of freedom and justice that have served as the beacons of our foreign policy, but be realistic and practical about what it takes to move the world in their direction.

Does the United States have the means to play this role? The military forces, foreign aid programs, and other instruments needed to play a great-power role are expensive. But with a GNP over $5 trillion, we have the resources to meet the challenge. As Herbert Stein has written, "America is a very rich country. We are not rich enough to do everything, but we are rich enough to do everything important."

We can afford the military forces necessary to ensure our security and defend our interests. But we must radically alter our force structure. The potential challenges of the next two decades are vastly different from those we confronted in the past. During the cold war, military planners spoke of building forces capable of simultaneously fighting one and a half wars—a major war in Europe and a minor war in a secondary theater. With the Soviet Union in a death spiral as a world power, those days are gone. To prepare for the wars of the future, we must overhaul the military forces we used to deter those of the past.

On the strategic level, we must recognize that we live in a dangerous world where the Soviet Union still has thousands of nuclear warheads targeted on the United States and where aggressive nations in the developing world will soon have nuclear programs and intercontinental ballistic missiles. Arms control has failed to neutralize either of these potential threats. Even if the START agreement and the additional Bush and Gorbachev weapons reductions are implemented, Moscow will have a more potent first-strike capability than it did when I signed the SALT I treaty in 1972. In addition, the Nuclear Nonproliferation Treaty not only failed to restrain Iraq's acquisition of nuclear technologies but its internationally mandated inspections even helped provide cover for its covert nuclear weapons program. The United States must commit itself to deploying by the end of the decade a limited space- and ground-based defense against ballistic missiles through the SDI. With nuclear weapons and their delivery systems proliferating, we cannot count on the chimera of arms control alone. We need defenses.

On the conventional level, we should put a premium on the flexibility of our forces. When the clear and present danger was Moscow's armies in Europe, we needed to build heavy forces dedicated solely to NATO's defense. In today's world, we need lighter forces and a smaller but more flexible force posture capable of responding to unforeseeable contingencies in other parts of the world. We must retain active forces adequate to respond to crises like the invasion of Kuwait and well-trained and -equipped reserves capable of reinforcing our allies in Europe and Japan in a major crisis. We must sharpen our technological edge. As the Gulf War demonstrated, this saves lives. But while we should vigorously research new technologies and develop new systems, we should not make the mistake we have too often made in the past of ordering huge numbers of new weapons that become obsolete before the final units roll off the assembly line.

Economically, we should not panic but must not become complacent. Our industrial productivity and technological innovation still lead the world. Our GNP leads that of our nearest rival by a factor of two. Our economy attracts more foreign investment than any other major industrial power. Although our advantage is narrowing, our per capita productivity is still higher than that of Japan, our closest competitor. But to stay ahead we must move ahead. To ensure we have the economic means needed to lead the world politically, we must seize the moment to renew and extend our commitment to the values of competition, education, and investment.

Instead of complaining about international competition, we should welcome it. Finland's Paavo Nurmi, the champion Olympic long-distance runner in 1924, had no competition. He had to run with a watch strapped to his wrist so that he could see whether he was running in championship form. He never broke four minutes in the mile. Had Nurmi faced strong competition, he would probably have broken the four-minute barrier thirty years before Britain's Roger Bannister did in 1954. Rather than hunkering down in the foxhole of protectionism or behind the wall of restrictive immigration, we should relish the opportunity to achieve excellence by competing with others. As St. Thomas Aquinas observed seven centuries ago, "If the highest aim of a captain were to preserve his ship, he would keep it in port forever."

America needs a National Economic Council with a status equal to the National Security Council. In our embassies abroad and our bureaucracies at home, economic issues must receive the same priority attention as political and military issues. Today they seldom get it. In Japan, government is an ally—and some say even an instrument—of business. Too often in America, government is an opponent of business. This does not mean that we should adopt a national industrial policy under which unqualified bureaucrats would dictate business decisions. Nor does it mean we should subsidize American industry to even the score with Japan or other industrialized powers. But it does mean that we must take steps to ensure that we have a coherent strategy to prevail in the global economic competition and that U.S. multinational corporations are enabled to compete on a fair and equal basis with their foreign rivals.

The United States will lose its economic and technological edge if we fail to do a better job of educating young Americans for the tasks they must perform as we move from an industrial to a high-tech economy. Over 25 percent of Americans do not graduate from high school, and many who do graduate lack the basic skills needed in a modern society. In the crucial disciplines of math and science, our teenagers trail those of virtually every other industrialized country. While some of our public schools perform well, many are less effective than schools in many countries of the underdeveloped world. Most school standards have become so lax that students no longer feel a need to work hard, with two-thirds of today's high school seniors spending an hour or less on homework, reading ten or fewer pages of text, and watching over three hours of mind-numbing television each day.

America is on a downward spiral toward scientific and technological illiteracy not because Americans have lost their aptitude for science but because the kind of discipline it requires has gone out of style. We are raising a new generation, both in inner-city slums and in middle- and upper-class neighborhoods, that might be characterized as the "MTV generation." The appalling ignorance of so many members of this generation is due not to their being less intelligent but because their intelligence is not used. They inhabit a world of hard-rock rhythms pounded at earsplitting volume, MTV images that flash across the screen in barely the time it takes the eye to follow, and sensual stimuli that appear in rapid succession. There is no room for ideas beyond the most banal. There is even less room for the information on which any sensible ideas have to be based. The once-ubiquitous bumper-sticker slogan has given way to the T-shirt slogan, but the content level has not improved.

To arrest this decline, we must move in six areas. We must reform the profession of teaching. At Whittier College in the 1930s, my classmates who were going into teaching almost universally complained about the boring, useless courses in education theory they were required to take. Teachers today share that frustration. School systems should place less emphasis on education theory and more on a teacher's knowledge of his substantive discipline. Teachers are taught how to teach but not enough about the subjects they are teaching —and a teacher who does not know his subject can neither teach it effectively nor convey enthusiasm for learning it.

We must raise the standards in schools. Students will deliver only as much as we demand of them. The erosion of standards—typified by policies of grade inflation and automatic advancement—has undermined the schools. Students will develop intellectual strength only by pedaling uphill. Unfortunately, in many school systems they can coast right through, with only students who seek admission into elite universities feeling any necessity to apply themselves fully.

We should focus more actively on motivation. Children are born with a vivid, innate curiosity—every child asks "Why?" until his parents' ears grow numb—but along the way too many fail to connect that curiosity to the wonders of science, the challenges of math, the insights of history, or the rich rewards of language. Instead of being turned on by the process of learning, they are turned off by it. The only classroom learning they absorb is what they are force-fed, and the force-feeding only turns them off further. Both inside the classroom and outside it, we need to do far more to catch their imaginations and to lead them—especially in those early formative years when attitudes are being so crucially and often permanently shaped—to want to learn. This means exciting them not just about the process of learning but about what there is to learn. They have to be wakened to the inherent fascination of history, science, and the other disciplines. Once they want to learn, they will learn.

We must break the monopoly of the education establishment over public schools and introduce competitive market forces into the system to improve its performance. I support public schools. I attended them until I entered college, and Mrs. Nixon was a teacher in an excellent public high school. But today the difference between the performance of public and private schools in America is shocking. Public high school seniors who took the Scholastic Aptitude Test scored significantly lower than the private school seniors who did so. Many public schools are top-heavy, spending excessively on bloated administrative bureaucracies concerned more about maintaining their monopoly on public funds than about improving their performance. As *The Economist* reported, "New York's public-sector schools employ ten times as many administrators per pupil as private schools do." Private schools ultimately must satisfy their customers—parents and students—by providing effective educational services. In this competitive environment, they must continuously strive to upgrade their programs or risk going out of business.

To improve the public schools, we should subject them to the same competitive pressures that have made our private schools the envy of the world. The money each state spends on education should be pooled and then disbursed to parents of students in equal individual vouchers that can be spent at any school, public or private. This so-called "choice" program has already transformed some school systems. Since 1973, in New York City's East Harlem district, it has boosted the graduation rate from under 50 percent to over 90 percent. When parents are given the power to choose, they become more involved in their schools and their children's education. When students bear responsibility for their own future, they apply themselves more and develop greater self-discipline. Choice will create market pressures that will break the stranglehold of the education bureaucracy on the system and will force the public schools to reorganize and measure up to the competition of private schools. If we do not move decisively, the battle for education reform will be lost in the school boardroom before it ever gets to the classroom.

We must dispel the patronizing and destructive myth that all young people need to go to college and develop alternate career tracks based more on modern-day apprenticeship than on classroom learning. Today, too many students unsuited to college and uninterested in it waste four years that could have been better spent gaining practical workplace experience. To accommodate the aptitudes of the unsuited, many colleges have loosened their standards. This exacerbates "degree inflation," which forces stronger students to spend more years "credentialing" themselves with graduate diplomas. Meanwhile, weaker students find that the first task an employer gives them is to enroll in a training program that will actually provide them with basic skills. Enabling all students to attend college might sound appealing in the abstract, especially to intellectuals, but for many young people hands-on training in workplace skills would be more appealing, more useful, and more appropriate. And we should recognize that a good carpenter is a lot more useful to society than a bad lawyer.

We must demand more of our universities. In recent decades, a silent conspiracy has developed between professors uninterested in teaching and students too lazy to study. Faculty, particularly at our best universities, often put first priority on their own research. Tenure and advancement are awarded on the basis of how many papers and books they publish rather than on what teachers do for their students. To reduce the burden of teaching, professors relax standards, often giving exams that demand little mastery of the material. Students, to a great extent, happily play along. The result is the paradox of declining competence of graduates amidst widespread grade inflation comparable to the currency inflation of Germany's Weimar Republic.

Members of the educational establishment reflexively insist that whatever the problem, the answer is more money. But the United States already outspends all other major industrial democracies on education per student, even while their schools outperform ours. The answer is not more spending but better-targeted spending. Countless studies have linked student achievement not to higher budgets but to such essentials as student motivation, active family involvement, and well-organized and disciplined schools. America does not need to make a greater financial investment in its educational system but rather to demand a greater return on its current investment. The 180-day school year is a ridiculous carryover from the time when children were needed to harvest crops in the summer months. Germany has a 195-day school year. Japan has a 225-day school year. Lengthening the school year will give our students more opportunity to learn and make more efficient use of our school facilities.

The decline of our human capital is matched by a potential decline in our industrial capital. The debate over whether the federal deficit matters misses the point. A deficit level of over 5 percent of GNP will not bring the apocalypse. But it does represent an important economic choice. Because the deficit is financed through the pool of private savings and foreign investment, we are siphoning off funds into short-term consumption that could have gone toward long-term capital investment. While sustainable, the deficit acts like water eroding the foundation of a strong economy.

We should address the deficit through spending cuts, not tax increases. The deficit exists not because the American people are undertaxed but because the U.S. government overspends. In fiscal year 1988, the federal budget topped $1 trillion for the first time in history. By fiscal year 1992, it reached $1.45 trillion, increasing 45 percent while the economy barely grew 10 percent. Taxes now claim a larger proportion of the GNP than at any time since World War II. To rein in spending, we must disabuse ourselves of the myth that much of federal spending is "uncontrollable." Apart from interest payments on the national debt, all spending derives from laws that Congress enacted and that Congress can change. To argue that we cannot tamper with the spending formulas for entitlement programs is to abandon any hope for bringing federal accounts into balance.

Savings and investment are central to our ability to finance industrial expansion and productivity growth. Capital gains taxes are taxes on savings. Payroll taxes are taxes on production. The sensible way to structure a tax system, if our goal is to increase prosperity for all, is to place the bulk of levies on consumption and to reduce the impediments to savings and production. This is essentially the way the value-added tax now used throughout much of the industrialized world operates. As we gear up to take on the global economic challenge, we should consider overhauling our tax system in this direction.

Now that socialism has so visibly failed abroad, we should not let the United States become the last surviving bastion of that discredited creed. In Eastern Europe, once-prosperous nations that were destroyed economically by their Communist captors are now struggling to make their way back to freedom and the prosperity that goes with it. We should help them, but we should also heed the lessons of their tragic experience. We must rededicate ourselves to the competitive, free-market values that have enabled us to become the world's only superpower. If we do so, we can maintain that power and continue to play a major positive role in the world.

Is the United States worthy to play a leadership role in the world? In a word, yes—and the world needs our example.

Western civilization is not just a condition but also a process. It is a process of striving toward the heights of freedom, creativity, and fulfillment. Through the centuries there has been one tragic setback after another on the way toward those heights. Some of the most highly developed nations have waged wars of conquest and committed some of the most grisly barbarities in the history of man. Those reversals provide dramatic proof that civilization itself is not a sufficient guarantor of freedom. We have to use the gifts that civilization offers and enforce the rules on which it rests.

One role of a great power is to enforce those rules on the world stage. Another is to set an example at home of what nations and people can achieve if they live by them. Unless the rules are enforced, the example will lose its luster and may itself become a casualty. And unless we set the example, we will throw away all that we have struggled to make possible for our own people and those of all nations. As Theodore Roosevelt observed fourteen years before he became President, "It is not what we have that will make us a great nation; it is the way in which we use it."

America preeminently represents three values: freedom, opportunity, and respect for the individual human being. These values transcend borders. They rise from the human spirit, and they speak directly to that spirit. They are inextricably linked with the virtues of individual responsibility, competitiveness, self-reliance, and compassion grounded in an understanding of human nature. America's dedication to these values and its practice of these virtues are what, through the years, has given such power and reach to the American idea. They are the source of our strength and cohesion at home. They also give powerful moral sanction to our voice in the councils of nations abroad.

American progress, based on these values, has been spectacular. We are the richest nation in the world. The very poor in the United States would be rich in three-quarters of the world today. We are the strongest military power in the world. We have the world's best universities. Americans have won more Nobel Prizes in the sciences than any other people have. We have the best medical care in the world, with those abroad who can afford it coming here for treatment rather than using their own countries' nationalized health care programs. We have the most advanced programs for protecting the environment. We have less racial prejudice and more opportunity for all in our society than virtually any other multiethnic nation. That is why the traffic is all one way. Those who want to leave America and live in another country number in the hundreds. Those who want to leave their home countries and live in America number in the millions.

It is vital to the democratic future of the world that the one nation preeminently associated in the minds of others with the democratic ideal should, in the course of this next generation, be an example visibly worth emulating. We have to show democracy not only working, but working well— not just to persuade others that the democratic way is the way to go, but also to demonstrate *how* a democracy can be made to work effectively. Even those who most hunger for democracy are still trying to figure out how best to achieve it. Ours must be an open laboratory that shows how the experiments can work.

In *Democracy in America,* Tocqueville stated that the principles on which the U.S. Constitution rests—"those principles of order, of the balance of powers, of true liberty, of deep and sincere respect for right"—were indispensable. As Europe moved into the democratic age, he urged, "Let us look to America." At the same time, however, he foresaw dangers inherent in democratic society. The universal obsession with materialism, the ruthless economic competition, the lack of enduring social bonds, and the shallowness of religious and philosophical thought, in his analysis, gave rise to the danger of a "new despotism." He feared that because of the lack of economic security in democratic society, individuals would eventually seek that security from the state—which, in turn, would render society dependent on a paternalistic government.

Today, we are witnessing the rise of that new despotism under the cover of "entitlements." We hear claims that by virtue of living in the United States, a person is "entitled" not only to subsistence amounts of food, clothing, and health care, but to more and more of the amenities of life as well. It is not just the poor who seek these entitlements. Farmers who demand a guaranteed price for their crops, steelmakers who demand tariffs to protect their market share, retirees who demand Social Security payments far exceeding their contributions into the system, students who claim a right to subsidized loans, and dozens of other special interests all seek a guaranteed place at the federal trough. Today, if entitlements continue to proliferate, we risk the demise of the virtues of self-reliance and individual responsibility and the triumph of the new despotism about which Tocqueville warned.

It is healthy for all Americans to strive for the amenities of life, but dangerously destructive to foster the notion that they are entitled to them. People are entitled to an opportunity to earn the good things in life. They are not entitled to receive them from the earnings of others. It is up to them to ensure that what they bring to the market equals in value what they want to get out of it. Entitlement is one of the most ruinous concepts in the philosophical lexicon of the modern American liberal. It saps incentive, builds resentment, and leads eventually to a corrosive sense of alienation and failure among those who are lured by its siren song into thinking that the nation owes them the good life without effort on their part.

There is an enormous difference between a right and an entitlement. We have largely lost sight of that difference in the rush toward a "risk-free" economy in which the government insures us against failure and an egalitarian society in which each is rewarded regardless of his contribution. A right permits us to work our way up, while an entitlement is something society owes us whether we earn it or not. Rights help a society and an economy grow, while entitlements slow its growth and erode its character.

The old hereditary nobilities were, in essence, built on the principle of entitlement. A person was born to privilege, and by virtue of birth alone was entitled to keep those privileges. It is essentially this concept of birthright entitlements that is corroding American society. Liberal egalitarians are trying to impose it on the United States, except they have applied it from the bottom up rather than from the top down. To the extent that they succeed, they reinforce society's other special pleaders in their quest for equality not of opportunity but of results.

America has other daunting problems at home, and because of them we are far less than we could be and should be. We must seize the moment of freedom's triumph abroad to make America not just a rich society but a good society.

—The richest country in the world cannot tolerate the fact that we have the highest per capita health care costs in the world and yet 38 million of our people are unable to get adequate medical care because they cannot afford it.

—The richest country in the world cannot tolerate the fact that America—with one-twentieth of the world's people—spends almost as much on illegal drugs as the rest of the world combined.

—The richest country in the world cannot tolerate the fact

that we have the highest crime rate in the world and that during the Persian Gulf War almost twenty times as many Americans were murdered in the United States as were killed on the battlefield.

—The richest country in the world cannot tolerate the fact that a permanent underclass has developed that is rapidly making our great cities unsafe and unlivable.

To address these problems, we need not new ideas but a renewal of faith in those that brought us to where we are. From the beginning, this has been a country in which people from every corner of the earth could reach their full potential because it was built on the rock of individual liberty, equality before the law, and opportunity for all.

It has become fashionable, especially in the news media, to measure every effort to deal with America's domestic needs in purely quantitative terms—and specifically to measure it solely by the number of additional federal dollars committed to federal programs that are labeled, however falsely, as cures. This is nonsense. It represents the sort of one-dimensional thinking that gave us the great failure called the Great Society. The Great Society was given a blank check. It bounced. While some of the poor advanced over the last twenty-five years, most who did so succeeded the old-fashioned way—by their own efforts. Most inner-city poor are worse off today than they were before President Johnson launched the Great Society.

If we are both serious and realistic about addressing the nation's key domestic needs, we must make two clear distinctions.

First, the most critical of our social problems—crime, drugs, dependency, education—center on values, attitudes, and behavior. These are not dependent on dollars, and programs to deal with them that are measured in dollars are often counterproductive. More than dollars we need direction—a clear, forceful set of values and norms that the community accepts and imposes.

Second, a vital distinction exists between a national response and a federal response. From the beginning, the secret of America's success has been that it has not depended on government, but rather has been achieved by private institutions and all the many centers of activity that make up our free society. In most matters that directly touch people, those organizations operate more effectively than the federal government would. And they have the energy, the resources, and the skill to get things done. If we depend on government, we force all concerned to follow the government's rigid prescriptions, on the government's timetable, and through the often impenetrable labyrinths of the government's bureaucracy.

This is not the way a free society is meant to work. And it is not the way a successful society does work. As Goethe observed two hundred years ago, "What is the best government? That which teaches us to govern ourselves."

One of the key roles of national leadership is to focus people's attention on what needs to be done and inspire them to do it. The more the federal government steps in and does things for people—whether for individuals, state and local governments, school boards, or communities—the less they are going to do for themselves and for one another. The best spur to initiative by the private sector is to let people know that if they want something done, they had better roll up their sleeves and do it. The best role for the federal government is to create conditions conducive to doing it.

Most of our current ills are the direct result of going down the wrong path—of flirting too much with the dreams and doctrines represented by statist, socialist ideals, and in the process eroding the unique and special values that have made

America a great nation. At a time when those who have tried socialism are turning our way, we should not turn their way.

To take one glaring example, we have made a mistake in addressing issues such as the exploding costs of health care in ways that removed market forces from the equation. We have erred by separating health care consumers from any concern about the costs of the care being provided. We need to work out a system that includes a greater emphasis on preventive care, sufficient public funding for health insurance for those who cannot afford it in the private sector, competition among both health care providers and health insurance providers to keep down the costs of both, and decoupling the cost of health care from the cost of adding workers to the payroll.

On another front, we will not gain the upper hand in the war against drugs until we shift the focus of our efforts from a supply-side battle in distant corners of the world to a demand-side battle at home. There is no way that the United States can seal its borders tight enough to stop drug trafficking. While budgets for drug interdiction have risen, the street price of drugs has dropped as traffickers devised ever-more-artful means to penetrate our defenses. Victory will only come if we reduce the demand for drugs through stronger legal sanctions, education, treatment, and most important, a radical change in community values. The current drug culture has its roots in the permissive attitudes of the 1960s, which glorified the use of both marijuana and hard drugs, and in the condoning of the "casual" use of drugs today. Unless we reach children early with knowledge of the consequences of drug use, and unless we reverse the tolerance and even glamorizing of drug use in the popular culture of Hollywood and the rest of the entertainment industry, we will stand no chance of winning the war on drugs. And unless we adopt and enforce strict gun-control laws—ones much tougher than the Brady bill—we will never succeed in stemming the violence spawned by the drug trade.

For years, it has been popular in many quarters to say that the answer to poverty in America is to give the poor money. This approach is tragically misguided. We should heed the old proverb, "Give a man a fish, and he has food for a day; teach him to fish, and he has food for a lifetime." There is a place for welfare payments and other purely financial aid, but only as a means of meeting temporary needs and only in conjunction with a structure of incentives—both positive and negative—designed to make the dependent independent. Dependency weakens the nation and destroys the individual, yet too much of our welfare system today merely institutionalizes dependency and perpetuates it from one generation to the next.

Attacking the pathology of the urban underclass is central to success in meeting the whole range of our domestic social needs. This underclass is primarily responsible for the plague of violent crime. It drains the resources of our state and local governments and of our social service institutions. It cripples much of our school system. It represents an enormous human waste: millions of people wasting away in slums could be productive members of the larger society, strengthening the nation in the global economic competition and adding to its reputation as a place of opportunity.

The underclass will be rescued only to the extent that its members can be induced to change their patterns of behavior. They suffer not so much from material poverty as from behavioral poverty—a vicious cycle of illegitimacy, broken families, lax work ethics, and welfare dependency. We have developed this vast and often predatory underclass precisely because we adopted policies that denied the individual's responsibility for his own condition and for the consequences of his own behavior. Too often, the most effective sanctions in the inner cities today are not against destructive behavior but against constructive behavior, as in the case of those students who try to study and, because of this, are shunned or even persecuted by their classmates for "acting white."

The worst thing that we could do would be simply to increase the present programs of welfare maintenance, which make no demands on the recipient and pay no dividends to society. Unless a program motivates the recipients to change their behavior, it cannot be considered a success. By those standards, 90 percent of the current welfare system is an abject failure. It not only perpetuates the behavioral pathologies, but also actively encourages them by making the decision to work or go on welfare purely a pragmatic one of which pays better, with welfare often the winner.

Liberalism holds as its central article of faith that society —"the system"—and not the individual is responsible for antisocial behavior. This approach has produced disaster in coping with the problems of the inner city.

The only way to lift people out of the underclass is to change their behavior. This requires national leadership. But above all, it depends on local and community leadership. It requires a wrenching, radical change in the systems of values that govern in the inner city. We must accept the fact that when people are poor because they choose not to make the effort or to accept the discipline needed to earn a living, it is not only appropriate but necessary that they suffer the consequences of that choice.

The threat of having to do without is central to a productive economy. Some people work because they want to, but most people work because they have to. If you eliminate the necessity, you remove the motivation. Even worse, you introduce a spiritual rot that eats at the foundation of society itself. Those who do work resent those who do not, and they also resent the system that rewards the lazy with leisure. Seeing the lazy rip off the system and get away with it, they are tempted to rip it off in their own ways. Society as a whole goes on a downward spiral of alienation and irresponsibility, which in turn fosters hostility, resentment, and even revenge.

An approach based on enforcing society's values will be fiercely rejected by most of the noisiest self-proclaimed tribunes of the poor, who have created a thriving poverty industry of their own. A lot of that poverty industry is built on the hustle. It is about getting and taking in the name of the poor but not for the benefit of the poor. It is about preserving the jobs and status of the welfare bureaucracies that ostensibly serve the poor but primarily serve themselves. It is the old, familiar shell game played out on a grand national stage.

The exploiting class in the black community today is every bit as despicable as those who lived on the slave trade. Their cynical manipulation of the fears, anxieties, and vulnerabilities of their black constituents is itself a form of psychological slavery. America's blacks will not be fully free until they free themselves from that exploiting class—until they learn that each of them can make it on his or her own and until they set out to do what it takes to make it on their own. As long as they give their allegiance to the loud wheedlers for alms, they will not have their independence. And without their independence, they will not truly have their freedom.

Almost anyone can lead a productive life. The basic distinction we must draw is between those who choose to do so and those who choose not to do so. Those who choose to do so but need help in getting started deserve that help. Those who through misfortune falter along the way and need a hand back up deserve it. But those who willfully fail to prepare themselves for a job or self-indulgently sink themselves into drugs have no claim on the community conscience.

Once we make this crystal clear, the numbers choosing life outside the productive economy will drop drastically. Crime rates will fall. Despair will diminish. Productivity and incomes will rise. Alienation will give way to pride and a sense of community. All of this requires one basic step: a radical change in attitude among those who live on the fringes of civilized society. Like behavior, attitudes are learned. Changing attitudes requires altering our social system of reward and punishment. It requires reinstilling that basic sense of personal responsibility that has been one of the prime casualties of the liberal era.

Racism will not be conquered with more welfare. It will be overcome when people no longer draw invidious distinctions among one another on the basis of skin color. The best way to speed that day is to get more blacks and other minorities climbing the ladder of opportunity. This requires ensuring that any remaining obstacles are removed. And it requires those at the bottom of the ladder to take the first step and then to make the climb.

What a person makes of that opportunity is, and should be, up to the person himself. The flip side of individual freedom is individual opportunity. In maximizing opportunity government has a key role in ensuring that individuals are able to take advantage of it. This means promoting educational achievement. It means motivating people to use the advantages available to them. It means knocking down barriers of discrimination that have historically held so many back. It means, in many cases, extending a helping hand to those who have the will to make the climb but have not found the way. This is more than a moral obligation. It represents an indispensable investment in the nation's future.

To be both strong and rich is not enough. We must also be an example for others to follow. After Nelson's victory at Trafalgar, William Pitt was toasted as the savior of Europe. He responded, "Europe will not be saved by any single man. England has saved herself by her exertions and will, I trust, save Europe by her example." To paraphrase, the victory of freedom will not be won by America alone. We can make freedom work by our exertions at home and enable freedom to win abroad by our example.

How should the United States exercise its leadership in today's world? The world needs U.S. leadership militarily, politically, and economically. Most of all, it needs our leadership in the critical arena of ideas.

Even within and among the countries of Western Europe, bitter conflicts have arisen over the extent to which markets should be controlled by the state and over the degree to which democratic choices of individual nations should be turned over to a new supranational bureaucracy. The danger that the united Europe after 1992 will become protectionist and socialist is real. This is one reason why a continued active American presence is essential to Europe, the United States, and the world. Our commitment to democracy and free markets could prove to be a vital counterweight to the forces trying to turn Europe inward and backward.

As the world's only complete superpower, the United States must exercise leadership without imposing its political and cultural values on others. This is a fine line to walk. But we can advance our values and ideals with restraint dictated by realism. We should cultivate the growth of democratic principles where a reasonable prospect exists for their success and where they would be supported by national traditions, customs, and institutions. We should not, however, engage in an indiscriminate global ideological crusade.

Traditionally, nations have chosen to wage war according to the logic of their interests. America is no exception, even though leaders such as Woodrow Wilson and Franklin D. Roosevelt skillfully couched their appeals to war in terms of the natural idealism of the American people. To a substantial extent, President Bush also followed this tradition in the Persian Gulf War. This approach should not be dismissed as cynicism. Our basic idealism is not only a defining characteristic and animating force of the United States but also a key facet of our own national interests.

America's concern for the Kurds, like its earlier concern for the victims of the Holocaust in World War II, was genuinely based on compassion rather than on a geopolitical calculus. But the plight of the Kurds, like that of the Jews in Europe under Hitler's rule, cannot be divorced from that equation. The hardheaded calculations of power politics do not exist in a vacuum. They must serve not just our security interests, but our wider values as well.

America's central national interest in the world today can be defined in terms of structure and process. In my administration, I spoke often of building a "structure of peace." By that, I meant a set of interlocking relationships, together with accepted processes for resolving differences and effective deterrents to aggression that would allow even antagonists to live together in a reasonable expectation that peace was secure enough to be maintained among them.

This kind of structure requires a decent respect for the norms of civilized behavior both among and within nations. Promoting—and, when necessary and possible, enforcing—such norms may seem idealistic. But it reflects a hardheaded assessment that practical idealism represents an indispensable component of realism in the modern world. While our short-term goals must be governed by the limits of our resources and our ability to shape a frustrating and intractable world, such constraints should not limit our long-term aspirations. Just as no man is an island, no nation lives in isolation. When freedom is denied in one country, it is diminished in all.

This does not mean that we should insist that other nations copy our particular form of government. Many countries are not ready for it. Each nation must develop its own institutions and advance at its own pace. Democracy literally means government by the people. It must come from the people. In contrast to the Bolshevik revolution of 1917, the peaceful revolution in Eastern Europe in 1989 and in the Soviet Union in 1991 were peoples' revolutions. They were not imposed from above by an elite few—a "vanguard." They welled up from below—from the people themselves. Democracy has to grow roots and branches in a society before it blossoms. We can and should work to speed this growth, but the process is vital to realizing the promise.

In the Soviet Union, after centuries of autocratic rule, the people have only recently had a chance to begin experimenting with the institutions of self-government. They face enormous challenges, but have shown themselves eager to learn and alert to the lessons of other countries. If they continue to go down this path, they will astonish the world with their achievements.

To say that we should be realistic does not mean that we should abandon our idealism. Practical idealism differs fundamentally from mere expediency. We should be circumspect about prescribing the political means chosen by others, but we should insist that those political means serve moral political ends. We seek to advance the cause of freedom, but we must recognize that in different cultures it will take different forms and advance in different ways.

The great danger in Eastern Europe and the Soviet Union is that the current high expectations, when not fully met, could themselves lead to impatience and disillusionment and ultimately a return to coercion and control. It is precisely when a faith appears to have been betrayed that a people are most susceptible to the lures of the demagogue. These coming years are critical to the future of Europe and the world. It is vital that the experiments in freedom now being tried should succeed, that those countries enslaved for so long should not stumble back into socialism or some other form of statist domination.

This means help. It means example. The revolution for freedom currently sweeping the world began with a spark of hope—what Dostoyevsky called "the fire in the minds of men." It is a testament to the human spirit that this fire continues to burn so brightly in so many places among so many people. As Americans, we carry part of the original flame. We must make sure it is never extinguished.

As I have traveled around the world during the past forty-five years, I have found that some hate us, some envy us, and some like us. But I have found that almost all respect us. All know that without the United States peace and freedom would not have survived in the world in the past and will not survive in the future. But the question that has arisen again and again has been whether the United States had the will to play a world role over the long haul.

We have demonstrated that will during the decades of the cold war, and we must sustain that will in the decades to come. We should commit ourselves to a world role not just to keep the world from becoming worse but to make it better. We need to restore our faith in our ideas, in our destiny, and in ourselves. We exist for more than hedonistic self-satisfaction. We are here to make history, neither to ignore the past nor to turn back to the past, but to move forward in a way that opens up new vistas for the future.

In his writings, legal philosopher Lon Fuller contrasted what he called a morality of duty and a morality of aspiration. A morality of duty requires only doing what is right in the sense of avoiding what is wrong. A morality of aspiration requires the full realization of our potential in a manner worthy of a people at their best. It is not enough to be remembered just as a good people who took care of ourselves without doing harm to others. We want to be remembered as a great people whose conduct went beyond the call of duty as we seized the moment to meet the supreme challenge of this century: winning victory for freedom without war.

There has never been a more exciting time to be alive and a better place to live than America in 1992. For centuries, people have dreamed of enjoying peace, freedom, and progress around the world. Never in history have we been closer to making those dreams come true.

The twenty-first century can be a century of peace. Because of the destructive power of nuclear weapons, there will not be another world war. Those who have nuclear weapons know that in a nuclear war there will be no winners, only losers. Although the twentieth century has been the bloodiest in history, the world's aggressors have suffered devastating defeats. Hitler's fascism was defeated in World War II. Soviet communism was defeated without war in 1989 and 1991. Saddam Hussein's brazen aggression was defeated in 1991. Because the world united to liberate Kuwait, international outlaws—large or small—will be less likely to launch aggressive wars against their neighbors.

The twenty-first century can be the first in history in which a majority of the world's people live in political freedom. Not only in Eastern Europe and the Soviet Union but also across Latin America, Asia, and even Africa, freedom has become the wave of the future. A revolution of free ideas and free elections is sweeping the world. This freedom comes not from abroad or from above but from within the people themselves. Woodrow Wilson sought to make the world safe for democracy. Today, many urge in his name that we export our particular form of democracy to other nations. This is not necessary. Dictatorship of the left and of the right has been discredited. The people have spoken: they want freedom. America's challenge is not to export democracy but to provide an example of how freedom can be secured through democracy.

The twenty-first century can be the first in which the majority of the world's people enjoy economic freedom. The twentieth century has taught us four great economic lessons: communism does not work. Socialism does not work. State-dominated economies do not work. Only free markets can fully unleash the creative abilities of individuals and serve as the engine of progress.

The twenty-first century can be a century of unprecedented progress. The technological revolution can provide the means to win the war against poverty, misery, and disease all over the world. Twenty years ago, futurist Herman Kahn predicted that the annual per capita income of the world's 5 billion people—now less than $4,000—would rise to $20,000 in the next century. His predictions, which seemed so unrealistic at the time, will almost certainly come true in a century of peace.

Only 5 percent of the world's people live in the United States. But what we do can make the entire world a better place. We are not mere passengers on the voyage of history.

We are its navigators. We have the opportunity to forge a second American century.

In his Iron Curtain speech in 1947, Winston Churchill said, "The United States stands at this time at the pinnacle of world power. It is a solemn moment for the American democracy. For with primacy in power is also joined an awe-inspiring accountability for the future." Those words are as true today as when he spoke them forty-five years ago. We hold the future in our hands.

This is not a burden to be grimly borne. It is a high enterprise worthy of a great people. We are privileged to live at a moment of history like none most people have ever experienced or will ever experience again. We must seize the moment not just for ourselves but for others. Only if this becomes a better world for others will it be a better world for us, and only when we participate in a cause greater than ourselves can we be fully true to ourselves.

AUTHOR'S NOTE

IN 1990, WHEN I BEGAN preliminary work on this book, I intended to address the U.S. role in the world after the historic collapse of Moscow's satellite regimes in Eastern Europe in 1989. I believed we faced an unprecedented opportunity to win victory without war in the East-West conflict. Since then, the world has changed dramatically. The United States orchestrated a global coalition to liberate Kuwait in the Persian Gulf War in 1990. Most momentous, the death of Soviet communism and the disintegration of the Soviet empire in 1991 revolutionized the global political landscape.

I believe that it is imperative that the United States seize this moment to secure peace and to advance freedom around the world. The conventional wisdom has been that we no longer need to play a major world role, that our mission was completed. I strongly disagree. The end of the cold war has made the world not simpler but more complicated. It resolved some conflicts, but it gave rise to new and more difficult ones. In my view, a central U.S. role became not superfluous but more important now than ever before. The first six chapters are about how the United States should exercise this leadership. The seventh chapter is about what we must do at home not only to have the means to lead through our actions but also to be worthy to lead through our example.

In preparing this volume, I received help from members of my staff and from experts in various fields. Carmen Tirado provided outstanding stenographic and secretarial support. Kathy O'Connor, my administrative assistant, ably organized my office staff and other affairs.

I wish to thank Walter McDougall, Jed Snyder, Herbert Stein, William Van Cleave, Jennifer Widner, and David Wigg for preparing insightful background papers. I also benefited from the views of James Billington, Fritz Ermarth, William Hyland, James Lilley, and Michel Oksenberg. I want to express particular appreciation to three longtime associates. Robert Ellsworth and Dimitri Simes not only provided me with their perceptive analyses of the situation in Europe and the Soviet Union but also gave me indispensable help and advice during my trip to the Soviet Union in March 1991. Ray Price, who served as chief of my White House speech-writing staff and who organized two of my previous book projects, contributed insight and wisdom about how we must confront our problems at home.

I am especially grateful to Monica Crowley and Joe Marx for their immensely helpful research and editorial assistance and to Marin Strmecki, who again served as my research and editorial director, for his wise counsel throughout the project.

—RN

Park Ridge, New Jersey
September 11, 1991

INDEX